The WOMEN'S ESTATE PLANNING

GUIDE

TECHNIQUES FOR PROTECTING YOURSELF AND YOUR FAMILY

ZOE M. HICKS, ESQ.

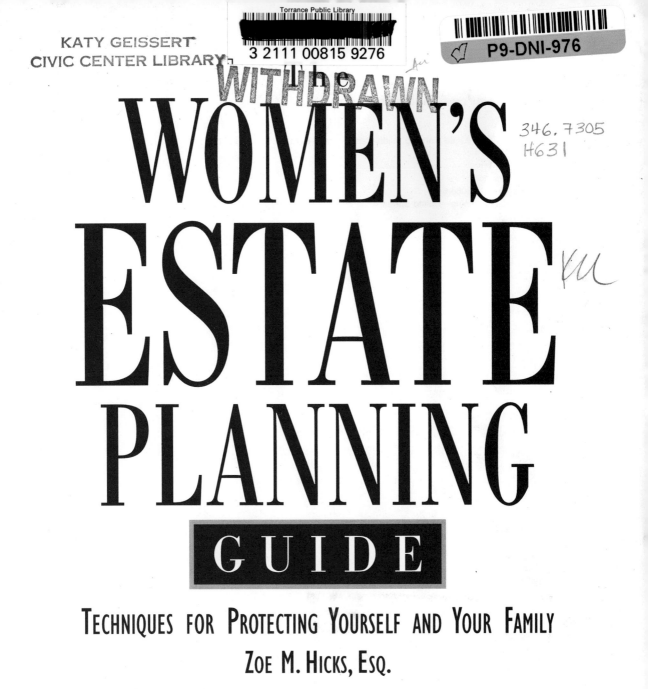

CB

CONTEMPORARY BOOKS

Library of Congress Cataloging-in-Publication Data

Hicks, Zoe M.
    The women's estate planning guide : techinques for protecting yourself and your family
/ Zoe M. Hicks.
        p.   cm.
    Includes index.
    ISBN 0-8092-3066-6
    1. Estate planning—United States.   2. Women—Legal status, laws, etc.—United
States.   I. Title.
KF750.Z9H53   1997
346.7305'2—dc21   97-38091
                                                             CIP

This book is intended to provide general information and is not intended as specific
advice for any particular reader. I have tried my best to be accurate, but I have found over
the years that I *do* make mistakes, and it is entirely possible (even likely) that I have failed
to produce an error-free manuscript. The reader should also keep in mind that tax laws
are constantly changing, and parts of this book may therefore become outdated.

Each reader should consult her own tax and estate planning counsel with respect to any
of the techniques discussed or information provided herein. Neither the author nor pub-
lisher shall have any liability to any person or entity for any loss or damage caused, or
alleged to be caused, directly or indirectly, by information contained in this book.

Cover design by Scott Rattray
Interior design by Nancy Freeborn

Published by Contemporary Books
An imprint of NTC/Contemporary Publishing Company
4255 West Touhy Avenue, Lincolnwood (Chicago), Illinois 60646-1975 U.S.A.
Copyright © 1998 by Zoe M. Hicks
Printed in the United States of America
International Standard Book Number: 0-8092-3066-6

19   18   17   16   15   14   13   12   11   10   9   8   7   6   5   4   3   2   1

To my husband, Charles, who touched the heart of God for this book,
and to the One who heard and answered, my source and strength.

Contents

Acknowledgments

No one writes a book alone, and this book could not have happened without the help and assistance of many people. I am deeply indebted to each and every one of them.

First and foremost, I thank my former associate and valued colleague, Elizabeth McCaw. Beth did the research and initial drafting for five of the chapters of this book—those on "legalese," disabilities, charitable giving, life insurance, and prenuptial agreements. Without her, I never would have been able to tackle a task of this magnitude. Her thoroughness and dedication were a constant source of encouragement to me. She approached every task with determination, hard work, and courage, and this book was no exception.

Judith Shur, an extremely talented attorney and a recent addition to the firm, provided valuable editing and proofreading assistance. Judi's eye for detail and delightful personality kept me calm through the home stretch.

My secretary, Linda Lee, is not only a remarkable and exceptionally fast word processor, but a writer herself. She often corrects my spelling, grammar, punctuation, and syntax. I look forward to the day when Linda writes a book of her own. For now, her tremendous assistance in processing this book, not to mention her emotional support, is greatly appreciated.

Other members of my staff—Sue Glass, Laura Tweedell, and Davita Milsaps—lent support and encouragement and held me accountable to our deadlines. Without them, I could not operate, and I am forever grateful to each of them.

I cannot give thanks enough to my friends and colleagues who reviewed chapters of this book for the invaluable time they donated. Each of them is an expert in an area covered by one of the chapters. These dedicated friends include: Jack Baker, CLU; Warren C. Budd, CLU; Natalie B. Choate, Esq.; Richard P. Kessler, Esq.; Clifton B. Kruse, Jr., Esq.; Ira Leff, Esq.; and Judith F. Todd, Esq. Their reviews helped keep me straight on some of the technical matters covered. I am also grateful to Christopher Consenza for all the information he provided.

No list of acknowledgments would be complete without thanking my family for their neverending support and encouragement. This book could never have happened without my husband, who has always believed I could do things that I would never have thought possible. I thank him for encouraging me to make my dreams come true and for entertaining me with his great sense of humor through it all.

My daughter, Alice, provided number-crunching assistance and, with her analytical skills, brought me back to center many times when I strayed too far to the left or right.

Mom and Dad, Edith and Bill McFee, are always there for me, always interested, always supportive, and always encouraging, as are my sister, Edith Lycke, and my brother, Bill McFee.

Finally, last, but certainly not least, I thank Contemporary Books for its invaluable editorial assitance and its commitment to getting this information out to women who need it to protect themselves and their families. Every person I talked with at Contemporary Books was courteous, supportive, and encouraging.

Why Bother?

The Benefits of Estate Planning

Dear Abby: *The letter signed "In the Dark in Canada" could have been written by my mother. She and Dad were married for 40 years when they found out that Dad had cancer. Chemotherapy was started immediately, but after 11 months, he died.*

Before his illness, my mother had never paid a bill or balanced a checkbook. She had never put gas in the car or checked the oil. Dad did everything for her. All Mother knew how to do was cook, keep house and raise children.

When Dad died, Mama got a crash course in reality. Abby, please print this. There are many women out there who need to wake up. —***Their Daughter***

Taken from the DEAR ABBY column by Abigail Van Buren. © Universal Press Syndicate. Reprinted with permission. All rights reserved.

I had been on the phone for 20 minutes, discussing estate planning possibilities with Al, a successful entrepreneur and CEO of his own company. Finally, I said, "Look, why don't you and Scotty [his wife] come in so we can review the options?"

"Scotty wouldn't be interested," Al replied. "She would forget everything 10 minutes after leaving your office. If I don't take care of it, it won't get done."

I knew Al to be a fair-minded, generous man. He actually regretted the fact that Scotty wasn't concerned about her financial future. He didn't want to exclude her, but being a realist, he knew he had to proceed with estate planning without Scotty's input if it was to get done at all.

Indeed, why should Scotty be interested? Al made a good living, and she didn't have to work. Certainly, there were more interesting things to do than sit down and think about one's own demise, or one's husband's for that matter. Scotty's life was full, both with her children's activities and with her own, and business was not her thing. Fortunately, Al realized the importance of good estate planning for Scotty's protection, as well as his children's. Unfortunately, Al is the exception, not the rule. It is a rare man who proceeds with estate planning in the face of total disinterest on the part of his wife.

If Scotty could have been a fly on the wall when Diane, an attractive young widow, found herself in my office, she would have realized the importance of good estate planning. Diane's husband, Stan, an engineer, had recently been killed while inspecting an underground storage facility for his company. An explosion during the inspection had caused the earth to cave in around Stan and two other men—an unbelievably horrible accident. Now Diane had two young children to support single-handedly. She and Stan had been married about nine years, and they had a house but very little else, except some insurance provided by Stan's company. Diane wanted to know how to put the house in her name now that Stan was dead. There were also a few other assets—a brokerage account and an automobile that had been in Stan's name—and she wanted to transfer title to these assets as well.

I began with some preliminary questions to ferret out basic information.

"Did Stan have a will?"

"No."

"Was there any insurance on his life other than that provided by his company?"

"No."

"Were there any retirement assets?"

"No."

"Were there any other employee benefits?"

"No."

"How old are the children?"

"Six and eight."

"Are you trained professionally in any way?"

"No."

At least she was young and had her health.

I had the unfortunate task of telling Diane that, because her husband had died without a will, she was not entitled to receive a full ownership interest in the house or any other asset in Stan's name. Rather, under state law, Stan's assets were to go one-third to her and one-third to each of her minor children. Furthermore, Diane would have to go to the county probate court and be appointed the guardian of her minor children. If she ever wanted to sell an asset, additional guardians (attorneys) would have to be appointed to represent her children in the sale. She would have to purchase expensive insurance policies called "bonds" and report to the probate court at regular intervals with respect to how she was handling the children's monies. The investment options for guardians are quite limited—insured certificates of deposit, government bonds, and money market funds. When each of her children turned 18, Diane would have to release to that child any assets in his or her guardianship account. Thus, even if she managed to do exceedingly well with her limited investment choices, Diane would be putting the results of her labor into the hands of an 18-year-old child, who just might decide to buy a new sports car or an electric guitar.

Diane was devastated by the news I gave her. She couldn't believe that Stan had not written a will. But, then again, neither had she. Before leaving my office that day, Diane instructed me to draw up a will for her, thus beginning her own estate planning for the benefit of her children.

About a year later, Diane returned to my office, this time with her fiance. The first thing she and her new husband were going to do after their wedding was execute new wills. "Never again will I go through what I went through when Stan died," Diane told me. "It was a horrible experience for me. I couldn't believe that I had to share ownership of our home with my children and actually get consent from an attorney appointed to represent them if I ever decided to sell it."

Diane's experience illustrates why every woman should concern herself with estate planning. If you are fortunate enough to have a husband like Al, who insists that everything be planned and taken care of for your protection, you might think that you needn't trouble yourself with such matters. But if you don't participate in the estate planning process, you will be giving up the right to help make crucial decisions that will affect your future and your children's future, such as the selection of a trustee and guardian. For the majority of women, estate planning can make all the difference in the world—by protecting minor children from their own immaturity, by avoiding expensive bonds and filing requirements with probate courts, by minimizing (or eliminating) estate taxes, and—most importantly—by ensuring financial security.

So why are women like Scotty and Diane uninterested in estate planning? The reasons include the belief that planning can always be done later (procrastination), a fear of meeting with lawyers, a tendency to allow the urgent to take precedence over the important in our lives, superstition, lack of knowledge, and expense. The list goes on. Yet, 9 times out of 10, it is women who benefit from good estate planning. Women outlive their husbands 90 percent of the time, and a woman's life expectancy exceeds that of a man her age by seven years. Good estate planning includes insuring adequate financial resources for one's life expectancy, whether one ends up spending that time alone, married, widowed, or divorced. Therefore, no group should be more interested in estate planning than women. Because women will, on the whole, live longer than men, they will generally be left with the family wealth to handle and plan.

PEACE OF MIND

Estate planning can be broadly defined as the building of an estate to achieve financial goals (such as enjoying a comfortable retirement and financing children's education) and the proper management and disposition of that estate to protect loved ones. Perhaps the greatest benefit to having prepared for your future disability and/or retirement through good financial and estate planning is the security and peace of mind achieved. Security is important to everyone, but particularly to women. We must assume the responsibility of having a plan in place for dealing with our own or a husband's disability, retirement, or death.

Assume responsibility for your family estate plan, and insist that it be done properly. Knowing that your future is secure will give you great peace of mind. Don't count on your husband or anyone else to initiate the process or do the job for you. In her book, *Feminine Force,* Georgette Mosbacher says, "Entrusting my financial security to anyone else is an unacceptable risk. *I* am responsible. . . ."

PROTECTING YOURSELF

When a husband or parent dies, a woman stands to gain (or lose) a great deal, depending on the adequacy of her husband's or parents' estate planning documents. Being involved in the planning stage is vitally important. If trusts are used (as discussed in Chapters 5 and 6), the selection of trustees and the terms of a trust can make your life either miserable or enjoyable. A good estate plan can dramatically reduce—and in most cases eliminate—estate taxes, professional fees, and other costs associated with the administration of an estate.

There can be no better investment of a woman's time than good estate planning. The top federal estate tax bracket, which is applicable to estates of $3 million or more, is 55 percent. The thought of a drain of that magnitude on the value of a parent's estate should motivate any daughter to encourage both of her parents to seek competent estate planning counsel. A married woman should make sure that her husband's estate plan takes full advantage of the deferral of estate taxes available through the federal estate tax marital deduction and the federal exemption available. That way, at his death, she will not have to turn over any of his assets to Uncle Sam, and taxes will be minimized or eliminated for her children at the time of her death.

PROTECTING YOUR HUSBAND

If your spouse is knowledgeable about money management and not a spendthrift, protecting him would be easy—*if* that were the only concern. You could simply, in your will, leave everything to him. As a good money manager, he would know how to invest the money and use it to provide for his lifetime needs.

Unfortunately, it's not that simple. First of all, protecting your husband is not your only concern. You also want to reduce taxes to the extent that you can, and you probably want to ensure that, when your husband dies (should he survive you), the assets you leave to him will go to your children and not a new wife or someone else. If your husband is not a U.S. citizen, leaving assets directly to him could cause taxation, which might otherwise be avoided through the marital deduction. You see, then, that protecting your husband is only one of several estate planning goals you might have. Your other goals might include making sure that property eventually winds up in the hands of your children, reducing estate taxes, and, if your husband is not a U.S. citizen, making sure that all taxes are deferred until his death.

In order to achieve all of these goals, a woman must use testamentary trusts in her estate planning documents. A testamentary trust is one established by a last will and testament or a revocable living trust that continues beyond death. A woman who predeceases her husband will want to take maximum advantage of laws that allow her to protect her estate from taxes. If she has an estate large enough to be subject to estate taxes, she will likely want to establish a trust giving her husband maximum flexibility in using the assets while keeping them out of his taxable estate. This technique is discussed in more detail in Chapter 5. Additional testamentary trusts will be necessary if a woman's husband is not a U.S. citizen or if she is concerned about her husband leaving her assets to a new spouse or anyone other than her children. These techniques are discussed in Chapter 8.

PROTECTING YOUR CHILDREN AND/OR GRANDCHILDREN

Mothers are naturally concerned for their children's welfare. While your children are minors, your main concerns are that the right person will care for them if anything happens to you and their father, and that there will be adequate financial resources to support them. Naming a guardian by will ensures that the parents' wishes for their children's future are carried out. Surely every mother can think of people she would not want raising her children. Unless the parents make provisions otherwise in their wills, a court might appoint the very person the parents do *not* want. And what about provisions to take care of the children's inheritance until they are old enough to take care of it themselves? In many states, without a will, the children will receive any assets inherited by them through guardianship proceedings at age 18. How many 18-year-olds really know how to manage money and protect it for their future?

A properly drawn estate planning document can nominate a guardian and a trustee. A *guardian* is a person appointed to take physical custody of the children and assume the responsibility of raising them. A *trustee* is a person appointed to manage the children's money. A child's guardian and trustee may or may not be the same person. A trust within the estate planning document may stipulate how the trustee will spend the money for the children and may authorize the trustee to make payments to the guardian to support the children. A trust can be as flexible or rigid as you wish. Furthermore, trust provisions may specify at what age the children will receive their funds.

If a child with special needs is involved, a trust can continue for as long as the child lives. Often, if there are several children but only one has special needs, more than the usual share will be placed in trust for that child, with specific instructions on how to care for the child. The care of an adult son or daughter with special needs is of particular concern to parents who have been caring for that son or daughter since infancy. That son or daughter, although an adult, may be unable to care for himself or herself without assistance, and parents may wonder what will happen in the event of their death. In such a case, a trust arrangement in the proper document, allocating the child's share to the trust, can provide care for that child after the parents' death and thus provide great peace of mind. Trusts for such children are discussed in Chapter 9.

For other children, a parent's concerns are generally that the children receive the parent's inheritance in an appropriate manner. Should a child predecease a parent, most people want their grandchildren, rather than the child's spouse, to receive the child's share. If the grandchildren are minors, their deceased parent's share can remain in trust for them as long as necessary.

TAX PLANNING

Parents will also be interested in their children, not the government, receiving their estates. If people only realized how much tax money could be saved by good estate planning, far more time and effort would be spent on the process. Transfer taxes (estate and gift taxes) are the highest taxes imposed on individuals. The first $600,000 (this is being increased to $1 million by the year 2006) of an estate is exempt from taxes, but then transfer taxes hit, beginning at a 37 percent bracket and quickly going to a 55 percent bracket for estates of $3 million and above. For estates of $10 million to $21 million (rounded), the top marginal bracket is 60 percent. Income tax rates are significantly lower than transfer tax rates, even at the highest income tax brackets. Furthermore, income taxes are far more difficult to avoid than estate taxes. One of the most painful situations in an estate planning practice is preparing estate tax returns where the executors must write out large checks to the Internal Revenue Service (IRS) and the State Department of Revenue when those taxes could have been avoided altogether with proper planning. If only the decedents had gotten some professional help in planning their estates, their children could have avoided huge tax burdens. Numerous techniques exist for shifting assets to children while reducing transfer taxes and even allowing the parents to retain control over the assets.

In many cases, the payment of large estate taxes at a parent's death is due to sheer ignorance. If I were to ask my clients whether they would rather have hard-earned dollars go to the IRS or to family members, they would look at me as if I were crazy. No one totally approves of the way the government spends money. (Conservatives think that the government spends their tax dollars on welfare, and liberals think it all goes to defense.) Yet, in many estates, the IRS is the major estate beneficiary because of lack of knowledge or interest or both.

PROVIDING FOR LIQUIDITY

Estate taxes are due nine months from the date of death and generally must be paid to the IRS in cash on that date. When estate assets consist of real estate or a family business, how can cash be raised to pay the tax liability on the transfer of these assets? Illiquid assets are often quite valuable and thus generate a high tax. Some of the questions that arise for the executor of an estate with such assets are:

- Do I sell the illiquid assets (perhaps in a depressed market) in order to pay the estate tax?

- Do I borrow money from a bank to pay off the IRS?

- Can I qualify the estate under the Internal Revenue Code for an extended payout of estate taxes (15 years for family businesses that qualify)?

The purpose of estate planning is not only to reduce taxes but also to *pay* those that are left.

Several provisions in the Internal Revenue Code permit payment of estate taxes over an extended period of time *if* an estate qualifies to take advantage of these provisions. (See Chapter 4.) It would obviously be disadvantageous for a family to have to sell assets in a "fire sale" context in order to raise revenue to pay estate taxes. Adequate liquidity is so important that many people purchase life insurance just to cover the tax liability.

Another concern is that a surviving spouse may need liquidity to maintain his or her standard of living. Illiquid assets may or may not be able to provide cash to continue financing a surviving spouse's lifestyle. (This must also be considered in overall estate planning.) If the decedent spouse was the primary wage earner, that spouse's death may mean a cessation of cash flow. Again, insurance is often considered in such situations.

PROVIDING FOR DISABILITY

Disability may be either temporary or permanent. If you or your husband becomes disabled, it is important to have a plan to manage assets for the disabled spouse for the benefit of both of you. This may be accomplished in several ways. If the disabled spouse has a revocable living trust (discussed in Chapter 5), provisions for disability may be included in the trust document. To the extent that assets have been transferred to the trust prior to the disability, the trustee would be able to use those assets for the benefit of the disabled individual. The trustee could pay bills, make decisions with respect to buying and selling assets, and distribute assets to or for the benefit of the disabled person.

If a living trust has not been established, a general durable *power of attorney* can be used. This is a way for an individual to grant authority to another to take care of assets in the event of a disability. A general durable power of attorney gives authority to buy and sell assets and make distributions of assets to the grantor of the power. Another popular document is the health care power of attorney, which authorizes an individual to make health care decisions for the grantor in the event that the grantor is unable to do so for himself or herself. The health care power of attorney may or may not include a *living will*. A living will provides that, in the event an individual is being kept alive only by heroic measures, the power holder should instruct the doctors and hospital to discontinue life support systems. Powers of attorney and living wills are discussed in Chapter 7.

PROVIDING FOR CHARITY, FRIENDS, AND COLLATERAL RELATIVES

State statutes governing the disposition of property in the event that a person dies without a will or a revocable living trust always provide for the immediate family alone to receive the estate. The only way for charities, friends, and collateral relatives to receive anything is for an individual to make provisions for such people and organizations in a will or revocable living trust. Small token remembrances or major bequests can be given to charities and collateral relatives. Furthermore, particularly if one is giving to a charity, specific instructions on how the money is to be spent may be included. For example, if you intend to leave half of the residue of your estate to a college, rather than have the money go toward general operation of the college, you may want to provide scholarships for a particular group of students, students planning careers in biomedical research, for example, or students who plan to become medical missionaries. Perhaps you want to leave a large bequest to a medical research facility. You may specify that the funds be used to conduct research on a disease from which a loved one suffered. By including such specific instructions in your estate planning documents, you can be certain that the funds you leave to your favorite charity will go specifically toward the cause you choose.

With respect to friends and collateral relatives, individuals sometimes wish to leave particular items of tangible personal property (the category of property that includes clothes, jewelry, and household effects) to close relatives or people who have expressed a desire for such property. These types of bequests are often made on a list attached to the will specifying who is to receive which property. The will must simply refer to this list. The advantage of such a list is that you do not have to go back to the attorney's office to make changes or additions to it. Check with a local attorney to make sure such a list is valid in your state.

SIMPLIFYING YOUR LIFE AND REDUCING EXPENSES

We have discussed the reduction of taxes as one advantage of good estate planning, but good estate planning also reduces expenses and red tape when a spouse or parent dies. Properly drawn and executed estate planning documents may eliminate some of the requirements state probate law otherwise imposes. For example, the personal representative of an estate (called the *executor* or *administrator*) will probably have to purchase a bond unless he or she is relieved from doing so by a provision in the decedent's estate planning documents. A bond is an expensive insurance policy that ensures against the personal representative handling the estate in a manner contrary to the will (or to state law if the individual died without a will). The expense of purchasing a bond is unnecessary in most cases but will be required unless there is a waiver. In most cases, the personal representative also will have to file reports with county probate courts unless the decedent's will relieves the personal representative from filing reports.

In some states, the attorney handling the probate and administration of an estate receives a percentage of the estate as his or her fee. Executors also may charge a percentage of the estate for their services. In states where attorneys typically charge a percentage fee or where the executor is going to charge a percentage of the estate, revocable living trusts are popular techniques to avoid such fees. An individual establishes a living trust and transfers assets to it during his or her lifetime. At death, the trust assets do not actually go through the probate process, which subjects assets to these fees. Rather, the assets remain in the living trust and are distributed according to the terms of the trust that become effective at the individual's death. In some states, probate fees are quite low, and revocable living trusts are less useful. Ask a local attorney for advice in this area.

PREPARING TO STEER THE FAMILY FINANCIAL SHIP

Because women outlive their husbands ten-to-one, in all probability a wife will be left with the responsibility of steering the family financial ship after her husband dies. Preparing now to be the captain of that ship can benefit not only you, but also your children, grandchildren, and great-grandchildren. If your husband typically manages the family investments and legal affairs, you should know where all legal documents, insurance policies, deeds, and other important papers are kept. You should also meet the family financial advisors and become familiar with what your husband is doing with the family assets. Of course, you may disagree with these advisors when it is your turn to steer the ship, but it will be highly advantageous for you to become involved with all aspects of the family financial plan and with the family financial advisors. This will make your life far easier if and when you become solely responsible for family decision making. Perhaps more important, if you feel you cannot work with one of the family financial advisors, you might persuade your husband to change advisors while he is still alive. If you are the spouse who typically manages the family's investments and legal affairs, it is likewise equally as important that you encourage your husband to meet with the advisors and know the whereabouts of your documents.

There are all kinds of people out there giving investment advice. Some of these advisors are very good, some do nothing but collect fees, and a small minority are actually crooks. Without some background and experience, you might find it hard to separate the sheep from the wolves. The more you can learn now, the better your family's financial ship will run now and later.

Emotional Blocks to Estate Planning

What Prevents Us from Taking Steps to Provide Protection?

We have met the enemy and [she] is us.

—Walt Kelly, "Pogo"

Estate planning is an emotionally charged activity. After all, estate planning concerns death and taxes, two subjects that evoke deep emotional responses in most of us. Anyone who has worked in the estate planning area for any length of time has witnessed these emotional responses firsthand. In my own practice, I have seen clients cry, yell at each other, and lash out at me. A client might break out in a cold sweat when discussing his will or become immobilized over emotional issues such as which child should run the family business when Mom and Dad die.

Estate planning is an unselfish act. Anyone who takes the time to plan for what will happen to assets when he or she is no longer around is thinking about others—family, relatives, friends, and charitable organizations. Those who plan their estates are planning and caring for others, distributing assets in a wise and helpful way, in order to do the most good for family, loved ones, and the community—a noble venture indeed.

FACING THE GRIM REAPER

The first emotional hurdle encountered in planning one's estate is facing the fact of one's own mortality. This is rarely easy for any of us, but it is more difficult for some people than others. The subject of death, while not exactly taboo, is often "soft-pedaled" in our culture. Consider the many euphemisms used to describe the end of life: "gone away," "departed," "passed on," "gone home," "gone to her reward," "gone to glory," "the product of negative patient care outcome" (nurses' lingo), "gone to that great hunting ground (fishing hole, golf course, etc.) in the sky," "kicked the bucket," "six feet under," "gone to heaven," "cashed in," "bought the farm," "pushing up daisies," "checked out," "departed." The list goes on. Many of us will go to great lengths to avoid using the word *death* to describe an event that is certain to occur in all of our lives.

The fact of the matter is: death is an unknown. None of us who are alive have experienced it, and we don't know exactly what to expect. There are stories, of course, of people who have survived near-death experiences. They tell of a tunnel, of approaching a bright light, and of being sent back to complete their task on earth. Some speak of the love that they felt while traveling toward the light, and some say they were even sorry they had to return. But even these people don't understand all that happens after death. Deeply religious people tend to be more open and willing to talk about death than others because, for people of faith, death is the doorway to a new and perfect body, a better life, a great victory and reward. Yet it still makes us more uncomfortable to consider our own personal death, as opposed to the concept of death in general.

Some people appear to believe that participating in the act of estate planning can actually accelerate the need for estate planning documents. This, of course, is nothing more than superstition, but it is a superstition that must be acknowledged and dealt with.

Anthony Robbins, a student of psychology and one of the great motivational speakers of our day, points out in his audiocassete series, *Personal Power*, that the two greatest people motivators are the avoidance of pain and the pursuit of pleasure. Furthermore, says Robbins, avoiding pain is a stronger motivator than pursuing pleasure. Coming to terms with our own death as part of the estate planning process can be a painful experience; therefore, many people choose to avoid the process altogether. Even though one's family will suffer later if there is no planning, if the pain associated with estate planning is perceived as too great, the entire process will be avoided. Robbins suggests that, to overcome the pain, we think of the consequences of *not* engaging in the painful act. In our case, consider the consequences our families would suffer if we did *not* participate in the estate planning process—confusion, conflicts, higher fees, higher taxes, broken relationships. For those of us involved in the estate planning process, our job is to make the experience as painless as possible.

GIVING UP CONTROL

The next emotional hurdle to overcome is the fear of giving up control of our assets. For both married and single women, this is a fear that must be faced in order to proceed. It might help a woman to consider the fact that the men in her life—husband, father, brothers—probably have even more difficulty with this issue than she does.

If you are married, you might fear your husband's putting assets into trust, thinking that you will have no control over the assets. This is not necessarily true, and I spend a fair amount of time explaining to couples that, in most cases, for testamentary trusts created in wills to save taxes, the wife may be the sole trustee with control over the assets (provided that the trust is drafted properly, as explained in Chapter 5). Generally, after learning how the tax-protected trust works, a woman will feel comfortable knowing that she (if she is named as trustee) is not giving up any control from a practical standpoint—which she would have if her husband had left the assets to her outright.

If you are the surviving spouse and have assets that will be subject to estate tax upon your death, you know that you must "do something" to avoid the estate tax. You want your children, not the IRS, to have your estate when you die, but in the meantime, you want to control and enjoy those assets. Several clients have told me stories about people who had given assets to their children only to have the ungrateful children refuse to give anything back to the destitute parents. These stories are probably repeated over and over in retirement communities, paralyzing individuals who should be doing estate planning.

Other clients believe that they can transfer legal title to assets while retaining control of the assets, and still have those assets excluded from their taxable estates. This is generally not true. Estate tax laws tax not only what you legally own, but what you control at death. For example, you cannot transfer legal title to your home to your children, continue to live in it rent-free for the rest of your life, *and* have the value of the home excluded from your taxable estate. The fact that you live in the home indicates that you are enjoying the use of it and controlling it while you are alive, despite the fact that the legal title has been transferred. Fortunately, there are several exceptions to this general rule, estate planning techniques that allow a senior family member to transfer value for estate tax purposes but still retain control of investment decisions and distributions. These techniques are discussed in Chapter 6.

FEAR OF DEALING WITH ATTORNEYS

For a woman, part of the fear of hiring an estate planning attorney may involve a fear of being thought stupid, uninformed, or silly. A woman may also have a fear of being patronized, gouged by fees, or not listened to, particularly if her husband is participating in the process with her. All of these concerns are valid.

If you are married, your first concern should be to decide whether you and your husband should retain the same estate planning attorney or seek separate legal counsel. Many factors enter into this decision. For example, if either you or your husband have children from a previous marriage, there may be a real need for separate legal counsel to protect those children. If you have children from a prior marriage but your husband does not, you have two concerns—your husband and your children. You may want to seek separate estate planning counsel to ensure that you are protecting the interests of both husband and children adequately in the best possible way. If you and your husband were to meet together with the same estate planning attorney, you might be less inclined to express your true wishes in front of your husband if those wishes would result in his receiving less than your entire estate or less than he expected to receive. In this situation, you might feel less constraint if you consulted with an attorney of your own choosing.

Even if you and your husband have been married for 40 years and have children only by each other, you might have other concerns. If your husband has been in the business world for those 40 years and you have not, you might fear being ignored in the estate planning process. Remember that there are plenty of estate planning attorneys out there, and your first meeting with any attorney should be viewed as an interview. Most estate planning attorneys are happy to meet with potential clients for half an hour to an hour at no charge to get acquainted, review the situation, and provide estimates of fees. During that interview, if you sense for any reason that an attorney is ignoring or patronizing you, then simply use a prearranged signal to let your husband know that it's thumbs down for this attorney. Thank the attorney for his or her time, then leave.

Perhaps you are afraid that an attorney will think your specific wishes and desires are silly. This fear usually comes into play with respect to pets and burial instructions. Particularly for single people and childless couples, pets are very special. People often care deeply about who will have custody of their pets and want to make sure that funds are provided for the lifetime care of their pets.

Likewise, a person might have very specific instructions regarding the disposition of his or her body or how the funeral should be conducted. These concerns should be as serious and important to an estate planning attorney as they are to you. You should not feel hesitant about expressing any such desires or concerns frankly. If an attorney you have chosen does not take such concerns as seriously as you do, look for another attorney.

FINDING AN ESTATE PLANNING ATTORNEY

Law is a highly specialized field today, and estate planning is a subspecialty of a general specialization in tax law. An estate planning attorney must have a good grounding in the particular area of the tax law that relates to transfer taxes (taxes imposed on the privilege of transferring assets from one generation to the next). Estate planning attorneys must also be trained in probate law and procedure, with a smattering of knowledge in real estate, family law, elder law, and perhaps tax-exempt organizations. While the services of an estate planning specialist are always desirable, they are essential in cases involving taxable estates, second marriages, or unorthodox estate plans. The closest analogy that can be made is with the medical profession. Would you allow your family doctor to perform bypass surgery on your husband or plastic surgery on your face? Of course not. In each case, you would seek the best specialist you could find. Law is no different from medicine. You may be thrilled with advice you receive from your company's corporate counsel, but keep in mind that he or she is a corporate attorney—schooled and trained and experienced in corporate law. To expect the same performance from an attorney trained and experienced in one area of law in a totally different area is no different from expecting your family doctor to be able to perform a facelift or bypass surgery. You need a legal specialist just as you would a plastic surgeon or a medical specialist.

So how do you go about finding an estate planning attorney? You might start your search with the recommendation of a friend or by calling a legal professional association.

Friends

If any of your friends have recently undertaken estate planning, find out who they used. Call the attorney's office and ask for some biographical information by mail. You already know that the attorney at least holds himself or herself out as an estate planning attorney, because he or she has already provided some estate planning services to your friend. At this point, you will want to verify that the attorney is in fact trained and qualified as an estate planning attorney. Most attorneys have resumes and brochures that they are happy to mail out to inquirers. Review this information, looking for activities that indicate the attorney is involved in the estate planning area. Such activities might include articles the attorney has written, organizations he or she is involved in, or presentations he or she has made. If, from the information you receive, you are satisfied that the attorney is involved in the estate planning area, then you may want to go to your local public library and consult the *Law Directory* (published by Martindale-Hubbell), a directory that rates attorneys. Attorneys listed in the *Law Directory* are rated by their peers. Attorneys with an "AV" rating have the highest rating of their peers, "BV" is good, and "CV" is average. Don't deal with an attorney who has no rating.

State Bar Associations

Call the bar association in your state and ask for the names and phone numbers of several estate planning attorneys in your city. Members of a state bar association may join sections of the bar relating to probate, tax, and estate planning (such as the "fiduciary section" or the "tax section"). Any of these would be possibilities. You should still do further investigations, however, because in some states, all an attorney has to do to join a section is pay an additional fee. After receiving names from the state bar association, you should follow the same procedures you would to verify the qualifications of an attorney referred by a friend.

American College of Trust and Estate Counsel (ACTEC)

ACTEC is a group of 2,500 estate planning attorneys, each of whom has a minimum of 10 years experience and has been elected to membership in the organization based on his or her expertise in and contribution to the estate planning field. Even an attorney with ACTEC credentials should be checked out, however. Call ACTEC at (310) 398-1888 and ask for a list of members in your geographic area.

If there is a local Estate Planning Council (The Atlanta Estate Planning Council, for example) listed in your phone book, call and ask for a list of members. Five years of experience in the estate planning area is required for membership.

Interviewing an Attorney Candidate

Having satisfied yourself that an attorney is technically qualified, the next step is to interview the attorney personally to see if the "vibes" are right. There are always personality issues involved in dealing with professionals, and you will want to ensure that the attorney you choose treats you with respect, concern, and fairness. When you call to make an appointment, ask if the attorney gives an initial complimentary interview. Most estate planning attorneys do, so you might choose to limit your interviews to three or four attorneys who will meet with you on a complimentary basis.

At the interview, be sure to ask how the attorney charges. Most estate planning attorneys charge on either a flat fee basis or an hourly basis. For documents which the attorney prepares regularly, a flat fee might be the norm. However, when an attorney does something out of the ordinary, an hourly basis is more common. Some attorneys (particularly in certain states) typically charge a percentage of the estate to administer it, but this can be negotiated at the outset—for example, to an hourly basis. If an attorney charges on an hourly basis, ask for an estimate of the number of hours it will take to get the job done. Also ask about additional charges for services such as copying, faxing, word processing, paralegal time, express mail, and so on. Most law firms charge for these services over and above the legal fees.

Many attorneys will send an engagement letter setting out the terms of your agreement regarding his or her services and fees. If the attorney does not mention such a letter during your interview, ask him or her to estimate the fee (including any additional expenses) in writing.

Be especially wary of attorneys who write themselves into your will as the estate's legal counsel. Sometimes these attorneys may charge very little (even nothing) for preparing the will, only to take a huge fee, in the form of a percentage of the estate, for acting as the estate's legal counsel later.

COMMUNICATING YOUR WISHES TO AN ESTATE PLANNING ATTORNEY

When you are interviewing attorneys, whether with your husband or alone, a few pointers from corporate trainer and executive speech coach Marian K. Woodall might help you avoid having an attorney patronize or ignore you. In her book, *How to Talk So Men Will Listen,* Woodall observes that women use language to build relationships, whereas men use language to exchange ideas. Therefore, for example, if a woman is dealing with a male attorney, she cannot be taken seriously if she rambles on (attempting to build a relationship) when he is simply trying to get to the bottom line quickly. Women have certain strengths as communicators, such as listening well, asking questions, facilitating group problem-solving, reading nonverbal cues, and reacting sensitively to the opinions of others. Women's weaknesses as communicators include using too many details, failing to distinguish between the important and the trivial, being indecisive, allowing interruptions, using an unassertive voice, and having inadequate eye contact.

Woodall's advice to women for getting men to listen to them and treat them as equals in any situation is:

- *Look like an equal.* Dress the part.

- *Act like an equal.* Sit up straight, look the other person directly in the eye, and if you are interrupted, either keep talking using a louder or firmer tone of voice, or say, "I'll be glad to continue when you finish."

- *Feel like an equal.*

Remember, you are the boss because you are paying the bill. You have every right to expect the attorney you hire to hang onto your every word. Woodall wisely urges all of us to get to the bottom line in a hurry and say less than we want to say.

She notes, "Powerful people know what they want to say. They say it in a concise, precise manner. They say it with force and emphasis in their voices. They say it with good idea contact. They say it with good posture. They say it with assertive behavior."

MAKING TOUGH DECISIONS THAT AFFECT THE FAMILY

After dealing with the fear of death, the fear of giving up control, and the fear of dealing with attorneys, you must face the tough emotional issues that affect the family. If there is a family business, an estate plan might involve having to select one of several children to ultimately control the business (and perhaps even own all or a majority of the stock). Other tough emotional issues arise when a child has deeply disappointed the parents by choosing a lifestyle of which they do not approve. Do the parents treat such a child the same as his or her siblings, or do they reduce—or even eliminate—that child's share from their wills? If one child is a world-class money manager and another constantly seeking loans, which should be appointed executor at the surviving parent's death? Which should be given the power of attorney and health care power of attorney? How much should be set aside for charities?

These are tough emotional issues, and in some cases, estates wind up in litigation for years because of the choices the parents make. Your attorney can educate you and suggest options, but you must ultimately make these tough decisions yourself. I recently met with a client who owns a very successful business with approximately 300 employees. His two sons are involved in the business, but his daughter, a spendthrift, is not. When the father prepared his will, he omitted his daughter from inheriting any part of his business. He then sat down and read the will to all three children. As he expected, his daughter was furious. But he told her, "Honey, you can't even manage your own finances. I certainly can't trust this business to you." He made other provisions for his daughter, and he wanted to look her in the eye and tell her exactly why he was doing what he was doing. After a month of silence, she was her old self again, much to her father's delight. This man loves his daughter, enjoys her company, and often helps her out financially. But with 300 jobs on the line, he couldn't risk giving her a share of the business.

My job as an estate planning attorney is to help my clients do what they want to do. I do not sit in judgment on whatever choices they make. They know far more about their children, their businesses, and their assets than I do. My job is to be a good listener, to provide advice and options, to try to help people work through emotional issues to reach their own logical conclusions and to help them keep the ball rolling. No matter how tough such decisions are to make, it's better than having someone else make them for you after your death. And that's exactly what will happen if you don't exercise your right to do it for yourself.

The Language and Tools of Estate Planning

Terms and Documents Used by Estate Planning Attorneys

"Legalese—an obscure language based on Latin, and hopefully destined for the same fate . . ."

—D. Robert White, Esquire
White's Law Dictionary

You have the choice of giving away your property in one of two basic ways: you may give gifts of property now, or you may designate persons to receive your property later. A *gift* is the voluntary permanent transfer of property from one individual to another without receipt of value in return for the gift. If you hand your son a check for $5,000 at graduation, title your old car in your daughter's name for her 16th birthday, forgive a $100 loan you made to your neighbor, or sell your $15,000 sailboat to your grandson for one dollar, you have made a gift. If you set up a joint bank account with your own money for yourself and your mother, you have made a gift to her if and when she withdraws money from the account.

A *beneficiary* is simply someone "who benefits from the act of another."[1] If you pay a neighbor's son $25 to mow your mother's yard every two weeks, you have designated your mother as the beneficiary of a contract with your neighbor's son and, in so doing, you have made a legal gift of the value of that service to her. If you name your husband as the beneficiary of your life insurance policy, you have made a gift to him of the value of that policy, which takes effect only at your death. In addition to outright gifts, your estate planning attorney may recommend that you use trusts, wills, and deeds to accomplish your goals and objectives. These tools will be defined later in this chapter.

WILLS

At your death, you have an opportunity to give away your property by your will. A *will* is a written instrument by which you indicate your wishes as to the distribution of your property after your death. It serves as your set of instructions regarding who gets your property after your death. A gift made by the terms of your will is called a *testamentary gift* and does not take effect until after your death. A *testamentary trust* is created by the terms of your will, but property is not transferred to a testamentary trust until after your death.

A will is revocable until your death. In other words, you may change the instructions in your will in any way at any time. To make these changes, you may wish to execute a whole new will or modify portions of your existing will by executing a codicil. A *codicil* is a written supplement or addition to a will which may revoke, explain, alter, amend, modify, and/or add to the provisions of the will.[2]

If you have a valid will when you die, you are said to die *testate*. The *testator* (male) or the *testatrix* (female) is the person who executes (or makes out) the will. A gift made by the terms of a will may be called a bequest, a devise, or a legacy. A *bequest* or a *legacy* is a gift by will of personal property (i.e., stocks, bonds, or cash). A *general bequest* is a gift paid out of the general assets of your estate.[3] For example: *I hereby give, devise, and bequeath one-fourth of the rest and residue of my estate to my son, William.* A *specific bequest* is a gift of a particular item. For example: *I hereby bequeath to my daughter Sharon my grandmother's pearl necklace.* A *devise* is a gift by will of real property. It is common to see the terms *bequest, devise,* and *legacy* interchanged.

A will is important not only because it sets forth your wishes as to the ultimate distribution of your property, but also because it serves as a tool for naming the important people who will carry out your wishes and take care of your property and the interests of your beneficiaries. In your will, you may name a *trustee* to hold property for the benefit of family members, friends, or organizations, or a *guardian* to hold the property of your minor children. You may also name a *guardian of the person* (and an alternate) of your minor children, who may or may not be the same individual as the guardian of the property. If both biological or adoptive parents are deceased, a guardian of the person is given custody of a minor child and has the duty of caring for and raising that minor child until he or she reaches the age of majority.

It is necessary for you to name an executor or executrix (and alternates) in your will. The *executor* (male) or *executrix* (female), as representative of your estate, is the person responsible for carrying out the wishes set forth in your will. Your executor or executrix will probate your will, pay any final debts, receive payment from any outstanding creditors, file any necessary tax returns and distribute your property to your trustees or beneficiaries. An *administrator* (or *administratrix*) is the person appointed by the court to handle your estate if you die without a will or fail to name an executor (or executrix) in your will.

Even if you have a will, you must be certain that you have properly executed it. All states have laws that tell you how you must execute your will. If you do not follow these laws, your will is not valid. An invalid will is the same as no will at all. Also, if you execute a will in one state and then move to another, you must check the laws of the new state to ensure that your will is still valid.

In order for a will to be valid, a few basic requirements (which are generally the same in all states) must be met. In most states, you must be at least 18 years old to make a valid will (in Georgia, however, you may be as young as 14, and in Wyoming, you must be at least 19). All states require that you have sufficient mental capacity (or *testamentary capacity*) to make a will. Typically, state laws will require that you be of "sound mind" to sign a will, although what it means to be of sound mind is rarely defined. In general, state courts have found persons to have sufficient mental capacity to make a will if they understand: (1) the nature and extent of their property (what it is and how much they have); (2) the persons who are the natural objects of their bounty (children, spouses, and other family members); and (3) the disposition they are making of their property (how they are giving it away and to whom they are giving it by the terms of their wills).[4] In addition, a person executing a will must have *testamentary intent*. This means that you must intend for the document you are writing to serve as your will or as the final disposition of all your property. Testamentary intent is usually clear from the language used in the document.

Other technical requirements for making a will valid include: (1) having at least one substantive provision in your will (one provision giving some, if not all, of your property away); (2) naming at least one executor; (3) dating the will; and (4) signing the will in the presence of at least two witnesses. A *witness* is someone who watches you sign your will and then signs the will himself or herself. In most states, a person not capable of making a will (due to mental incapacity or being a minor) is also not capable of witnessing a will. In addition, many states will not permit as witnesses blood relatives of the testator or testatrix or any individual named to receive property under the will.

Most states require that your will be typewritten or printed from a computer. A few states recognize *holographic wills*, wills that are wholly handwritten by the testator or testatrix. Although holographic wills must be entirely handwritten, signed, and dated by the testator or testatrix, they do not have to be witnessed.

A will does not have to be signed and stamped by a *notary public* in order to be valid. (A notary public is an individual who has been authorized by the state to administer oaths and to attest, by his or her signature and official seal, to the authenticity of signatures.[5]) Some states permit the testator or testatrix (and his or her witnesses) to sign a notarized affidavit that makes his or her will *self-proving*. To probate a will, states require that at least one of the witnesses to the will offered for probate be located for the purpose of testifying as to the validity of the will and the signatures thereon. A self-proving affidavit serves as this testimony and thereby avoids the delay and expense of locating the witnesses at the time of probate.

In California, Maine, Michigan, New Mexico, and Washington, *statutory wills* are recognized as valid wills. Statutory wills are preprinted documents with boxes to check and lines to complete. They are called statutory wills because they are authorized by state law (or state statute).

A few states also accept *oral wills* or *nuncupative wills* if such wills are made under special circumstances, such as by a soldier dying on the battlefield. However, the one to whom the will is "told" may be required to later write down the provisions spoken to him or her.[6] In addition, state law may require that a testator "tell" his will in the presence of at least two individuals.[7] Videotaped wills are not valid in any state.

Two individuals, usually a married couple, may wish to have one will. Such *joint wills* are signed by both individuals. A joint will usually directs that the survivor is to receive all property upon the death of the first spouse. A joint will also contains provisions controlling the ultimate disposition of the couple's property upon the death of the survivor. The reason a couple may wish to have a joint will is to prevent one spouse from disinheriting the couple's children in favor of a second husband or wife after the death of the first spouse. However, a joint will may cause transfer tax problems and cloud the title to property, thereby restricting the transferability of the property until the second death.

If you have a revocable or living trust, as explained later in this chapter, you may choose to execute a *pour-over will*. The distributative provisions of a pour-over will direct that any property remaining in your estate at your death should be distributed to the trustee of your revocable living trust.

TRUSTS

A *trust* is a tool that can be used before or after your death. A trust can be created by an agreement you sign (like a contract) or by a provision in your will. If you transfer property to a trust you have created, you are making a gift to the beneficiaries of that trust. Generally, a trust is an arrangement by which one person transfers property to a second person to hold and administer for the benefit of one or more beneficiaries. The property transferred to the trust is the *trust corpus, trust res,* or *trust principal.*

The transferor of the property to the trust is known as either the *grantor, settlor,* or *trustor* of the trust. Each of these terms refers to the same person, and they may be used interchangeably. The person holding and administering the property in the trust is called the *trustee.* The trustor and trustee may be the same person. In addition, the trustor may be a beneficiary of his or her own trust.

If a trust agreement is in writing, it is an *express trust.* An express trust must clearly show that the trustor intends by the writing to create a trust.[8] Trusts may be revocable or irrevocable. A *revocable trust* may be revoked, amended, or changed in any way and at any time by the trustor. In creating a revocable trust, the trustor does not give up total control over the trust property during his or her lifetime, because he or she can always revoke the trust and regain possession and control of the trust property. A revocable trust is used by residents of some states to minimize the amount of property passing through probate. An *irrevocable trust* may never be revoked, amended, or changed in any way without a court order.

As will be explained in detail in Chapter 5, a revocable trust may also be called a *grantor trust.* For income tax purposes, the trustor of a revocable trust (or grantor trust) is treated as the owner of the trust property as if he or she had never given it to the trust. In addition, there is no gift of any of the revocable trust property from the trustor to any beneficiary until the beneficiary actually receives a distribution from the trust.

Example: On December 24, Marianne transfers 5,000 shares of IBM stock to her son, David, as trustee of an irrevocable trust for the benefit of her granddaughter, Sally. David is instructed to pay the trust income to Sally at the end of each year and is to distribute all of the stock held in the trust to Sally on her 30th birthday. Marianne is the *trustor* or *grantor* of the trust. Sally is the trust's *beneficiary*. David is the *trustee*. The stock is the *trust corpus* or *res*. Because stock earns dividends, the dividends paid by IBM to the trust constitute the income of the trust. Because the trust is irrevocable, Marianne can never get the stock back and cannot designate anyone other than Sally as the beneficiary of the trust. From a legal standpoint, because the trust is irrevocable, Marianne has made a gift of the value of the stock to the trust on December 24. If the trust had been revocable, Marianne would not have made a gift of the stock until the trust terminated and David transferred all of the stock outright to Sally.

A *revocable living trust* is a revocable trust that you create during your lifetime. Property you transfer to a revocable living trust is removed from your probate estate, although it is not removed from your taxable estate. Living trusts may be used to:

- avoid probate

- manage property for the benefit of yourself and other family members who may not be able to do so for themselves due to their minority, mental incapacity, immaturity, or inexperience

- ensure privacy at your death, because a trust, unlike a will, does not have to be filed with the local probate court, which makes the will public record

Common trusts created by wills are *marital trusts* and *credit shelter trusts*. These trusts also may be created at the time of your death by the terms of your revocable living trust. A marital trust is a trust created for the benefit of your spouse if he survives you. The surviving spouse will usually have a life income interest in the trust property, and then at the surviving spouse's death the property passes to the children. A credit shelter trust (also sometimes referred to as the *family* or *residuary trust*) is created to receive the $600,000 amount (increasing to $1 million by 2006) that is exempt by law from federal and state taxation in the estate of the first spouse to die. (See Chapter 4 for a complete explanation of the transfer tax system.) Placing this exemption amount in the credit shelter trust further protects it from taxation in the survivor's estate at his or her death. The credit shelter trust may be created for the benefit of the surviving spouse, children, grandchildren, other family members, and/or charitable organizations.

DEEDS

Deeds are frequently used in estate planning. A deed is simply a written document by which one person transfers property to another. A deed may be used for personal property (*a deed of gift*) as well as for real property. A deed usually contains the name of the *grantor* (the person transferring the property), the name of the *grantee* (the person receiving the property), a description of the property being transferred, and the date of the transfer. The grantor is required by law to sign the deed, and in some instances (such as when a taxable gift of personal property is being made) the grantee should probably sign the deed as well. In all states, real property deeds must be notarized and recorded in one of the courts of the county in which the property is located.

A *warranty deed* is a type of deed in which the grantor warrants that he or she has "good title" to the property that he or she is transferring (or conveying). By warranting that he or she has good title, the grantor is promising: (1) that there are no liens or other encumbrances upon the property about which the grantor has not provided notice to the grantee; and (2) that no third parties have any rights with respect to that land which would interfere with the grantee's possession and use of it at any time. The grantee who receives a warranty deed has received the maximum security available against claims by third parties.

A *limited warranty deed* reduces the grantor's liability for defects in the title. Defects in title may be encumbrances placed on the property or claims of better title in existence prior to the purchase of the property by grantor. What the grantor promises when he or she executes a limited warranty deed is that *he or she* did nothing that might interfere with the grantee's right to the possession or use of the land. The grantor, however, is not willing to guarantee that no prior owner did the same.

A *quitclaim deed* passes title to land as effectively as does a warranty deed.[9] However, a quitclaim deed does not include any warranties.

If property is being transferred from an estate to a beneficiary, the executor will sign an *executor's deed.* The provisions of an executor's deed state that:

- The property being transferred by the deed belonged to the decedent at the time of death.

- The decedent's will has been probated.

- All debts of the estate have been settled.

- The property is free from any claim.

- The property is now ready for transfer to the beneficiary.

If the property is being transferred to the decedent's *heirs at law* (legal heirs) because there was no will, the deed used to transfer the property is called an *administrator's deed*. A transfer from a trust to a beneficiary is accomplished by means of a *trustee's deed*.

A *security deed* or *deed to secure debt* transfers land that is security for a debt owed by the grantor to the grantee. A true security deed, unlike a mortgage, passes actual title to the land, even if repayment of the debt will cause the land to be reconveyed to the grantor, who is the debtor.[10]

STATUTORY INHERITANCE

If you choose *not* to give your property away yourself during your lifetime or to leave instructions to someone else to give it away after your death, your state of residence has already decided how to give your property away for you. If you do not have a valid will when you die, you are said to die *intestate*. Every state has a set of laws—called *laws of descent and distribution*, *intestacy laws*, *laws of intestate succession*, or *rules of inheritance*—controlling the manner in which your property is distributed after your death if you have failed to provide for distribution by the execution of a valid will.

Under the terms of these laws, your *heirs at law* are entitled to share in the distribution of your property after your death. Heirs at law (or legal heirs) are simply those individuals designated by state law to share in the distribution of the property of a person who dies without a valid will.[11] They are not necessarily the blood relatives of such person. Spouses and adopted children may be heirs at law even though they are not blood relatives. Under some state statutes the term *next of kin* also may be used in the same manner as "heirs at law" or "legal heirs," although next of kin also may mean those closest blood relations of the person who has died.

Most intestacy laws establish degrees of inheritance. As an example, under the rules of inheritance of most states, the first rule is that if a man or woman dies without lineal descendants but with a surviving spouse, the surviving spouse is entitled to the entire estate of the deceased person.[12] *Lineal descendants* are those persons in the direct line of descent, such as a child or grandchild.[13] *Collateral descendants*, such as nieces and nephews, are more distantly related. However, if there is no surviving spouse, but there are children living, state laws generally provide that the children will inherit equally all property of the deceased.[14] Brothers and sisters and the parents of the deceased generally stand equally to inherit if there are no children or grandchildren. Maternal and paternal grandparents, then uncles and aunts (or their children if they are no longer living) come next in line for the inheritance.[15]

Most states have laws that protect a surviving spouse from being disinherited or left with very little property, even if the deceased spouse's will expressly excludes the surviving spouse from inheriting anything. These laws actually trump the terms of a will, although if you have provided even a small amount for your spouse in your will, your spouse may have to choose between taking the inheritance provided for him under the terms of your will or taking that which is provided for him by the state law. These laws protecting spouses were developed from old English concepts that were created to prevent the disinheritance of surviving spouses and adopted by early American courts. Under the old common law, *dower* was the right of a widow to her husband's property after his death, and *curtesy* was the right of a widower to his wife's property after her death. Today most states have adopted laws that provide modified forms of dower and curtesy. These laws usually give the surviving spouse the right to an *elective share* of the deceased spouse's property. The term *elective share* is used because the surviving spouse must usually elect to take against the inheritance left to her under her husband's will in order to be entitled to the share set aside by the state law. The size of the share varies from state to state, usually ranging from one-third to one-half of the deceased's spouse's estate. In addition, the size of the share usually varies according to the number of minor children, if any, who also survive, because they may also be entitled to a share.

MORE ESTATE PLANNING LEGALESE

Before deciding who gets what and how and when, it is important to understand what assets you have and their value. Your *estate* is the equivalent of your *net worth* (i.e., your assets minus your liabilities). Your *taxable estate* is the portion of your estate subject to the federal estate tax. Your taxable estate is computed by subtracting from the value of your estate (also called the *gross estate* by the Internal Revenue Code) certain deductions permitted by the IRS (discussed in Chapter 4).[16]

Your *probate estate* is not the same as your taxable estate. *Probate* is the legal process by which a deceased person's will is filed with the probate court of the county in which he or she lived at the time of death. Then, under the supervision of that court, the executor or administrator of the estate will proceed to pay the deceased individual's debts, receive payments from his or her creditors, take possession of his or her property, and distribute such property by the terms of the will. Thus, your probate estate consists of that property that must pass through probate before it is distributed by the terms of your will to your beneficiaries. Property that passes to selected beneficiaries at the time of your death by virtue of the instructions set forth in a contract (i.e., beneficiary designations) such as a life insurance policy or a living trust agreement is not part of your probate estate. Property that passes automatically by law to a surviving joint tenant is not part of your probate estate either. (Joint tenancy is discussed later in this chapter.)

Example: Linda has no debts and owns property worth $1 million at the time of her death. This property includes an insurance policy with a $500,000 face value, a house worth $200,000, and stocks worth $300,000. Linda had named her sister, Sue, as the beneficiary of her life insurance policy. In her will, Linda has left all of her property to her mother, Jean. Linda's taxable estate is $1 million. Her probate estate is only $500,000 (the combined value of her house and stocks), because the proceeds from her life insurance policy pass by contract designation to Sue. If Linda had designated her estate (the Estate of Linda Smith) rather than Sue as the beneficiary of her life insurance policy, then the proceeds of the policy would have been paid to her estate and would have been part of her probate estate as well as her taxable estate. Furthermore, under the terms of her will, the estate would have distributed the proceeds to her mother rather than to Sue.

WHO'S WHO IN WILLS AND TRUSTS

Usually the most important personal decision you make in estate planning is choosing which family members, friends, and organizations (such as churches, schools, and charities) will get your property (and which will not). The persons and organizations you designate to share in the distribution of your property are your *beneficiaries.* You may designate beneficiaries by will, by trust, or by contract. A person to whom you give real property by your will is called a *devisee.*[17] A person to whom you give personal property by your will is called a *legatee.*[18]

It is common for an individual to have concerns about how to include provisions for the proper care of his or her spouse in an estate plan (although, as alluded to earlier, the question may sometimes actually be one of exclusion). A very few states (among them Alabama, Colorado, District of Columbia, Idaho, Iowa, Kansas, Montana, Oklahoma, Pennsylvania, Rhode Island, South Carolina, and Texas), recognize the concept of *common-law marriage*.[19] In these states, a man and woman will be considered legally married if they have lived together for a certain number of years, have intended to be husband and wife, and have held themselves out to others as husband and wife.

After your spouse, it is likely that your children will be your next concern when planning your estate. Legal restrictions may affect the ability of your children to own your property if they are minors at the time of your death. A *minor* is any person who is under the age of legal competence.[20] In most states, a person is no longer a minor if he or she is at least 18 years of age. (However, in some states he or she may not be able to legally own property until age 21.) *Posthumous children* are children born after the death of a parent. A state's laws of intestate succession may permit these children to share in the estate of the deceased.[21]

Most states have laws permitting *pretermitted heirs* to claim a share of the deceased parent's estate (or grandparent's estate if the parent is deceased) even if it reduces the shares passing to the surviving spouse or other descendants. Preterermitted heirs are those children (or children of a child who has predeceased you) whom you fail to expressly mention in your will. Thus, if you intend to disinherit a child, you should name him or her in your will and then either leave that child a small sum (say, a dollar) or expressly state your intention to disinherit that child. Otherwise, your estate may be subject to a lawsuit brought by that child on the grounds that you forgot the child in executing the will.

You may wish to treat your *adopted children*, if any, the same as your natural-born children in the final distribution of your property. State laws of descent and distribution which control intestate succession may or may not include adopted children among the classes of individuals who will share in the distribution of the estate of an individual who dies without a valid will.[22] In interpreting the specific language of wills, courts have debated for years over whether the term *children* includes adopted children as well. Therefore, if you have adopted children, it may be particularly important for you to not only have a valid will, but also to expressly mention in the will that you desire for your adopted children to be treated the same as your natural-born children for purposes of the will. On the other hand, if your children have entered into second or third marriages and have adopted the natural-born children of the second or third spouse, you may wish to expressly exclude such adopted grandchildren from sharing in the distribution of your estate.

As with adopted children, it is important to clarify your intentions as to *children born out-of-wedlock* or *illegitimate children*. Most states agree that, for purposes of the rules of inheritance, a child born out-of-wedlock may inherit from his or her mother or from any relatives or other children of his or her mother as would any legitimate child.[23] However, by law, a child born out-of-wedlock usually may inherit from his or her biological father only if the father has legally acknowledged that he is the child's father (such as by written statement or signature on the child's birth certificate) or if paternity has been conclusively established by a court of law.[24] In some states, if the father takes the child into his home or later marries the mother, such actions will also establish paternity for inheritance purposes.

WHATIZIT?

Some people have more and others have less, but all estates are made up of property—tangible property, intangible property, real property, or a combination of the three. *Tangible personal property* is property that may be touched or felt.[25] It includes jewelry, cars, antique furniture, china, silver, clothing and furs, television sets and stereo equipment, and stamp and coin collections. Tangible personal property may also be referred to as *personalty*, *personal effects*, *household effects*, or *household goods*. *Intangible property* is property that has no intrinsic and marketable value but is representative of value.[26] Examples of intangible property include stock certificates, bond certificates, promissory notes, patents, trademarks, copyrights, royalty rights, and franchise rights. Patents, trademarks, and copyrights may also be known as *intellectual property*. Cash, checking accounts, savings accounts, money market accounts, and certificates of deposit as well as stocks and bonds traded on the securities exchanges—all of which may be called your *liquid assets*—also are part of your property.

Real property and *real estate* are the same thing. Real property or real estate is land and anything that is affixed to or erected upon the land.[27] These *fixtures* include such things as buildings, fences, barns, and greenhouses, as well as items affixed to such structures such as lightposts or mailboxes. The term *real property* may also include things growing on the land (crops or timber) or rights derived from the land (water, mineral, oil, or gas rights).

There are several different ways you may own real and personal property. The way in which you own property will dictate what part of it (if any) you may give away. State law defines the various types of ownership. If you own real property, the laws of the state in which that real property is located are applicable to your real property even if you do not live in that state. As for your personal property, the laws of the state in which you live or are *domiciled* will be applicable. Your *domicile* is the place you permanently live and where you intend to return even if you are residing elsewhere.[28] You may have more than one *residence*—for example, a foreign residence if you are studying abroad for a year, a vacation residence if you spend the summer at your beach home, or a country residence if your family owns a horse farm—but for purposes of property ownership, you can only have one domicile.

The deed to your house or your Coca-Cola stock certificate may say that you and your husband own that property as "*joint tenants,*" as "*joint tenants and not as tenants in common,*" or as "*joint tenants with rights of survivorship.*" A *joint tenancy* is created when two or more persons purchase or are given property at the same time. Each joint tenant owns an undivided interest in the whole property and each has the equal right to use, enjoy, possess, occupy, or rent the property. The *right of survivorship* means that, upon the death of one of the joint tenants, the property does not pass through probate but automatically belongs to the surviving tenant or tenants by operation of law. Therefore, a provision in your will that attempts to give away property that you own as a joint tenant with right of survivorship will have no effect on the transfer of that property at your death.

Tenancy by the entirety is a form of joint tenancy created between a husband and wife and is recognized in only a few states (Arkansas, Delaware, District of Columbia, Florida, Hawaii, Maryland, Massachusetts, Mississippi, Missouri, Oklahoma, Pennsylvania, Tennessee, Vermont and—for real estate only—Alaska, Indiana, Kentucky, Michigan, New Jersey, New York, North Carolina, Oregon, Virginia, and Wyoming). If a couple owns property as tenants in the entirety, then, without the consent of the other, neither party can mortgage, transfer, or otherwise deal with the property in any way that would affect the rights of the other. Dissolution of the marriage changes the tenancy by the entirety to a tenancy in common.[29]

A *tenancy in common*, which is the most common form of property ownership in most states, is created when two or more persons own property together but also own separate titles in the property. Property owners who own property as tenants in common may or may not own the same percentage of the property. One may own 25 percent of it and the other 75 percent. There is no right of survivorship in a tenancy in common, and each owner may do as he or she wishes with his or her interest in the property—such as sell it, mortgage it, or give it away—without the consent or even the knowledge of the other owner or owners.

Some states, which are called *community property states*, have special laws defining how you own property if you are married. These laws affect your ownership of both personal property and real property and dictate what portion of your property you may give away. The community property states are Arizona, California, Idaho, Nevada, New Mexico, Louisiana, Texas, and Washington. (Wisconsin has adopted the Uniform Marital Property Act, which is similar in many respects to the laws of the community property states.) In a community property state, the law provides that any property purchased or earned by a married couple during the course of their marriage is owned equally by each. Salary earned by one spouse at his or her job is deemed to be owned 50-50 by both spouses. Property purchased by one spouse with money he or she earned during the marriage is owned 50-50 by both spouses. A house one spouse owned before the marriage but which she transfered by deed into her name and her husband's name is owned 50-50 by the two of them. Property one spouse receives as a gift or a bequest, however, is not community property, and property one spouse owned before the marriage and that he or she has kept segregated from the community property during the marriage (in a separate bank account or in a trust) is generally not community property, but *separate property*.

TIMING IS EVERYTHING

In estate planning, not only do you get to choose who gets your property and what property they get, but you also get to decide how they will own it and when they will actually get it. The most common and most simple way to transfer property is to do so as an *outright gift* or *bequest*. This simply means that you have transferred property to another person without placing any restraints or restrictions on his or her ownership of the property. The person to whom you have transferred the property immediately takes full and absolute possession of the property. A *transfer in trust*, as previously explained, is when you give property to one person, the trustee, to hold for the benefit of another person or persons, the beneficiaries. The trust agreement you sign with the trustee will set forth the restrictions on ownership you wish to place upon the property. For example, the beneficiary may not be permitted to use the property until he or she is a designated age, or the beneficiary may receive only the income earned by the property each year.

An estate planning attorney may refer to a gift made during your lifetime as an *inter vivos* gift. *Inter vivos* means, literally, "between the living" or "from one living person to another."[30] An inter vivos gift takes effect during your lifetime. If you create an inter vivos trust, you intend for the trust to take effect during your lifetime.

You may be concerned about the complexities or expenses related to creating a trust for one of your family members, but due to the family member's age or mental capacity, you still would nevertheless like to delay or avoid his or her outright ownership of the property. As previously mentioned, the age of majority in most states is 18. However, most states limit the amount of property a child under the age of 18 may own or prohibit a child from owning property outright until he or she is 21. Therefore, a child under the age of 21 typically must have an adult managing and supervising his or her property. In legal terms, this adult, if not one of the child's legal parents, is the child's *custodian*, or *property guardian*, or *guardian of the property*.

All states except Connecticut, Delaware, Michigan, New York, Pennsylvania, South Carolina, Texas, and Vermont have adopted a law called the *Uniform Transfers to Minors Act* (*UTMA*), albeit modified to some extent by each adopting state. UTMA permits you to give property by either will or trust to a *custodian* who manages such property for your child. In addition, during your lifetime, you may transfer real estate or securities to the custodian for the benefit of your minor child under UTMA. There is one major drawback to using UTMA if your estate is large and you desire long-term management. In Arkansas, Maine, New Jersey, North Carolina, and Virginia, the UTMA custodianship ends when your child reaches age 18, which means that the child becomes the outright owner and gets full use and possession of all property held by the custodian when the child turns 18. In Alabama, Arizona, Colorado, Florida, Georgia, Hawaii, Idaho, Illinois, Indiana, Iowa, Kansas, Maryland, Massachusetts, Minnesota, Mississippi, Missouri, Montana, Nebraska, New Hampshire, New Mexico, North Dakota, Ohio, Oregon, Tennessee, Utah, Washington, West Virginia, Wisconsin, and Wyoming, the UTMA custodianship ends when your child reaches age 21. Under the version of UTMA adopted in Alaska, California, and Nevada, you may select the age (between the ages of 18 and 25) at which your child's custodianship will end.

Regardless of whether you leave someone property outright, in trust, or through a custodianship or guardianship, you may further restrict how they own that property. If you give your son a *life estate* in property, you have given him the right to use that property as if it were his during his lifetime. However, the person holding the life estate must protect and preserve the property and is not permitted to do anything to it that would irreparably damage or permanently injure the property.[31] Furthermore, the person holding the life estate may not sell the entire property. All he or she may sell is his or her life estate. These restrictions are placed on the life estate because every life estate is followed by a *remainder interest*. If you give someone a *remainder interest*, you have given that person the right to own the property after someone else has been allowed to use it for life or for a term of years. Instead of giving away the remainder interest, you may choose to have the property return to you or to your estate (in the event you die prior to the end of the life estate) after the life estate. What you have reserved for yourself or your estate is not a remainder interest in the property but a *reversion* (or *estate in reversion*).

A life estate, a remainder interest, and a reversion may be created by deed, by will, or by contract. Thus, you may give someone a life estate in property other than just real estate. If your will gives your daughter a right to receive the dividends from your IBM stock for her lifetime and further directs that, at her death, your grandson is to be given the stock outright, you have given your daughter a life estate and your grandson a remainder. However, when indicating that someone is to receive the income from certain property for life, we usually refer to that person as the *life income beneficiary* (or *income beneficiary*) and to what they have received as an *income interest*. The person who receives the *remainder interest* after the death of the income beneficiary is the *remainder beneficiary*.

DIVIDING UP THE PIE

When drafting your will, you may be concerned about property passing on to your grandchildren if any of your children should predecease you. Many times an individual will direct that, should a child predecease him or her, then the descendants of that child should take their deceased parent's share. However, if you have several children and each child has several children, you should note that you have two choices for dividing the property between all of them should a child predecease you. If you direct by will that your deceased child's share should pass to his or her descendants *per stirpes* (pronounced "stir peas"), what you mean is that your child's share will be divided equally among his or her descendants. Literally, the term *per stirpes* means "by roots or stocks"; in a legal sense, it means "by representation."[32]

Example: Item V of your will states: "I give, devise, and bequeath the remainder of my estate equally to my sons John and James. Should either of them predecease me, then such deceased child's share shall be distributed to his descendants then living *per stirpes*." John has two sons, Luke and Mark. John predeceases you, but your son James and grandsons Luke and Mark are living at the time of your death. Your will first directs that your estate should be divided as follows: one-half to your son James and one-half to your son John. Since John has predeceased you, however, Luke and Mark are to get their father's share. Therefore, your estate actually is divided as follows: one-half to James, and one-quarter to Luke, and one-quarter to Mark.

Although it is not as common to find such language in a will, laws of descent and distribution may direct that property pass *per capita* to the descendants of a deceased individual. Being the antithesis of *per stirpes*, the term *per capita* means "by the heads or polls" or "share and share alike."[33]

Example: Item V of your will states: "I give, devise, and bequeath the remainder of my estate equally to my daughters May and April. Should either of them predecease me, then such deceased child's descendants shall share in my estate *per capita*." May has two daughters, June and Sarah. April has two sons, Bobby and Benny. May predeceases you, but her daughters, June and Sarah, are living at your death. Your will first directs that your estate should be divided as follows: one-half to your daughter May and one-half to your daughter April. Since May has predeceased you, however, June and Sarah are to share in the distribution of your estate. Therefore, since you have chosen *per capita* distribution, your estate is divided as follows: one-third to your daughter April and one-third to your granddaughter June and one-third to your granddaughter Sarah—"share and share alike." (Remember from the previous example: If you had directed distribution to be made *per stirpes*, then April would have received one-half and the granddaughters would have received only one-quarter each).

Now that you can speak legalese, we can continue with our discussion of estate planning techniques.

NOTES

1. *Black's Law Dictionary*, 6th ed. (1990).

2. *Id.*

3. *Id.*

4. McGovern, William M., Jr., et al., *Wills, Trusts and Estates* (1988).

5. *Black's Law Dictionary*, 6th ed. (1990).

6. See O.C.G.A. (Official Code of Georgia Annotated) § 53-2-49 (requiring that the "substance of the testamentary dispositions of a nuncupative will must be reduced to writing within 30 days after the speaking of the same, or the will shall be invalid.")

7. See O.C.G.A. § 53-2-48(1) (requiring that the terms of a nuncupative will be proved "by the oaths of at least two competent witnesses who were present at the making thereof.")

8. O.C.G.A. § 53-12-20(b)(1).

9. See Pindar, George A. and Georgine S. Pindar, *Georgia Real Estate Law Practice and Procedure*, Vol. 2, 4th ed. (1993).

10. Pindar at § 19-10.

11. *Id.*

12. See O.C.G.A § 53-4-2(1).

13. *Black's Law Dictionary*, 6th ed. (1990).

14. See O.C.G.A. § 53-4-2(4).

15. O.C.G.A. § 53-4-2(5), (6), (8), (9), and (10).

16. I.R.C. § 2051.

17. *Black's Law Dictionary*, 6th ed. (1990).

18. *Id.*

19. Georgia courts recognized common-law marriages until such marriages were expressly prohibited by statute, O.C.G.A. § 19-3-11, effective as of July 1, 1996.

20. *Black's Law Dictionary*, 6th ed. (1990).

21. "Posthumous children shall stand upon the same footing with children in being upon all questions of inheritance." O.C.G.A. § 53-4-2(4).

22. As an example, under the Georgia rules of inheritance, adopted children are only mentioned in O.C.G.A. § 53-4-2(5), which states in part that "brothers and sisters adopted by a mutual parent of the intestate shall stand in the same degree and inherit equally from each other." Thus, there is no provision for the adopted children of the intestate, although his adopted brothers and sisters may receive a share of his or her estate.

23. "A child born out of wedlock may inherit in the same manner as if legitimate from and through his mother, from and through the other children of his mother, and from and through any other maternal kin, whether collateral or lineal." O.C.G.A. § 53-4-4(b).

24. See O.C.G.A. § 53-4-4(c).

25. *Black's Law Dictionary*, 6th ed. (1990).

26. *Id.*

27. *Id.*

28. *Id.*

29. *Id.*

30. *Id.*

31. O.C.G.A. § 44-6-83.

32. *Black's Law Dictionary*, 6th ed. (1990).

33. *Id.*

Federal Estate and Gift Taxes

What Is Taxed When We Leave This World?

Death and taxes and childbirth! There's never any convenient time for any of them.

—Margaret Mitchell, *Gone with the Wind*

The federal government imposes a tax on the privilege of transferring assets from one individual to another. These taxes are called estate taxes, gift taxes, and generation-skipping taxes. These transfer taxes (when they apply) are the highest taxes the government imposes on individuals.

HOW THE FEDERAL TRANSFER TAX SYSTEM WORKS

In 1997, the federal government allows an exemption from transfer taxes of $600,000 for every individual. Thus, in 1997, if the value of your federal taxable estate exceeds $600,000 at your death, your estate could owe federal estate tax. Federal estate tax rates are now higher than federal income tax rates. The marginal estate tax rates (the rates at which every dollar over $600,000 of estate assets will be taxed) start at 37 percent and rise to a maximum of 55 percent (plus an additional 5 percent tax on net taxable estates between $10,000,000 and $21,040,000, designed to create a maximum average overall rate of 55 percent for those leaving a taxable estate in excess of $21,040,000).

The exemption has been increased by the Taxpayer Relief Act of 1997. For years 1998–2006 the exemption is:

1998	$625,000	2003	750,000
1999	650,000	2004	850,000
2000	675,000	2005	950,000
2001	675,000	2006	1,000,000
2002	700,000		

When we talk of the exemption from this point on, it's the exemption as increased by Congress.

The federal transfer tax on the first $600,000 can be offset by the unified federal gift and estate tax credit in the amount of $192,800. (This is the amount of tax imposed on the transfer of the first $600,000 of your estate.) This credit offsets both gift and estate tax liabilities. To the extent that the credit is used to offset the tax on lifetime transfers, it is reduced and cannot be used to offset the tax on transfers at death. Consequently, unless your federal taxable estate exceeds $600,000, no federal estate tax will be owed (assuming that none of your $192,800 credit has been used previously to offset otherwise taxable gifts).

The federal estate tax rates are applied against your federal taxable estate. The taxable estate is basically the net value of all the property that you own at the time of death reduced by various deductions. The net taxable estate includes all property (1) which the decedent owned in whole or in part, and (2) over which he or she exercised control at the time of death. Examples of property included in the taxable estate are:

- life insurance policies *owned by the decedent* (whether on the decedent's life or the life of another, but if on the decedent's life, the face value of the policy is included);

- one-half of joint tenancies with right of survival which the decedent owned with a spouse;

- the portion of joint tenancy property owned with a nonspouse beneficiary that represents the percentage of property the decedent contributed to its acquisition;

- the decedent's retirement plan assets;

- property transferred by the decedent in which he or she retained an interest or a measure of control.

ESTATE TAX WORKSHEET

ASSETS

Cash (bank accounts, CDs, etc.) $_____

Personal residence (market value) $_____

Stocks, bonds, partnerships $_____

Closely held business $_____

Vacation home (market value) $_____

Investment real estate (market value) $_____

Other investments $_____

Qualified retirement plans (profit sharing, IRAs,
defined benefit, Keogh, etc.) $_____

Home furnishings (furniture, appliances, art, china,
jewelry, clothing, etc.) $_____

Automobiles, boats, other vehicles $_____

Other personal property $_____

Life insurance on husband (face value) $_____

Life insurance on wife (face value) $_____

Other assets $_____

Total assets $_____

LIABILITIES

Personal residence mortgage (balance) $_____

Other real estate mortgages (balance) $_____

Installment loans (balance) $_____

Other loans (balance) $_____

Credit cards $_____

Other liabilities $_____

Total liabilities $_____

NET WORTH (assets less liabilities) $_____

After the total value of the net taxable estate is computed, certain items are deducted before the tax is calculated. These deductions include:

- funeral expenses
- executor's fee
- legal and accounting fees
- debts of the decedent
- probate court fees
- expenses of estate administration (insurance, appraisals, investment counsel, real estate commissions, and upkeep on property fees)

The following worksheet can be used to calculate the amount of the net assets potentially subject to estate tax.

FEDERAL ESTATE TAX

Because the federal estate and gift tax is always a significant factor in estate planning decisions, a more detailed discussion of the way this tax operates is in order. Prior to January 1, 1977, there were separate estate and gift tax rates. Not only were there two separate rates, but with respect to each bracket, the gift tax rate was only three-fourths the estate tax rate for the corresponding bracket. In addition, for each tax there was a separate exemption. The federal estate tax exemption was $60,000, and the gift tax exemption was $30,000. This structure, where appropriate, permitted an individual to remove his or her assets from the highest estate tax bracket and have them taxed at the lowest gift tax bracket.

The Tax Reform Act of 1976 eliminated the separate rate schedules and imposed a cumulative unified transfer tax on all transfers, whether by gift during lifetime or at death. Today the estate tax is imposed on the sum of the taxable estate plus adjusted taxable gifts.

TAX RATES

The rates in the case of decedents dying and gifts made in 1994 or thereafter are as listed in the following table.

If the amount with respect to which the tentative tax to be computed is:	*The tentative tax is:*
Not over $10,000	18 percent of such amount
Over $10,000 but not over $20,000	$1,800, plus 20 percent of the excess of such amount over $10,000
Over $20,000 but not over $40,000	$3,800, plus 22 percent of the excess of such amount over $20,000
Over $40,000 but not over $60,000	$8,200, plus 24 percent of the excess of such amount over $40,000
Over $60,000 but not over $80,000	$13,000, plus 26 percent of the excess of such amount over $60,000
Over $80,000 but not over $100,000	$18,200, plus 28 percent of the excess of such amount over $80,000
Over $100,000 but not over $150,000	$23,800, plus 30 percent of the excess of such amount over $100,000
Over $150,000 but not over $250,000	$38,800, plus 32 percent of the excess of such amount over $150,000
Over $250,000 but not over $500,000	$70,800, plus 34 percent of the excess of such amount over $250,000
Over $500,000 but not over $750,000	$155,800, plus 37 percent of the excess of such amount over $500,000
Over $750,000 but not over $1,000,000	$248,300, plus 39 percent of the excess of such amount over $750,000
Over $1,000,000 but not over $1,250,000	$345,800, plus 41 percent of the excess of such amount over $1,000,000
Over $1,250,000 but not over $1,500,000	$448,300, plus 43 percent of the excess of such amount over $1,250,000

Over $1,500,000 but not over $2,000,000 . . . . . . $555,800, plus 45 percent of the excess
of such amount over $1,500,000

Over $2,000,000 but not over $2,500,000 . . . . . . $780,800, plus 49 percent of the excess
of such amount over $2,000,000

Over $2,500,000 but not over $3,000,000 . . . . . . $1,025,800, plus 50 percent of the excess
of such amount over $1,000,000

Over $3,000,000 . . . . $1,290,800, plus 55 percent of the excess
of such amount over $3,000,000

During 1982, a total credit of $62,800 was available to offset the estate or gift tax that would otherwise be paid. This credit translated into an "exemption equivalent" of $225,000, meaning that the first $225,000 escaped taxation. The balance of taxable transfers were then taxed at the applicable rates, beginning at the 32 percent bracket. This credit was increased over each of the next several years until it reached $192,800 in 1987. During the phase-in period, the applicable credits and corresponding exemption equivalents were as follows:

YEAR	UNIFIED CREDIT	EXEMPTION EQUIVALENT
1982	$62,800	$225,000
1983	$79,300	$275,000
1984	$96,300	$325,000
1985	$121,800	$400,000
1986	$155,800	$500,000
1987	$192,800	$600,000[1]

However, for estates exceeding $10 million, the Revenue Act of 1987 phased out the benefit of the unified credit and the lower brackets by adding a 5 percent surtax from $10 million to $21,040,000.[2]

As previously noted, the 1997 Taxpayer Relief Act increased the exemption equivalent amount to $1 million by the year 2006.

As a result of the unification of the previously separate estate and gift tax rates, the estate tax liability is computed differently under present law than under prior law. An estate tax is computed on the total of the taxable estate *plus* adjusted taxable gifts and any gift tax paid on gifts made within three years of death. From this tax on the total of lifetime and testamentary transfers is subtracted the credit previously described, as well as any gift tax actually paid because of gifts made during one's lifetime.[3]

MARITAL DEDUCTION

One of my law school professors, who taught an estate and gift tax course, used to call the marital deduction the "pearl of great price." Use of the marital deduction permits an unlimited deferral of tax on amounts left to a spouse until the death of the surviving spouse.[4]

In arriving at the taxable estate, the value of property passing to (or for the benefit of) the surviving spouse is deducted from the gross estate, provided that it passes in a manner that qualifies for the estate tax marital deduction. To qualify for the marital deduction, property may be given outright to the surviving spouse. This type of gift can take the form of an outright distribution of estate assets to the spouse. It also can take other forms. Examples include the designation of the surviving spouse as the beneficiary of insurance proceeds or naming the surviving spouse as a joint tenant with right of survivorship so that the property automatically passes to the spouse upon the decedent's death.

The deduction is also available, under certain strict circumstances, if property is placed in trust for the benefit of the surviving spouse. Before 1982, if the trust vehicle was chosen, the trust had to provide (with certain exceptions) that the surviving spouse would be the only income beneficiary, that he or she would receive all trust income at least annually, and that he or she would be given either the power to withdraw all trust assets during his or her lifetime or the complete power of disposition by will over the trust assets remaining at the time of his or her death. Alternatively, under prior law, the trust would have qualified if (1) all income was either paid to the spouse or accumulated, and (2) trust principal and accumulated income were paid to the estate of the surviving spouse upon his or her death.[5] These trusts continue to qualify for the marital deduction under current law and are typically referred to as general power of appointment marital deduction trusts and estate trusts.

Beginning in 1982, a new type of trust, called the *qualified terminable interest property trust* (or QTIP trust), qualified for the marital deduction. This type of trust requires only that (1) the surviving spouse receive all of the income at least annually; (2) no person have a power to appoint any part of the trust property to any person other than the surviving spouse; and (3) an election be made to qualify the trust for the marital deduction.[6] If these requirements are met, and if the subject property (or a specific portion thereof) has passed from the decedent, the trust may qualify for the marital deduction even though the surviving spouse is not given the power to dispose of remaining trust corpus during his or her lifetime or upon his or her later death. This trust is particularly important for second marriage situations.

A final, although seldom used, type of marital deduction trust is the estate trust. This trust need not give the surviving spouse anything during the spouse's lifetime, but the trust assets do at least have to be distributed to the spouse's estate at the spouse's death or the spouse must be given a power to appoint all of the property by will to his or her estate.[7]

Before 1982, the marital deduction was limited to the greater of 50 percent or one-half of the adjusted gross estate. Since January 1, 1982, an unlimited marital deduction has been available.[8] The unlimited marital deduction eliminates any estate tax, regardless of the size of the estate, upon the death of the first spouse to die. The price of this deduction is that the property may be subject to transfer tax when the surviving spouse dies.

The 1988 Tax Act imposed a new requirement with respect to the application of the marital deduction to bequests to non-citizen spouses. In order to receive the tax benefits of the federal estate tax marital deduction, an individual married to a non-citizen is required to make a transfer to his or her spouse through a so-called "qualified domestic trust," which is discussed in Chapter 8.

Example: Fred and Fran are concerned about the impact of estate taxes on their wealth after they are gone and want to pass on as much of their wealth as possible to their three children and six grandchildren. They currently have "simple" wills leaving everything to each other. Fred and Fran have asked about the federal estate tax liability at each of their deaths under their current wills.

FRED AND FRAN
STATEMENT OF ASSETS AND LIABILITIES

ASSETS

Cash (joint accounts)	$ 25,000
Stocks and bonds (held as joint tenants with right of survival)	200,000
IRA (Fran) (Fred is beneficiary)	160,000
Residence (Fran's name)	150,000
Commercial building (Fred's name)	300,000
Farm (Fran's name)	500,000
Note receivable from Fred's company (Fred's name)	50,000
Insurance on Fred's life (Fran is beneficiary)	1,000,000
Personal assets (joint)	50,000
Total Assets	**$2,435,000**

LIABILITIES

Mortgage payable on home (by Fran)	($100,000)
Total Liabilities	**($100,000)**

NET WORTH	**$2,335,000**

The survivor of Fred and Fran will wind up owning everything with their current wills, beneficiary designations (they name each other), and joint property. The estate tax liability on the estate of the first to die is zero because the unlimited marital deduction shelters it. The estate tax liability at the survivor's death is $752,150.

In Chapter 5, we will look at relatively simple techniques to substantially reduce Fred and Fran's estate tax liability.

CHARITABLE DEDUCTION

A decedent's estate is permitted an unlimited estate tax deduction for interests passing to charitable organizations approved by the IRS.[9] An unlimited gift tax deduction is available for outright gifts to qualified charitable organizations.[10] Estate and gift tax charitable deductions are available for qualified gifts in trust where the charitable beneficiary is given a present interest in the trust income or a remainder interest in the trust principal.[11] Creative estate planning is often done using special charitable techniques. These techniques are discussed in Chapter 10.

SPECIAL USE VALUATION OF FARMS AND REAL PROPERTY USED IN A CLOSELY HELD BUSINESS

When certain tests are met, the fair market value of certain property includable in a person's gross estate, including farms and real property used in a closely held (family) business, can be significantly reduced—by as much as $750,000.[12] The Taxpayer Relief Act of 1997 has indexed this for inflation for decedents dying after December 31, 1997. If the value of the business (or farm) is at least 50 percent of the adjusted gross estate, and the value of the real property is at least 25 percent of the adjusted gross estate, this special use valuation might be available.

FAMILY-OWNED BUSINESS EXCLUSION

For decedents dying after December 31, 1997, the estate may elect to exclude up to $1.3 million in value attributable to a "qualified" family-owned business interest by using a combination of the unified credit and the new family-owned business exclusion (new Internal Revenue Code § 2033A). Example: Henry dies in the year 2000 with a qualified family business worth $2 million. Henry may use his $675,000 exemption *plus* another $625,000 of exemption (totalling $1,300,000) to offset the tax on the business.

PAYMENT OF ESTATE TAX ATTRIBUTABLE TO CLOSELY HELD BUSINESS

Highly beneficial rules allow the payment of estate taxes attributable to a closely held business in installments over a period of years and at low interest rates on the unpaid balance in certain circumstances. If the value of a closely held business exceeds 35 percent of a person's adjusted gross estate, the estate taxes attributable to the business may be deferred for up to 15 years, with the estate making annual interest payments for the first five years, and thereafter paying the balance in up to 10 annual installments of principal and interest. The interest rate on the estate taxes attributable to the first $1 million in value has been reduced to 2 percent by the Taxpayer Relief Act of 1997. The interest rate on the balance is equal to 45 percent of the normal interest rate charged by the IRS after 1997. However, the law provides for the acceleration of payment of the deferred tax balance if payment of any installment is delinquent or if 50 percent or more of the decedent's interest in the closely held business is disposed of or withdrawn.[13]

ALTERNATE VALUATION DATE

Normally, the property includable in a person's estate for estate tax purposes is valued as of the date of the person's death. However, the federal estate tax laws provide an optional date for valuing the property required to be included in the gross estate. In general, an estate may elect to value the estate assets on the date six months following the decedent's death, instead of the date of death. However, the alternate valuation date election may be made only where the election will reduce both the value of the decedent's gross estate and the federal estate tax liability.[14] Furthermore, the executor must elect to value all assets on either the date of death or six months from the date of death.[15] There can be no picking and choosing—one asset on the date of death and another six months from the date of death.

GIFT TAX PRESENT INTEREST
ANNUAL EXCLUSION

Although the federal estate and gift taxes have been unified, and adjusted taxable gifts are included in the taxable estate, it would be erroneous to conclude that lifetime gifts are without benefit in the estate planning process. Gifts can be particularly useful for reducing the taxable estate (by using the gift tax annual exclusion discussed below) as well as for "freezing" estate assets (because assets given away are included in estate tax computations at their values as of the time of transfer without any appreciation occurring after the gift). Also, if a gift is made and a gift tax is actually paid more than three years before death, the gift tax itself is removed from the computation of estate tax liability.

The federal gift tax exclusion for gifts of a present interest is $10,000 per year per donee.[16] The 1997 Taxpayer Relief Act has indexed this for inflation beginning in 1998. Under prior law, this exclusion was limited to $3,000 per year per donee. In addition, if certain requirements are met, there is an unlimited gift tax exclusion for the direct payment of tuition and medical expenses for the benefit of descendants.[17]

A husband and wife can consent to treat gifts made by either of them as though half of the gift had been made by each.[18] This permits a husband and a wife to transfer jointly, each year, up to $20,000 to each of as many beneficiaries as they wish even if the $20,000 transferred was owned solely by one of them. (Such opportunities will be discussed in more detail in Chapter 5.)

NOTES

1. I.R.C. § 2010(a).
2. I.R.C. § 2001(c)(2).
3. I.R.C. § 2012(a).
4. I.R.C. § 2056.
5. I.R.C. § 2056(b)(5).
6. I.R.C. § 2056(b)(7).
7. Treasury Regulation § 20.2056(c)-2(b)(1)(iii); Rev. Rul. 72-333, 1972-2 C.B. 530; Rev. Rul. 68-554, 1968-2 C.B. 412.
8. I.R.C. § 2056(a).
9. I.R.C. § 2055(a).
10. I.R.C. § 2522(a).
11. I.R.C. §§ 2055(e), 2522(c).
12. I.R.C. § 2032A(a).
13. I.R.C. § 6166.
14. I.R.C. § 2032.
15. Treasury Regulation § 20.2032-1(d).
16. I.R.C. § 2503(b).
17. I.R.C. § 2503(e).
18. I.R.C. § 2513(a).

SAMPLE FORM FOR FUNERAL ARRANGEMENTS

Name_____ Date _____

These are my wishes concerning my funeral:

  I. A.   That there be no public viewing of the body _____

          or

      B.   That there be a public viewing of the body _____

  II. A.   That the service be held in church with the body present _____

          or

      B.   That a memorial service be held in the church or synagogue some time after burial

          or cremation _____

          or

      C.   That the service be held in a funeral home _____

          Funeral home I prefer is _____

  III. A.   That the following hymns be sung:

          _____

          _____

      B.   That the following scripture be read:

          _____

          _____

      C.   Other instructions concerning the service:

          _____

          _____

      D.   That the following preacher or rabbi conduct the service:

          _____

IV. A.   That internment be in _____

Deed for cemetery can be found in _____

or

B.   That I be cremated _____

That my ashes be _____

V. A.   That costs be held to a minimum _____

or

B.   Other instructions on costs of funeral:

_____

_____

_____

VI.   That, in lieu of flowers, family and friends may make contributions to

_____

_____

VII.   That _____ is to have final authority
concerning my funeral and has the right to change any of the above arrangements
if necessary.

VIII.   Other special instructions:

_____

_____

_____

_____

Signed _____

Social Security Number _____

Classic Estate Planning

Basic Techniques

Let's choose executors and talk of wills.

—William Shakespeare, *King Richard II*

"Classic" estate planning techniques are used to plan most estates. Most estates will not need the more sophisticated techniques discussed in Chapter 6. Most estates are not in excess of the federal exemption and do not involve disabled beneficiaries, creditor protection, non-citizen spouses, or other unusual situations. Most estates can be well planned using the techniques discussed in this chapter. These techniques can be used if you want to do (more or less) the usual thing—protect a spouse and then leave property to children with minimum tax drainage. These estates do not exceed (at least by very much) $600,000 ($1 million by 2006) if you are single, or $1,200,000 ($2 million by 2006) if you are married. Therefore, your tax planning can be done with a good will or revocable living trust. Most tax planning in the estate area is done with a combination of a will (or revocable living trust used as a will substitute) and the proper titling of assets between spouses.

THE LAST WILL AND TESTAMENT

The *last will and testament* is the cornerstone of an estate plan. There are many reasons why virtually everyone needs a will. A woman with minor children, for example, will be particularly concerned that the right person raise her children. Therefore, she will want to name an appropriate guardian. If her husband survives her, she will probably want to leave her assets in a way that will take care of her husband for life and then go to her children in the event of his remarriage. She will want to ensure that her personal effects (her jewelry, valuable clothing, family heirlooms, and collectibles) go to the people whom she wishes to have these treasures. She will want to ensure that the right people manage and distribute her estate and handle monies placed in trust for loved ones. She may want to include non-relatives or charities in her will, and she may even want to exclude one or more family members. None of this can occur (or at least there is no guarantee that it will occur), without a valid last will and testament. Without a will, the law of the state where you reside controls what happens to your property (and your children) at your death. Most states have laws providing that, in the event you die without a will, your spouse, if he survives you, will receive a certain percentage of your estate. For example, in many states, the spouse receives one-third outright, and the children divide the remaining two-thirds. The local probate court would name the person to handle the estate and distribute the assets. Without a will, this person would typically be called an administrator or personal representative. In other words, a woman who dies without a will is giving up valuable rights to select people to be in charge of her estate and to determine where her property goes.

Wills can be as long and complicated or as short and simple as a situation warrants. I often receive phone calls from prospective clients who begin by telling me that they need a will and then start describing their situation. Regardless of the complexity of the situation, the prospective client always says that he or she needs a "simple" will. Wills that involve tax planning, children by prior marriages (if there has been a remarriage), the exclusion of immediate family members, or provisions for disabled beneficiaries are by definition not simple wills. More precautions must be taken, and great care in drafting of tax planning trusts and asset protection trusts (for disabled beneficiaries) is required.

When preparing a will, some of the most important things to a woman will often be her personal effects. Women tend to have more interest in jewelry, furniture, and household effects than men do. Women may spend a great deal of time, for example, agonizing over which daughter (or daughter-in-law or granddaughter) should receive which ring, bracelet, or brooch. In many states, a list (which is simply referred to in the will) may be attached to the will. Such a list indicates who receives the personal effects (legally called the "tangible personal property"). On this list attached to your will, you may list your jewelry, furniture, and other household and personal effects, indicating who is to receive each item. As long as state law formalities are adhered to (for example, the list is signed, dated, and witnessed by two individuals), it will become a part of the will. Check with an attorney in your state to find out what your state law says concerning this type of arrangement.

In my experience, it is often the tangible personal property (I have started affectionately calling this the "stuff") that causes splits in a family when a parent dies. For this reason, it is extremely important to have a plan in place so that your children cannot argue about who gets which ring or other heirloom. Over the years, I have had many interesting arrangements proposed. For example, some clients use the "pull the number out of a hat" technique. In this arrangement, the children draw numbers out of a hat. The child drawing number one gets first choice of all the stuff. Then the child drawing number two chooses an item, then number three, until each child has selected one item. Then the process begins again, with child number one selecting his or her next item.

Another arrangement is the auction technique. In this arrangement, each item of property is auctioned to the children. The children bid, and the child who bids the most receives the item. This is then, in effect, charged to that child's share of the estate. For example, if there were two children and $100,000 of stuff, and one child effectively won the bid on everything, receiving all $100,000 (which was the total amount bid), and the total estate (including the $100,000 of stuff) was $1 million, then the second child would receive $500,000 in cash, and the first child would receive the stuff plus $400,000 in cash. This is perceived to be fair and equitable by many parents. In another arrangement, the parent simply predetermines who gets what. The idea is that at least the children will not be mad at each other, and it will not matter if they are mad at the deceased parent.

It should be noted that, under state law, certain events will generally revoke a will. Marriage (where the will is not written in contemplation of the marriage), divorce, the birth of a child not contemplated by the will, and moving to another state which has different requirements for the proper execution of a will are all events that may revoke a will. I recently met with a client who had seven children. The seventh was a surprise. The couple had signed wills after the sixth child was born and mentioned all six children by name. No mention was made of after born children. When I reviewed the will and realized that child number seven was not mentioned or contemplated in the will, I told the parents the will was void under state law. They, of course, were shocked and instructed me to prepare new documents immediately.

MINIMIZING TAXES IN EACH SPOUSE'S ESTATE

For couples whose net worth exceeds $600,000, it is important to ensure that each spouse may take advantage of the $600,000 exemption from transfer taxes which the 1997 law currently provides (although Congress has increased the $600,000 phased in over nine years to $1 million, we will use the 1997 exemption in our examples). Suppose, for example, George and Carol's combined assets in 1997 equal $1,200,000. If George dies first and leaves everything to Carol, she will have a net worth of $1,200,000 at her death. The first $600,000 in her estate is exempt from taxation, leaving the other $600,000 fully taxable in her estate. The federal estate tax attributable to the $600,000 is $235,000, meaning that the government gets this much before George and Carol's children receive the rest.

George and Carol should sign wills providing that when the first spouse dies, that spouse's property, instead of going outright to the survivor, will go into a testamentary (created by will) trust. The survivor, as sole trustee, is able to use the money for his or her health, support, maintenance, and education for life, and the assets only go to the children at the survivor's death. The assets in the survivor's name *as trustee* will not be included in the survivor's estate. So, for example, if we effectively divided the assets so that $600,000 of the assets were in George's name and $600,000 of the assets were in Carol's name, and George's will provided that the first $600,000 of his assets went to Carol as trustee of a residuary (also called family or credit shelter) trust, then George's $600,000 would be offset by George's credit and not included in Carol's estate. Carol could leave her $600,000 tax-free to her children, meaning that no estate tax would be due. This is a very easy way to protect the first $1,200,000 of assets in a couple's estate from taxation with virtually no trade-off involved.

One of the most important issues in estate planning is control. The beauty of the technique just described is that if the trust (called the residuary, or credit shelter, or family trust) is drafted properly, the surviving spouse may be the sole trustee without pulling assets into the surviving spouse's estate for estate tax purposes later. Generally, in order for the surviving spouse to be the sole trustee, two requirements must be met. First, the surviving spouse must be "limited" to taking property out of the trust only for her health, education, support, or maintenance.[1] This is what the Internal Revenue Code calls an "ascertainable standard" and is enough of a limitation to keep the surviving spouse from being deemed to own the property for estate tax purposes.

Next, the surviving spouse must be prohibited from using the trust property in favor of her estate, her creditors, or the creditors of her estate.[2] This means that the trust language must include provisions saying, basically, that the survivor (sole trustee) cannot use property to fulfill any legal obligations of hers or exercise any tax elections favoring her (or those dependent on her) and cannot appoint the property to herself, her creditors, her estate, or the creditors of her estate.

If the first spouse to die has more than $600,000 of assets, then the remainder can go either outright or in a marital trust to the surviving spouse and qualify for the unlimited marital deduction in the first estate. Remember that the marital deduction is only a *deferral* of tax until the surviving spouse dies. Hence, if George's estate was $1 million and Carol's was $600,000, then George would leave $600,000 to Carol as trustee of the family (credit shelter or residuary) trust and the remainder to her outright or in a marital trust. This means that no tax would be due at George's death, but the $400,000 Carol received tax-free because of the marital deduction would be added to her assets and taxed later in her estate. However, the marital deduction provides a deferral of tax. If Carol were to live 20 years longer than George, she would have the use of those marital deduction dollars for 20 years before any part of them had to go to the government in taxes.

The two most popular forms of marital deduction gifts are probably the outright bequest (not in trust, no strings attached) and the *qualified terminable interest property* (QTIP) trust. The QTIP (pronounced "Q-tip") trust provides an arrangement whereby a spouse can enjoy the property over his or her life, but at the spouse's death, it is controlled by the will of the first to die and can, by that spouse's will, be directed to the children of the first spouse to die (or to anyone whom the first spouse to die selects). In other words, the surviving spouse does not have the power to direct the property by will. This is particularly helpful in second marriage situations. If property goes other than outright to a surviving spouse, then, generally speaking, the spouse must receive all the income from the trust for her lifetime (distributed at least annually) and the spouse must be the sole beneficiary of the trust during her lifetime (in other words, the children cannot be added as beneficiaries, even permissible beneficiaries).[3] The spouse may also be the sole trustee of the QTIP trust or other marital trust. The marital trust most frequently used when a QTIP trust is not used gives the spouse the power to appoint the property in the trust by her will to whomever she desires. This is called a general power of appointment marital trust.[4]

PROPER TITLING OF ASSETS

In order for the will to control the assets, the assets must be properly titled. Suppose, for example, that the assets in our preceding example were divided between George and Carol so that Carol owned everything. In other words, George owns nothing and Carol owns $1,200,000. If George dies first, even if he has the tax planning residuary (or credit shelter or family) trust in his will, nothing can go into it because everything is in Carol's name. In order to ensure that, no matter who dies first, the first to die may leave $600,000 to the other as trustee, $600,000 must be owned by each spouse.

One of the most common mistakes spouses make in estate planning when the combined assets exceed $600,000 is owning everything as joint tenants with right of survival. This is a type of ownership that passes outside of the will by operation of law. For example, suppose Carol and George have an account worth $500,000 at the Bulls & Bears Brokerage Firm which they own as joint tenants with right of survival. The rest of their assets are equally divided in their respective names. If George dies first, then the $500,000 joint account with right of survival immediately belongs to Carol. No part of it (not even George's "half") can go into the tax-protected trust George's will creates. This is why many times estate planning attorneys have to advise clients to undo assets previously titled jointly with right of survival. The solution to this problem is either to place half of the joint account with right of survival assets in the husband's name and half in the wife's name or retitle them as tenants in common, which is a type of joint ownership that effectively places half in each spouse's name in a way that allows each spouse's half to be controlled by his or her will.

BENEFICIARY DESIGNATIONS

Assets that pass by contract (such as insurance and most deferred compensation arrangements including IRAs, 401(k) plans, pension plans, and profit sharing plans) are not controlled by the will either; they pass outside the will by contractual arrangement. It is essential that these assets be coordinated with the will. A simple way to make the will control these assets is to simply make them payable to the estate of the insured or the participant in a retirement plan situation. However, for reasons discussed later in this book, this is almost never desirable. Making insurance payable to the insured's estate causes the insurance to be subject to estate taxation and creditors. With respect to retirement plans, many valuable tax deferral benefits are often lost if the assets are made payable to the decedent's estate. Protecting life insurance from estate tax will be discussed in the following section. Chapter 12 will discuss coordinating retirement assets with the will.

I cannot emphasize enough the importance of proper titling of assets and beneficiary designations in estate planning. I will never forget the time I sat down with a couple who had just moved to Atlanta from Chicago. I looked at their wills and marveled at the quality of the legal work. They were beautifully drawn and perfectly executed. I then started discussing with the couple their assets and learned that they had a large stock portfolio, all of which was titled as joint tenants with right of survival. I could not believe that an attorney who could draft such fine wills would overlook proper titling to make sure that the wills could actually act upon the couple's assets. Those wonderful wills were not controlling their assets and giving them the tax planning they were designed for. The couple was understandably dismayed, but we quickly rectified the situation by retitling the assets as tenants in common.

PROTECTING LIFE INSURANCE FROM ESTATE TAX

After taking advantage of the $600,000 exemption amount in your estate (or, if you are married, in your estate and in your husband's estate), the next step in tax protection, if you or your husband own life insurance on your lives, is to transfer ownership of the insurance policies so that they are not subject to estate tax. Remember that the face value of insurance is included in the owner's estate. The face value is generally quite high compared to the cash value (what you would get if you cashed in the policy). The policy's cash value is its value for gift tax purposes. Therefore, the policy then can be transferred at a small value for gift tax purposes compared to what it would be worth in the decedent's estate for estate tax purposes.

Insurance is one of the easiest assets to remove from the taxable estate and yet still be made accessible to a surviving spouse. For example, if your husband is insured for $500,000 and you are the beneficiary of his policy, then with no further planning, you will receive the $500,000 at his death; his estate will take a marital deduction because you, his wife, received the benefits; and, to the extent you do not use the funds during your lifetime, they will be included in your taxable estate later. Or, should your husband survive you, the $500,000 will be included fully in his taxable estate.

One easy way to avoid inclusion of the policy proceeds in both estates but still have the proceeds available to you is for your husband to transfer ownership of the life insurance to an *irrevocable life insurance trust*. The terms of this trust, if you are the sole trustee, would be the same as the terms of the residuary (or credit shelter or family) trust discussed earlier in this chapter. You can have access to the proceeds for your health, support, maintenance, and education, as well as for your children (subject to a restriction that you cannot use the funds to fulfill your legal obligations, including the parental obligation of support under local law). In reality, these are legal and tax limitations but not practical limitations. Most parents do far more for their children than the law requires. From a practical standpoint, you would basically have full use of the proceeds for your needs and those of your children. You should consult with your local attorney concerning any state law limitations.

Transferring ownership of an insurance policy to a trust is a simple thing to do. Once the insurance trust is drafted by a competent estate planning attorney, you simply obtain transfer of ownership and transfer of beneficiary forms from the insurance company and complete them, naming the trust as the owner and beneficiary of the policy. The trust will have a federal tax identification number (similar to an individual's social security number) assigned by the IRS. Most attorneys who do a lot of estate planning work can assign these numbers to the trusts they draft.

After the transfer to the trust (by you or your husband, whatever the case may be), it is important that the insured retain no incident of ownership in the policy transferred. An "incident of ownership" includes the power to change the beneficiary, cancel the policy, assign the policy, revoke an assignment, pledge the policy for a loan, or the right to any other economic benefit of the policy.[5] Despite the transfer to the trust (or to an individual, for that matter), retention by the insured of an incident of ownership will cause the policy to be included in the insured's estate.

The tax law also provides that, if an individual transfers a policy that he or she previously owned, then for a period of three years after the transfer, the policy proceeds are brought back into the insured's estate, notwithstanding the transfer.[6] Generally, the only way to ensure that this problem will not occur is to make sure that the insured never owns the policy to begin with. This is accomplished by having the trust (or someone other than the insured) acquire and maintain the policy from the outset.

One issue that comes up when looking at insurance in an individual's estate is whether ownership of the policy should be transferred to a trust or to an individual. For example, if you and your husband have grown children, all of whom are responsible, capable people, and if the policy is a joint and survivor policy (paying off only when the survivor of you and your husband dies), then you may simply wish to transfer ownership to your adult children and let them own the policy. This has the advantage of avoiding the trust mechanism (with some attendant red tape and expense in the initial drafting) and, as long as the children remain competent and capable (and do not have spousal problems in terms of undue influence or divorce), the arrangement would work quite well. However, even where the children are competent and capable, some parents prefer the trust arrangement for joint and survivor policies to protect from divorcing spouses or spouses who may exercise undue influence. If you are single and have a policy on your own life, you may simply want to transfer ownership of the policy to your children. This will remove the face value from your taxable estate just as placing it in trust would.

Perhaps the main advantage of the trust arrangement is when one spouse alone is insured. The trust allows the other spouse to enjoy the insurance proceeds for life and then pass them on to the children free of taxation in either spouse's estate.

Although insurance trusts are very powerful planning techniques, they must be drafted properly. This is no place for do-it-yourself drafting. A competent estate planning attorney must be consulted to draft an irrevocable life insurance trust. After the trust has been drafted, premium dollars paid on the policy must be placed in a trust bank account. If the husband is the insured and the wife is the trustee of the trust, then the husband would typically write a check out of his separate account to the wife as trustee. She would put it in the trust bank account. Then the beneficiaries of the trust must be notified that a contribution to the trust has been made and that they have a reasonable amount of time (at least 30 days) to withdraw the funds from the trust. This is the mechanism through which contributions to the trust are converted into what the tax law calls "present interest gifts," thus qualifying them for the $10,000 per donee per year present interest gift exclusion.[7] Obviously, this type of trust is not a technique for the detail-impaired. Adherence to formalities is essential in the event of an IRS audit later. If a life insurance policy is transferred directly to children, the parents would thereafter make gifts to the children which the children would use to pay the insurance company for the premiums.

Another advantage of choosing the trust arrangement over individual ownership (even though it is more complicated in some ways) is creditor protection. The trust arrangement may provide significant protection from the claims of creditors for the insured, the insured's spouse, and the children of the insured. Creditor protection will be discussed in more detail in Chapter 11.

The trust is also a flexible tool for managing and distributing assets. For example, if there are minor children, the trust provides a way for their money to be managed for them until they are older. Moreover, the trust can provide a means whereby all of the insurance proceeds are available until the last child is educated, and then the "pot" of money may be split and divided among the children. The trust arrangement can also be useful when there is a disabled beneficiary. The proceeds will be held for a disabled child's lifetime and then distributed to the insured's other descendants. Finally, the goals for which the insurance was acquired can be insured through a trust. For example, if the insurance was acquired for payment of estate taxes, the trustee of the trust can be given the authority to lend money to the estate of the insured or to buy assets from the estate of the insured. If the proceeds are in the trust, and if the trustee has this authority, then the trustee can exercise his or her authority and get the cash to the insured's estate when the time comes to pay taxes. If the children own the policy outright, on the other hand, one of them may decide to do something else with the proceeds to the detriment of the others.

If a surviving spouse is a trustee of an insurance trust holding insurance on her spouse's life, it is important that she not make any contributions to the trust herself. If this were to occur, it could cause inclusion of the trust proceeds in her estate.[8] This most often occurs when the property contributed to the trust for the payment of premiums is treated as belonging in whole or in part to the spouse/beneficiary/trustee because it comes from community property or some other type of commonly owned assets. The safest way to avoid this problem is to have the insured spouse (the grantor of the trust) set up a separate bank account and make premium payments from this separate account to the trust.

Although the spouse of the insured may be the trustee of an insurance trust, it is more difficult for the insured himself or herself to be the trustee. Although the IRS has relaxed its position on this issue somewhat, the better practice is to prohibit the insured from being trustee of the trust which owns insurance on the insured's life.

As a final note, unless neither spouse is the trustee of the trust, second-to-die insurance policies should not be placed in the same insurance trust as insurance on the life of only one of the spouses. If this is done, it could cause inclusion of policy proceeds in the survivor's estate.[9]

REVOCABLE LIVING TRUSTS

Perhaps no estate planning technique has received more press than the revocable living trust. "Living trust" means the trust is created while you are alive, and "revocable" means that you can revoke or change it at any time for any reason. This, of course, gives people a great measure of comfort. Revocable living trusts have been touted as the way to avoid all estate planning and administration evils, including exorbitant probate fees, exorbitant legal fees, estate taxes, creditors, adverse spouses—the list goes on and on.

The first thing to consider when listening to the benefits of revocable living trusts is the source of the information. There are many people with very few qualifications who call themselves estate planners, including some who are really using the revocable living trust as gimmick to gain control of a prospective client's investments. Regardless of whether an individual really needs a trust, these people want to *create* the need in the mind of the prospective client so that they gain the client's ear to sell what they are really selling.

The next thing to keep in mind about revocable living trusts is that, tax-wise, they do not do any more for you than a proper will can do. As we have already seen, a will with a credit shelter (or residuary or family) trust can protect $1,200,000 from estate tax. A revocable trust can do the same—no more and no less. For income tax purposes (as well as estate tax purposes), the revocable trust is as if the client personally owned the property.

Why then do some attorneys promote the trust as something that every client needs in order to "avoid probate"? The viewpoint of an attorney is colored by the law of the state in which he or she practices. In some states (Florida, for example), attorneys who probate assets (probate, remember, is the process through which assets are transferred from the name of the decedent into the names of those receiving them at the decedent's death) receive a percentage of the probate assets under state law. Although this can be negotiated by the executor with the attorney, many executors simply do not know this; as a result, attorneys take advantage of the state law that grants them a percentage of the probate estate. In these states, therefore, it is very important to either have a prearranged fee agreement with an estate planning attorney or to have assets in a revocable living trust so that the attorney is not paid this statutory percentage.

The other substantial fee typically encountered in the probate area is the executor's fee. If a professional executor is used (such as an attorney, a bank, or an accountant), this fee could be quite large. Again, most state laws award a percentage of the estate to the executor for serving. This fee could be quite unreasonable, however, if, for example, the estate is all marketable securities and quite easy to administer. On the other hand, if a family member is named as executor, that family member may not charge a fee at all. If that is the case, and if the state is not a state in which attorneys receive a percentage of the estate simply for probating assets (which is the case in the majority of states), then probate fees could be quite low. In Georgia, for example, I have probated many estates for less than $500. Because it costs more than $500 to set up a revocable living trust, using such a trust does not make sense in Georgia *just to avoid going through probate.*

Are there any other advantages to a revocable living trust aside from avoiding probate? The answer is yes. Perhaps one of the most compelling reasons is that a revocable living trust is a private document, as opposed to a will, which is a matter of public record. Every will that is probated is filed with the local probate court, and anyone who cares to may obtain a copy. If you use a revocable living trust, however, then a short "pour-over" will is used that simply says, "I leave everything to my revocable living trust that I didn't put in it prior to my death." The only thing anyone obtaining a copy of the will would know about the estate plan would be that there was a trust and everything went to the trust. No one would know where the trust property went.

For a person who wishes to keep his or her estate plan private, this option has real advantages. For a woman who is leaving more to charity than her children might approve, or leaving more to one child than the others, or doing anything out of the ordinary, the privacy aspect of the revocable living trust has great appeal. Another reason for establishing a revocable living trust is to provide ongoing management of assets in the event of disability. Although this can be handled through properly drafted financial powers of attorney (discussed in Chapter 7), some people prefer the revocable living trust because successor trustees can be named. Generally, when a revocable living trust is established, the grantor (the person establishing the trust) serves as her own trustee. Only if she is unable to serve does someone else step in, typically a spouse first, and then an adult child. You may name as many successor trustees as you wish. If you have children who are not very good at managing money, a good way to prevent them from doing so in the event of your disability is to establish a trust and name an advisor or friend who is good at managing money as successor trustee.

One further advantage of a revocable living trust is to avoid going through probate in states where you own out-of-state real estate. For example, suppose you reside in a state with low probate fees, and a family member is going to serve as executor of your estate without charging. You own a very valuable condominium in Florida, however, plus a mountain home in Colorado, and you also inherited some property from your great aunt in Alaska. If you establish a trust in your state, and have the Florida, Colorado, and Alaska properties contributed to the trust while you are alive, your executor will not have to deal with going through Florida, Colorado, and Alaska probate (filing papers with the probate courts in three other states to get the real estate transferred). This will make it a great deal easier on the individual serving as your executor and is often in itself reason enough for someone to establish a revocable living trust.

Are there any disadvantages to establishing a revocable living trust? Believe it or not, the answer is yes. First, there is the expense, which is a very minor disadvantage in estate planning scenarios. A revocable living trust is more expensive than a will because it requires not only the trust document, but also a companion pour-over will and the attorney's assistance in transferring assets to the trust during your lifetime. (However, these expenses should not deter anyone from doing a revocable living trust if she needs one.) Following are some tax disadvantages to doing a revocable living trust.

- Trusts must have a calendar year. This means that every trust, including the revocable living trust, must file a tax return based on a year-end of December 31. Estates, however, may select the last day of any month of the year as their fiscal year-end. This means that property held in an estate (and not in a revocable living trust) may file a tax return based on a year ending January 31, February 28, March 31, etc. This allows for deferral of the payment of tax, an opportunity not available for assets in a revocable living trust.

- Estates enjoy a $600 per year exemption from income tax; most trusts enjoy only a $100 exemption.

Most banks have a type of revocable living trust that, in reality, is simply an arrangement whereby the bank is engaged to invest assets and pay bills of the individual establishing the trust. These trusts provide that, at death, the property in the trust is turned over to the executor of the individual's estate. They do not avoid probate. Rather, this is simply a way for the bank to manage things while you are alive. This has a particular attraction for older single women who are childless or women whose children either live out of state or are not handy at assisting with financial affairs. An example of this type of revocable living trust can be found at the end of this chapter.

GIFTING

After protecting $1,200,000 (assuming you are married) through having credit shelter (family or residuary) trusts in your will and your husband's will, and after transferring any life insurance on either of you so that it will not be taxed in either estate, you still may be over $1,200,000 (in 1997). If you're not too much over, you might be able to utilize present interest gifts to eliminate your estate tax. The Internal Revenue Code provides that anyone may give $10,000 (indexed for inflation by the 1997 Taxpayers Relief Act) to as many people as he or she desires every year without reporting it to the IRS.[10]

The IRS does not tax these gifts because it does not want to keep up with smaller gifts. Otherwise, people would have to report birthday presents, Christmas presents, and cash given to adult children on gift tax returns. To qualify for this exclusion, a gift must be a "present interest" gift, which means that the recipient must have a present (as opposed to future) right to enjoy it. As with the insurance trusts discussed earlier in this chapter, premium dollars paid to the trust are converted into present interest gifts by notifying the beneficiaries of the trust that they have the right to withdraw contributions made to the trust.

For a woman who has several children and grandchildren, this can be an incredibly valuable tax-reduction technique. If you will recall, in Chapter 4, we discussed Fred and Fran whose taxable estate was $2,335,000. With no estate tax planning, the estate tax, at the survivor's death, was $752,150. Fred and Fran have three children and six grandchildren. By transferring the $1 million of life insurance on Fred's life to an insurance trust, correct titling of assets between the two of them, and utilizing a credit shelter trust in each will, the taxable estate is reduced to $235,000. With a total of nine children and grandchildren, Fred and Fran could each give each of their children and grandchildren $10,000 each year. In other words, in one year they could give their children and grandchildren $180,000! This means that, in no more than two years, all estate tax could be eliminated on the estates of Fred and Fran.

Even if a husband and wife have property titled in only one of their names, the propertied spouse may give $20,000 each to as many individuals he or she desires with the other spouse simply agreeing on a properly filed gift tax return that he or she will let the other spouse use his or her $10,000 per donee per year present interest gift exclusion.[11]

When the subject of gifts is being discussed, people often ask which assets are best for giving. From a strictly tax standpoint, high basis assets that are the most likely to appreciate are the best assets to give to children and grandchildren. Assets with a very low basis (basis meaning general cost) in the hands of the parents will get a stepped-up basis if the parents die with those assets. If assets get a stepped-up basis, this means that the children can sell them without the payment of capital gains tax.[12] In addition, if the most rapidly appreciating assets are placed in the hands of the children or grandchildren, then neither the appreciation nor the assets given will be taxed in the parent's estate.

The tax law also considers any amount paid on behalf of any person as tuition to an educational organization or to any person who provides medical care with respect to an individual to be a tax-free gift (not even coming within the $10,000 per donee per year limitation). In other words, good Samaritans who pay medical bills on behalf of individuals (even individuals not related to them, and even medical bills running into several hundreds of thousands of dollars) need not report these gifts to the IRS.[13] This is a great way for a grandparent to increase the amount transferred to his or her grandchildren. By simply paying a grandchild's tuition, a grandparent makes a tax-free gift.

When parents and grandparents make gifts to minor children, several options are available. First, the parent or grandparent, in order to preserve simplicity, may establish a *custodial account* under state law. A *custodial account* is simply an arrangement whereby property is transferred to a minor for whom a custodian is named. The custodian will manage the property for the minor until the minor is 21 years old (or other applicable state law age), at which time the property is turned over outright to the minor. The child's social security number is used to establish the account, and no attorney is needed. The parent or grandparent simply gets in touch with the stockbroker or bank and instructs the broker or the bank to set up a custodial account. If the parent of the child (or the grandparent) is the custodian of the account he or she establishes, then inclusion in the parent's or grandparent's estate (if the parent or grandparent dies before the child is age 21) occurs.[14] Nonetheless, most parents or grandparents act as custodians for their minor children's and grandchildren's custodial accounts.

Another way to give property to minor children is to establish a *minor's trust*. A minor's trust is a very simple trust, which simply provides that, before the minor is age 21, the trust property (corpus and income) may be spent for the benefit of the minor and, to the extent not so spent, will pass to the minor on his or her attaining the age of 21 and, in the event of death prior to age 21, will be paid to his or her estate. This type of trust is considered a present interest gift even though a minor may receive no income from the trust for years (the years prior to college, for example).[15] The advantage of this type of trust is that it is very simple to draft and automatically qualifies as a present interest gift, meaning that it is eligible to receive $10,000 per donee per year gifts from parents and grandparents with no requirement to notify the trust beneficiary of contributions made.

The final type of trust used for minors is more complicated. Here, the terms may be any terms the parent or grandparent desires. For example, if the parent believes that a child should not receive property outright until he or she is 40, then the trust may so stipulate. However, contributions to this type of trust do not qualify as present interest gifts eligible for the $10,000 per donee per year present interest gift exclusion without certain provisions in the trust document. These provisions, discussed previously, require the notification of beneficiaries and the allowing of reasonable time to withdraw any contributions made. Otherwise, the gifts will not qualify for the $10,000 per donee per year exclusions, and the parent or grandparent will have to file a gift tax return and report to the IRS that gifts were made and part of the $600,000 exempt amount was used.

Any time parents or grandparents make gifts in excess of the $10,000 per donee per year excluded amount, then the one-time (usable either during life or at death) $600,000 exempt amount is diminished to the extent of the excess.

NOTES

1. I.R.C. § 2041(b)(1)(A).
2. I.R.C. § 2041(b)(1)(C).
3. I.R.C. § 2056(b)(7).
4. I.R.C. § 2056(b)(5).
5. I.R.C. § 2042(2).
6. I.R.C. § 2035(d)(2).
7. I.R.C. § 2503(b).
8. I.R.C. § 2036(a)(1).
9. I.R.C. § 2036(a)(1).
10. I.R.C. § 2503(b).
11. I.R.C. § 2513(a).
12. I.R.C. § 1014(a)(1).
13. I.R.C. § 2503(e)(2).
14. I.R.C. § 2038(a)(1).
15. I.R.C. § 2503(c)(1),(2).

SAMPLE BANK TRUST AGREEMENT

I, _____, of _____, West Carolina, hereby transfer to XYZ BANK, as Trustee, the property identified in the attached Schedule of Property. The trust property so identified, any property added to the trust in accordance with the provisions of this instrument, and all investments and reinvestments thereof (hereinafter referred to as the "trust principal") shall be held upon the following terms:

ARTICLE I

Commencing as of the date of this instrument and during our joint lives, the Trustee shall administer the trust principal and any net income thereof as follows:

A. The Trustee shall distribute to me or apply for my own or my spouse's (if I am married) benefit such amounts of net income and principal, even to the extent of exhausting principal, as the Trustee believes desirable from time to time for my or my spouse's health, support in reasonable comfort, best interests, and welfare, considering all circumstances and factors deemed pertinent by the Trustee. Any undistributed net income shall be accumulated and added to principal, as from time to time determined by the Trustee.

B. In addition, the Trustee shall distribute to me or others such amounts of net income and principal as I may from time to time direct. My direction(s) shall be confirmed by the Trustee's periodic accounting sent to me.

ARTICLE II

A. As of the date of my death, the Trustee shall distribute the remaining trust principal to the personal representative of my estate.

B. Despite the foregoing paragraph, the Trustee may retain and pay over such sums as it, in its sole judgment, determines necessary to satisfy any or all income, gift, estate, generation-skipping, or other taxes, however identified, for which the trustee may, directly or indirectly, be liable to any taxing authority.

ARTICLE III

A. I give to the Trustee and incorporate by reference those powers set out in West Carolina General Statutes Section 32–27 (except for those powers set out in Section 32–27(29)), subject to the restrictions of Section 32–26, in effect at the signing of this instrument and those powers set out in West Carolina General Statutes Section 36A–136 (except for those powers set out in Section 36A–136(21). In addition, I direct the Trustee to retain and vote (to the extent voting is permitted by law from time to time) any security issued by it or the bank holding company of which it is a part, until such time as it shall receive written instructions to the contrary. I relieve the Trustee from any and all liability it may incur for retention of any security issued by it or the bank holding company of which it is a part. In addition, I give the Trustee the power to allocate receipts and disbursements between income and principal of the trust in such manner as it, in its sole discretion, may determine even if such allocation is contrary to West Carolina's Principal and Income Act.

B. The powers granted in this Article may be exercised even after termination of this trust until actual distribution of all trust principal.

C. To the extent that such requirements can legally be waived, no Trustee hereunder shall ever be required to give bond or security as Trustee, or to qualify before, be appointed by, or account to any court, or to obtain the order or approval of any court respecting the exercise of any power or discretion granted in this instrument.

D. The Trustee's exercise or nonexercise of powers and discretions in good faith shall be conclusive on all persons. No person paying money or delivering property to any trustee hereunder shall be required or privileged to see to its application. The Certificate of the Trustee that the Trustee is acting in compliance with this instrument shall fully protect all persons dealing with a Trustee.

E. This instrument and all dispositions hereunder shall be governed by and interpreted in accordance with the laws of the State of West Carolina.

F. The compensation of the Trustee shall be in accordance with its published schedule of fees as in effect at the time the services are rendered. Such compensation may be charged to principal or to income or partly to each in the discretion of the Trustee. In the event my estate is not subject to probate and no personal representative is appointed, the Trustee shall prepare and file, or cause to be prepared and filed, the federal estate tax return and such other returns as may be necessary. For any such extraordinary services, the Trustee shall receive additional compensation.

ARTICLE IV

A. Any Trustee may resign at any time by giving prior written notice to me.

B. During my lifetime, I shall have the following powers:

(1) To remove and replace the Trustee by written instrument delivered to the Trustee;

(2) To approve the accounts of the Trustee with the same effect as if the accounts had been approved by a court having jurisdiction of the subject matter and of all necessary parties; and

(3) To appoint successor Trustee(s) in the event any Trustee shall cease to act as Trustee for any reason.

Should I not be competent to so act, my spouse shall have the powers listed in 2 and 3 (but not 1) above.

ARTICLE V

I reserve the right from time to time during my life, by written instrument delivered to the Trustee, to amend or revoke this instrument in whole or in part; provided, however, that no amendment may substantially increase the duties of the Trustee or decrease Trustee compensation without the written consent of the Trustee, and if this instrument is completely revoked, all trust property held by the Trustee shall be transferred and delivered to me or as I may otherwise direct in writing.

ARTICLE VI

The parties agree that any dispute arising out of or relating to this Trust Agreement, or the breach of it, shall be settled by binding arbitration administered by and pursuant to the Commercial Arbitration Rules of the American Arbitration Association and judgment on the award rendered by the arbitrator(s) may be entered in any court having jurisdiction of the subject matter. Such arbitration shall be held in Townville, West Carolina.

I now sign this Trust Agreement on _____, _____.

_____
Settlor

The trust created by the foregoing instrument is accepted as of the day and year last above written.

XYZ BANK

By: _____

As its:_____

SCHEDULE OF PROPERTY

This schedule is attached to and forms a part of that certain trust agreement executed by _____ and identifies the initial trust property held subject to the trust thereunder.

Sophisticated Estate Planning

Tax Planning Techniques for Larger Estates

Any one may so arrange [her] affairs so
that [her] taxes shall be as low as possible . . .
there is not even a patriotic duty to increase one's taxes.
Judge Learned Hand

—*Halvering v. Gregory,* 69 F.2d 809 (2nd cir., 1934)

For the woman who is fortunate enough to have an estate well over $600,000 ($1 million by the year 2006) if she is single or $1,200,000 ($2 million by the year 2006) if she is married, and for whom making $10,000 (as indexed by the Tax Reform Act of 1997) per donee gifts to children and grandchildren will not eliminate the estate tax, this chapter will consider more sophisticated tax planning techniques. Generally, these techniques involve some combination of lifetime giving, insurance, charitable transactions (discussed in Chapter 10), and value reducing techniques. When these techniques are combined, substantial reduction in estate and gift taxes can be achieved.

The choice of techniques to use in any given situation depends on many factors, including the age and health of the individual at the time the estate plan is being prepared, whether everything is going to children or some is going to charity, the size of the estate, and even the gene pool (the longevity of the individual's ancestors). This is where estate planning crosses the line from science to art. If we had a crystal ball, we could do perfect estate planning. Since we don't, many educated guesses must be made.

This chapter will examine various estate tax reduction techniques for larger estates. But before looking at sophisticated trust or partnership arrangements, let's first consider the advantages of simple inter vivos gifting beyond the $10,000 (as indexed) per donee per year exclusion.

TAX ADVANTAGES OF GIVING BEYOND THE $10,000 PER DONEE PER YEAR EXCLUSION AMOUNT

Once I had a client with several million dollars in Coca-Cola stock. She and her husband, both in their 60s, had never given beyond the $10,000 per donee per year present interest gift exclusion to their children. However, in December 1993, they decided to establish a trust for their children and give $1,200,000 of the Coca-Cola stock to the trust. The trust lasts until the survivor of them dies, and then it is distributed equally to the children. In order to give $1,200,000 to their children in one year, they each had to use the full $600,000 exemption amount, meaning that there is none left to use on their estate tax return. They filed a gift tax return, reporting that they had fully used their exemptions. No gift tax was paid. Coca-Cola stock split in 1996. Today, the $1,200,000 of Coca-Cola stock they gave to the trust is worth approximately $3,000,000. This means that $1,800,000 has already escaped estate taxation (the current value less the $1,200,000 that they reported as taxable gifts). In all likelihood, the survivor of them will live another 25 years. What will the stock be worth then? Probably many times over what it was worth in December 1993. In other words, simply by giving the stock away during their lifetimes, they avoided tax on *all* of the appreciation from the date of gift to the date of the survivor's death. Remember, the best assets to give away are those with a high cost basis relative to fair market value or those that are likely to appreciate most rapidly.

Another reason to not only give assets but give in excess of the $600,000 (as indexed) exemption amount ($1,200,000 [as indexed] if you are married) and pay gift tax is that gift tax is a cheaper tax than estate tax. The rates are the same, but a gift tax is calculated on a tax-exclusive basis, while an estate tax is calculated on a tax-inclusive basis. A simple example will illustrate the difference. Suppose you have $1 and you are in a 50 percent gift tax bracket and a 50 percent estate tax bracket. With this $1, you have to pay your tax and give the rest to your children. If you die with the $1, you must pay 50¢ to the IRS, and the remaining 50¢ may go to your children. However, if you take the same $1 and give as much as possible to your children during your lifetime and then use the rest to pay the gift tax, you may give your children 66⅔¢ and pay the government only 33⅓¢. This is the difference between paying estate tax on the estate tax dollars themselves and not paying gift tax on the gift tax dollars—a very significant difference in large estates. Sam Walton, the founder of Wal-Mart, for example, gave millions to his children during his life, paying the gift tax.

There is one catch, however. If you actually pay a gift tax, in order for the gift tax dollars not to be deemed part of your taxable estate, you must live three years beyond the date of the payment of the tax.[1]

One other benefit of actually filing a return, paying a gift tax, and "making" the three-year period (during which the government may audit the return) is that, once the statutory three-year period is up, the government is then barred from revaluing the gifts for gift tax purposes.[2] (This is important for hard-to-value gifts.) According to more than one former IRS agent, the government is far less likely to audit gift tax returns than estate tax returns. Therefore, the time period during which the government *may* audit is likely to expire.

A final benefit of making gifts of certain types of assets, such as closely held stock, is the way the courts have looked at these gifts and awarded discounts for minority interests. Let's say you own 100 percent of The Great American Apple Pie Company, a closely held company worth $3 million. You have other assets worth $3 million. You have three children and would like to give the stock to your three children who assist you in the business. You are in a 55 percent estate tax bracket, meaning that if you were to die today and leave the stock of The Great American Apple Pie Company to your children by will, your executor would first have to turn over $1,000,000 to the government. The government, in other words, would get more than any child of yours. However, if you were to decide that you had been baking apple pies long enough and wanted to retire, and you were ready to simply give away the stock to the children because you had other assets to support yourself, you could give one-third of the stock to each child. If no discount were available, each third would be worth $1 million for gift tax purposes. However, because you are giving a *minority* interest to each child, a substantial minority interest discount (as well as a marketability [i.e., it's hard to sell] discount) could be taken. In order to compare apples with apples, let us assume that the $3 million value for estate tax purposes takes into account the marketability discount. Your appraiser tells you, however, that a 25 percent minority interest discount is reasonable for gift tax purposes. Therefore, each block of stock is now worth only $750,000. This means that you can value the three gifts (for gift tax purposes) at $2,250,000. If your husband graciously allows you to use his $600,000 exemption, you can offset the gifts by $1,200,000 of exemptions, and you have taxable gifts of $1,050,000. Your children, thrilled to receive the stock so soon, agree to pay your gift tax (a so-called net gift),[3] and with bonuses they will give themselves by virtue of now owning the Company, they can well afford to do so. The point is that, in valuing gifts of minority interests in certain types of assets, such as closely held stock, the courts look at what each recipient is *receiving* rather than the entire block of stock being given.[4] On the other hand, if you retain the entire block until death, the courts look at what is being *transferred,* and no minority interest discount is available. This technique can be invaluable in reducing the transfer tax costs of certain types of assets.

INSURANCE

For reasons obvious to everyone, insurance is very useful in estate planning. Term insurance can provide a younger woman with security for herself and her children if something happens to her husband (or to her if she is single), particularly before the children are fully educated. Insurance can also provide immediate liquidity upon the death of a business owner. If the business (or any illiquid asset for that matter) is a major asset in the estate and is causing most of the estate tax, it is especially important to provide adequate liquidity to pay the taxes. Although there are relief provisions in the Internal Revenue Code that allow your executor to pay taxes attributable to a closely held business over a 15-year period (as long as the business equals at least 35 percent of your estate), the IRS does charge interest.[5] It is nice to be in a position to pay off all the tax immediately. Insurance can put you in a good position to do so.

What we really want to consider here is whether it makes sense, from a purely economic standpoint, to buy insurance to pay estate taxes. It is common knowledge that an insurance company will not even issue a policy unless it believes the insured is going to live to a ripe old age. In short, if you have significant health problems, you don't get the coverage. The company won't take a risk on you if it doesn't think you're going to reach your life expectancy (or it will rate you, which increases the cost). Obviously, if the insurance company is wrong—if you buy the policy, pay the premiums, and get hit by a truck—then you have made a great investment. For you, the insurance made economic sense. But this is not what you're counting on. You're counting on living to your life expectancy. Is there, then, any rationale for purchasing life insurance if you're counting on paying the premiums for as long as you live?

There may be. The beauty of insurance is that you can take dollars that would otherwise be fully taxed in your estate (assume that you are in the top estate tax bracket of 55 percent) and convert them, through using the $10,000 (indexed) per donee per year exclusion from gift tax, into estate tax-free dollars by having the insurance policy owned either by a trust or by adult children. For example, suppose that you and your husband paid $1 million in insurance premiums to an insurance company over a 20-year period. Had you not sent this money to the insurance company, you would have invested it and would have had, at the survivor's death, $2 million after tax. At a 55 percent bracket, the children would get to keep $900,000 after the government received its 55 percent cut. If, instead, over the 20-year period $50,000 per year had been contributed to an insurance trust with at least five beneficiaries (your children and grandchildren), then the $50,000 paid in premiums each year could be transferred gift tax free. At the survivor's death, the $1 million in policy proceeds would come into the trust with no estate tax to be paid. This means that your children would have $1 million as opposed to the $900,000 had you not purchased the insurance. Of course, you need to make your own analysis. Many factors enter into whether this technique will pay off economically. One of the most important factors is how savvy an investor you are. If you excel at investing money, then you are going to be better off in almost all circumstances by not giving your money to an insurance company. However, if you hate investing and your usual practice is to buy CDs or municipal bonds, then take a close look at whether an insurance product can pay off for you.

Let's change the facts slightly. Assume that, instead of leaving the $2 million to your children, you want to leave it to your grandchildren. Furthermore, let's assume you are single. As we discussed in Chapter 3, you may leave $1 million (indexed by the 1997 Taxpayer Relief Act) to your grandchildren without the imposition of the generation-skipping tax. However, the second $1 million would be subject to two taxes, the 55 percent estate tax and a 55 percent generation-skipping tax, for an effective combined tax rate of *79.75 percent*. This means that your grandchildren would get to keep $450,000 of the first $1 million and only $212,500 of the second $1 million for a total of $652,500. On the other hand, if you had transferred $50,000 per year for 20 years to an insurance trust, you would have used up the $1 million (indexed) exemption protecting the trust from generation-skipping taxes, and there would be no tax imposed on the $1 million coming into the trust for your grandchildren. In this scenario, the grandchildren would come out $347,500 better off than without the insurance.

DYNASTY TRUSTS

One technique advocated by estate planners and insurance agents alike is the dynasty trust, a trust drafted to avoid taxation in the insured's children's estates, the insured's grandchildren's estates, the insured's great-grandchildren's estates, and so on—for as long as the state law will allow the trust to run. Most states have laws that prohibit perpetual trusts. These laws, called *rules against perpetuities,* generally prohibit a trust from lasting much beyond 90 years. In a dynasty trust, the assets avoid estate taxation at several generational levels for as long as the trust can run, then the trust must terminate and be distributed to the insured's descendants. If it weren't for the dynasty trust, the trust property would be taxed in the estate of each generation.

With the help of an insurance agent, a former law partner of mine used the following illustration to explain how a dynasty trust could assist a client (and the client's spouse) in estate planning.

Example: Sally and Bill have a large estate. They could leave their entire estate to their children with the expectation that they will leave it to their children and each successive generation will leave it to the next generation. Sally and Bill each have a $1 million exemption from the generation-skipping tax, but let's assume they don't take advantage of it.

We'll concentrate on $2,306,000 of their estate in 1997, because if Sally and Bill transferred $2 million to a trust for all succeeding generations for as long as the law would allow the trust to last, they would have to pay a gift tax of $306,000 (assuming neither of them had used any of their $600,000 exemption amount previously). Thus, a total of $2,306,000 would be removed from their estates.

Let's further assume that this amount would appreciate at an after-tax rate of 6 percent, that none of the income earned on this amount would be spent by succeeding generations, but would rather be reinvested, that Sally and Bill would live another 15 years, and that each succeeding generation lives 25 years beyond the death of their parents. How much would this $2,306,000 be worth at the end of 90 years? Assume that the state rule against perpetuities says a trust can last until the later of 90 years or 21 years after the death of the last surviving beneficiary of the trust who was living when the trust was established, which we will estimate to be 99 years.

With no trust, at the death of the survivor of Sally and Bill in 15 years, the $2,306,000 will have grown to $5,526,463. After paying an estate tax of $2,157,555, $3,368,908 will be left for their children. When their children die 25 years later, $7,058,513 ($14,458,918 less $7,400,405 in estate tax) will pass to the third generation. This continues until the expiration of 99 years, when the trust amount distributed to the descendants has grown to $44,481,999. Although this sounds like a lot of money, with a 4 percent inflation rate, the inflation-adjusted value is only $915,975. Using this approach, their original $2,306,000 has shrunk significantly in value by more than 50 percent.

Let's compare this to transferring property worth $2 million into a dynasty trust that provides for all income to be accumulated until it terminates at the expiration of the maximum period allowed. Sally and Bill still pay the gift tax of $306,000 out of their separate property. They fully utilize their $2 million generation-skipping exemptions on the property transferred to the trust. Therefore, all property in the trust and all future appreciation will be exempt from both estate tax and generation-skipping tax at each generational level until the trust terminates. If the property in the trust appreciates at a 6 percent after-tax rate, how much will the original $2 million be worth at the end of 99 years? Because it will avoid three generations of estate and gift tax, at the end of 99 years, it will be worth $640,192,620—more than 14 times as much as it would be with the no-trust approach. Assuming the same 4 percent inflation rate over the period, Sally and Bill have beat inflation by almost six times!

Finally, instead of simply investing the $2 million placed in the dynasty trust, let's assume Sally and Bill use it to purchase a second-to-die life insurance policy. Assume that the $2 million will buy a projected death benefit of $8,333,333, and the survivor of Sally and Bill lives another 15 years. At the expiration of the 99 years, assuming a 6 percent after-tax growth rate on the policy proceeds paid at the death of the survivor, the original $2 million put into the trust will be worth $1,113,041,700, more than 25 times the no-trust approach, beating inflation by approximately 12.5 times.[6]

VALUE REDUCING TECHNIQUES

The value-reducing techniques take advantage of two concepts to reduce the value of assets prior to your transferring them to your children. The first concept is based on timing. If your children receive something after a period of time (several years), that asset is worth less than if they were to receive it outright immediately. If someone were to ask you whether you would rather receive $1 million today or 10 years from today, you know what you'd say. You know intuitively that the $1 million is worth more to you if you receive it now than if you receive it 10 years from now. In other words, use of the money for a 10-year period is a valuable asset in and of itself, because it earns interest or dividends during that time. The tax law acknowledges this concept and allows us to reduce the value of something given through a trust to children after a period of time. The *grantor retained income trust,* the *grantor retained annuity trust,* and the *qualified personal residence trust* all take advantage of this principle.

The other way to reduce a property's value is by putting restrictions on the property. We all know that real estate that is virtually unrestricted (where one could build a factory or store or gas station if one desired) is more valuable than restricted real estate (restricted by zoning to single-family residences, for example). In order to create restrictions on property prior to transfer, you may use a family partnership. The partnership agreement places restrictions on what the limited partners can do with their interests, thus reducing the value of those interests for gift tax purposes. The IRS test for what something is worth is what a willing buyer and willing seller would negotiate, both being fully aware of all relevant facts. The idea is that, with all these restrictions, a willing buyer would not pay the underlying value of the assets, because he or she would not be able to sell his or her interests on the market, demand distributions from the general partner, or be able to liquidate the interests at will.

Grantor Retained Income Trust

The *grantor retained income trust* (GRIT) is an irrevocable trust where the grantor transfers property to a trustee to be managed by the trustee for a term of years. During the trust term, the trustee pays all the income from the property (whether it is a little or a lot) to the grantor. At the termination of the trust, the property goes to whomever the grantor has named in the trust document, typically the grantor's children.

Up until 1990, this was a great technique for a parent to use to give assets to children. Parents would put low-income-producing property into the trust, simply receiving the income and letting the trust appreciation go to the children at the termination of the term. The parents would file a gift tax return reflecting a gift of a remainder interest to the children. This gift, however, does not qualify for the $10,000 (indexed) per donee per year present interest gift exclusion, because it is a future interest gift rather than a present interest gift. The value of the remainder interest is only a fraction of the full value of the property transferred to the trust. The fraction is dependent upon two things—the length of the trust and the "applicable federal rate" on the date the property is transferred to the trust. The *applicable federal rate* (AFR) is an assumed trust rate of return that the IRS publishes on a monthly basis and which must be used in valuing interests in trusts.[7] Your accountant or estate planning attorney will be aware of these rates and can assist you in calculating remainder interests in the trusts described in this chapter.

The IRS never liked GRITS because parents would put rapidly appreciating, low-yielding property in a GRIT and receive very little out of the trust during its term, a practice the IRS considered abusive. As a result, in 1990 the IRS persuaded Congress to enact legislation addressing this abuse.[8] After passage of this legislation, no longer did the old GRIT work if the remainder beneficiaries were family members.[9] "Family members" were defined as "the grantor's spouse, any ancestor or lineal descendant of the grantor or the grantor's spouse, any sibling and the spouse of any such person."[10] The notable exceptions were nieces and nephews. So, if you would like to set up a GRIT, leaving a remainder to your niece or nephew, you may still do so.

Example: Dorothy, a successful businesswoman with no children of her own, adores her niece, Amy. Dorothy establishes a GRIT that lasts for 10 years, remainder to Amy. Dorothy is 65. Dorothy places low-yielding but rapidly appreciating stock in the trust, which is worth $1 million. If Dorothy dies during the trust term, it comes back into her estate. Dorothy creates the GRIT when the AFR is 8.2 percent. The value of the $1 million stock to Amy is $334,946. If, during the term of the GRIT, the stock triples in value, then Amy will receive $3 million at the end of the trust term, although Dorothy reported a gift of only $334,946.

In order for this technique to work, Dorothy must live through the trust term. If she dies during the trust term, the property comes back into her estate.[11] But to the extent she used her exemption on her gift tax return, she may reuse that exemption on her estate tax return.[12] So the technique is a no-lose technique. Dorothy does not gain its benefit if she dies during the 10-year term, but if she lives, she has transferred a great deal of property to Amy, levering her exemption amount.

Qualified Personal Residence Trusts

Although GRITs are wonderful estate planning techniques, the inability to use them to transfer assets to family members is a decided drawback. Fortunately, there is one notable exception, but a little background is in order first.

One's house or personal residence (even one's vacation home) has always been a tax-favored asset. You already know the advantages in terms of income tax. You may sell your house and roll over the proceeds tax-free into a new residence, as long as the new residence costs more than the old residence. You and your husband may also avoid paying capital gains tax on $500,000 (after 1997) if you sell your residence at age 55 or above (the figure is $250,000 if you are single). In the transfer tax area, one's house has been given a special exclusion from the rule that a common-law GRIT cannot terminate in favor of a family member.[13]

With respect to one's personal residence and one other vacation residence, a GRIT may be established with the remainder to a child or grandchild. This is called a *qualified personal residence trust* (QPRT, pronounced "Q-pert"). There are very strict rules governing these trusts and what may be placed in them. Generally, QPRT may hold the personal residence, one other residence if used primarily as a residence, cash required to pay up to six months of expenses, cash intended to be expended for improvements within six months, sale or insurance proceeds for up to two years pending the replacement or repair, and an insurance policy on the residence. No other assets may be placed in a QPRT.[14]

As with the common-law GRIT, for the QPRT the value of the interest going to the children or grandchildren for gift tax purposes is the value of the entire trust less what the parent retains. This is the sum of the value of the income interest (in a QPRT, the right to use the house during the term) plus the value of the contingent right to receive the house back if the parent dies during the term.

Example: Bob and Jane, ages 55 and 54 respectively, have a $1 million residence and are in a 55 percent estate tax bracket. They realize that, at some point in their lives, they will want to downscale and move into a condominium. They establish a 20-year QPRT. Because Jane has the longer life expectancy, they first transfer the residence to Jane and let her transfer it to the QPRT, which runs for 20 years. During the 20-year term, they continue to live in the residence and enjoy it. At the termination of the trust, the residence goes equally to their children. At that time, Bob and Jane figure, they will be ready for a smaller place with less responsibility. The AFR is 8.2

percent when the trust is established. A gift to the children of $137,576 has been made, and Bob and Jane may treat this as a gift made one-half by each of them on a gift tax return. If Jane lives through the trust term, then the technique worked for estate planning purposes. If Jane dies during the trust term, the value of the residence comes back into her estate, and she may pass the residence by her will. She will get back the amount of credit she that she used on her gift tax return.

One question that comes up when QPRTs are established is how much land can be included with the residence. I have had several people ask about contributing a house that sits in the middle of 200 acres to a QPRT. Unfortunately, only a limited amount of land (generally not more than five acres) is deemed to be residential land and can be transferred.[15]

Another concern is that, at the termination of the QPRT, the parents may decide that they want to continue living in the residence, even though it will belong to their children. If the children are cooperative and agree that the parents can continue to live in their house, the parents must pay fair rental value to the children in order for the transaction to be respected by the IRS. Of course, if the parents have major estate tax problems anyway, this is just another way to give money gift-tax-free to the children. However, there may be a psychological hurdle to paying rent to live in one's own house. If there is some concern that the children might not allow you to live in your house at the termination of the QPRT, then at the creation of the QPRT, you may enter into an agreement with the children stating that they will rent the residence to you at fair rental value after the termination of the QPRT.[16] Or you may have, as a remainder beneficiary, a trust for the children with a friendly trustee you know will rent the home to you after termination of the QPRT.

The real benefits of the QPRT are that it obtains a significant discount for transfer tax purposes; allows you to continue to live in your home throughout the trust term; requires no annual filing of trust income tax returns (because the residence doesn't generate income); and, even after termination, allows for gift-tax-free transfers of rental income to children.

Grantor Retained Annuity Trusts

If you have a residence to pass to your children, or if you have no children and wish to pass any type of assets to nieces, nephews, or nonfamily members, GRITS and QPRTs are great. However, if you have stocks and bonds you wish to pass to your children, GRITS and QPRTS are not available. One possibility, if you find yourself in this category, is the *grantor retained annuity trust* (GRAT).

A GRAT is, like the QPRT, an irrevocable trust lasting for a specified term and terminating in favor of children or grandchildren. However, instead of simply requiring that all the income (or the use of the property if it generates no income) go to the grantor of the trust during the term, a fixed dollar amount (an annuity) must be retained by the grantor throughout the term. When Congress enacted the tax laws applicable to QPRTs and GRATs, and prohibited GRITs from being available for family members, it perceived that there was abuse when parents transferred property generating very little income to GRITs, and then had the GRITs terminate in favor of the children. The calculated value for gift tax purposes of what went to the children was far less than it should have been because parents typically transferred very low-yielding assets to the old-style GRITs. Therefore, Congress required that the parent retain a yield from the trust that actually reflected the value of the parent's interest versus the remainder interest going to the children or grandchildren.[17]

The grantor may determine the payout from the GRAT. As already explained, the IRS determines the applicable federal rate (AFR) used to calculate the value of the interest going to the children or grandchildren. The AFR is published monthly by the IRS in an announcement called a Revenue Procedure and is reflective of interest rates in general. Typically, the higher the AFR, the greater the value of the remainder interest going to the children.

As a transfer tax planning technique, the GRAT is simply not as effective as QPRTs and GRITs, because only one discount is achieved with the GRAT compared with two discounts achieved with QPRTs and GRITs. The only discount achieved is for the right that the parent retains to receive the annuity. In other words, only a present value discount is available.

Example: Let's assume that Dorothy wishes to establish a GRAT for Dottie, her child, instead of a GRIT for Amy, her niece. We will assume the same AFR of 8.2 percent, the same trust term of 10 years, and a payout equal to the AFR of 8.2 percent of the initial fair market value of the trust assets. If Dorothy transfers $1 million to the GRAT, she makes a gift to Dottie of $454,702 (compared to a gift of only $334,946 with the GRIT). Notice how much more leverage Dorothy achieves with the GRIT.

The GRAT may be helpful if you have fully used your exemption amount and don't want to pay gift tax. For example, suppose you have just discovered an opportunity to get in on the ground floor of a great new company. You purchase the stock and expect it to sky-rocket in the next two years. You already have a taxable estate and would like to pass this great opportunity on to your children. Suppose you establish a two-year GRAT. If the AFR is 10 percent, then a two-year GRAT must pay a 57.6 percent annuity for two years to result in a zero remainder interest. Suppose the stock appreciates 100 percent over the two-year period. If you invested $1 million, it has now grown to $2 million in value. With the trust paying you an annuity of $576,000 each year for the two-year period, then after two years you will be able to transfer $848,000 gift-tax-free to your children ($2 million—two annuity payments totaling $1,152,000).

Family Discount Limited Partnerships

GRITs, QPRTs, and GRATs take advantage of a timing discount. That is, children must wait for a period of time, during which the parent receives income from, the use of, or an annuity from the trust property before they, the children, receive anything. The family discount limited partnership achieves its discount not from timing, but from restrictions placed on the assets transferred to the partnership before they are given to the children in the form of limited partnership units. The partnership, therefore, has an advantage over the other techniques in that it is immediately effective for transfer tax purposes, whereas the trusts we have been discussing, are not effective until the parent survives the trust term.

With the family discount partnership technique, the senior family member transfers assets into a newly created partnership, receiving in exchange two types of units—general units and limited units. The transfer of assets in exchange for partnership units is tax free.[18] Typically, a very small percentage of the total units are general units. For example, in the partnerships we use in our office, 1 percent of the units (10 out of 1,000 issued), are allocated to the general units. The general units carry *all* of the control in the partnership. The remaining 99 percent of the units are limited units, and these are the units the parents will transfer to the children and grandchildren (retaining the general units).

The partnership is designed so that the limited units are quite restricted. This is done intentionally so that discounts can be achieved in valuing the limited units. Limited partners have no management rights over the partnership; rather, the general partner (or partners) controls the partnership. The general partner alone has the right to make all decisions regarding distributions of profits or other property from the partnership to the partners. This provision also tends to reduce the value of the limited partnership units.

- The limited partners are prohibited from amending the partnership agreement without the consent of the general partner. However, the agreement may give the general partner the authority to amend the partnership agreement in certain respects without the consent of the limited partners.

- Limited partners are prohibited from transferring their limited units without first giving all other partners a right of first refusal (right to buy the partnership units before offering them to anyone else).

- A purchaser of a limited partner unit will not be admitted as a limited partner without the consent of the general partner.

- While the partnership agreement typically requires the consent of all partners, general and limited, to liquidate or dissolve the partnership, a limited partner is prohibited from withdrawing from the partnership and receiving the value of the partnership interest.

All of these restrictions reduce the value of the limited units.[19]

After the partnership is drafted, an appraiser is hired to value the limited partner units. Appraisers typically award a 30 to 60 percent discount depending on several factors, including how conservative the appraiser is, the underlying assets contributed to the partnership (assets such as restricted stock may cause a higher discount than marketable securities), the number of restrictions placed on the limited units by the drafting attorney, and recent court decisions involving size of discounts.[20]

One of the attractive features of the discount partnership is that, if you are the general partner, you may receive a salary from the partnership for running it. This gives you the opportunity to retain income even after you have given away all of the limited partnership units. The amount of income you receive must meet the IRS test of "reasonableness." Of course, this test of "reasonableness" is subjective with opinions varying widely from person to person, but even so, there are general parameters. For example, if you place income-producing real estate into a partnership, you may take a fee for managing the real estate as well as a fee for performing the general administrative function of the partnership.

It is important that the partnership have a business purpose and that it be stated in the agreement. Some of the valid business purposes for establishing a family partnership include:

- Maintaining control of family assets
- Consolidating fractional interests in family assets

- Increasing family wealth

- Establishing a method by which annual gifts can be made to children and grandchildren without fractionalizing family assets

- Continuing the ownership of family assets and restricting the right of nonfamily members to acquire interests in family assets

- Protecting family assets from claims of future creditors against family members. (The family partnership is also effective as a creditor-protection technique. See Chapter 7.)

- Preventing the transfer of a family member's interest in the partnership as a result of a failed marriage

- Providing the family flexibility in business planning

- Facilitating the administration of and reducing the costs associated with probate (important in some states)

- Promoting knowledge of and communication about family assets among family members

The IRS may take the view that, if you don't have a valid business purpose for establishing a family partnership, then you are doing it purely to reduce your estate taxes. Therefore, the partnership entity may be disregarded by the IRS for tax purposes.[21] That is why it is important for all family members to understand your partnership's business purpose.

Example: Becky is a widow, age 78, with three children, six grandchildren, and an estate of $2 million. Her estate consists of her house ($200,000), a duplex which she rents ($300,000), and marketable securities ($1,500,000). Becky wants her estate to go to her three children and six grandchildren rather than to the government. She establishes a family discount limited partnership, into which she puts her duplex and $1,100,000 of the marketable securities. She keeps $400,000 of stocks and bonds and her $200,000 residence in her name, because she can leave $600,000 with no estate tax. The total value of assets going into the partnership is $1,400,000.

Becky's attorney sends the partnership agreement and a list of assets contributed to a securities appraiser. The securities appraiser writes a report and says that the limited partnership units receive a 50 percent discount. When the partnership is created, 1,000 units are issued—10 general units and 990 limited units. Becky will keep the 10 general units and give away the limited units. As general partner, she may take a salary from the partnership. She will give the limited units (worth together almost $700,000) to her nine children and grandchildren over a period of roughly the next 10 years. She can give her children and grandchildren combined $90,000 per year (9 × $10,000). If she lives until her mid-80s she can give most, if not all, of the limited units away, getting the value out of her estate for estate tax purposes. As the underlying stocks, bonds, and duplex increase in value, then the value of the limited units in the partnership will also increase on an annual basis, but Becky will be able to apply the 50 percent discount to that increased value prior to giving the units to her children and grandchildren.

Such a partnership must be designed and drafted by a competent estate planning attorney. Creation of a family discount limited partnership is to law what a heart transplant operation is to medicine: it is not a job for a general practitioner. If you live in a small town, you will probably need to go to a larger city in your state to have such a partnership done. The tips in Chapter 2 for choosing an estate planning attorney should help you locate the right person.

Gifts of Fractional Interests in Real Estate

If you own 100 percent of a piece of real estate, giving even a small percentage of it to your child or children can achieve a discount in value for transfer tax purposes. For example, let's assume you own a tract of land that is quickly becoming more valuable as the nearby city expands outward. You inherited this land from your mother, who died some time ago, and its current value is estimated at $1 million. You have one son, and your estate planning attorney recommends that you give that son a 10 percent interest. You would be entitled to a discount on this gift provided that you could prove that an undivided interest in real property is not readily divisible and marketable. Fortunately, this should be easy to do. Justifications for the discount include the facts that:

- both you and your son must agree on matters affecting the property.
- Procedural burdens involving delays and costs in partition and severance proceedings are involved.

- A minority undivided interest in the property would be difficult to sell.[22] Generally, discounts range from 10 to 20 percent. Your estate would wind up with a 90 percent interest in the real estate, and your executor could make the same arguments for discount of your 90 percent on your estate tax return.

MULTIPLE DISCOUNTS

While any one of the techniques discussed in this chapter is effective, but we really get dramatic results when we combine the techniques to achieve multiple discounts. For example, let's assume that Elizabeth, age 88 (but in good health for her age), has no children and wishes to leave everything to her nieces and nephews. She has an estate of $2 million, and she first establishes a family discount limited partnership and places her $2 million (mostly income-producing real estate) into the partnership. Her appraiser awards a 50 percent discount, so she now has an estate value, for transfer-tax purposes, at roughly $1 million. She places all of the limited units into a common-law GRIT (discussed above), remainder after four years to her nieces and nephews. At the time she establishes the GRIT, the AFR is 8.2 percent. The value of the remainder interest going to the nieces and nephews is 37.4 percent of the value of the assets transferred to the GRIT (in this case, 37.4 percent of roughly $1 million, or $374,000). This means that, in effect, Elizabeth has transferred $2 million of value into $374,000 of value for purposes of transferring it to her nieces and nephews. As general partner of the partnership, even after the GRIT terminates, she may still retain (reasonable) compensation for running the partnership. Through the double discount achieved through the partnership and the GRIT, she is able to avoid estate tax altogether.

Although estate tax is the highest tax imposed on individuals by our government, it is also the easiest tax to avoid. The techniques discussed in this chapter are very effective at reducing transfer taxation, but they must be done properly. Qualified estate planning attorneys, accountants, and appraisers are essential if these transactions are going to stand up to audits of gift and estate tax returns. Not only must the initial transaction be handled properly, but the accounting from the transaction to date of death must also be done properly in order for the IRS to respect the techniques.

NOTES

1. I.R.C. § 2035(c).

2. I.R.C. § 2504(c).

3. A net gift is a gift in which the donee agrees to pay the donor's gift tax liability.

4. See, e.g., *Estate of Bright v. United States*, 658 F.2d 999, 1002-03 (5th Cir., 1981).

5. I.R.C. § 6166.

6. Appreciation is expressed to John ("Jack") Baker and to David A. Montgomery for their design and review of this illustration.

7. I.R.C. § 7520(a).

8. The result was Chapter 14 of the Internal Revenue Code §§ 2701-2704.

9. I.R.C. § 2702(a)(2)(A).

10. I.R.C. § 2701(e)(2).

11. I.R.C. § 2036(a)(1).

12. I.R.C. § 2001.

13. Treas. Reg. § 25.2702-5.

14. Treas. Reg. § 25.2702-5.

15. Private Letter Rulings 9328040 and 9442019.

16. Private Letter Ruling 9425028.

17. I.R.C. § 2702(a)(2)(B).

18. I.R.C. § 721(a).

19. Typically, these discounts fall into the categories of minority interest discounts and lack of marketability discounts.

20. Examples of court cases awarding discounts for lack of marketability include:

    a. *Bernard Mandelbaum*, et. al. 69 TCM 2852 (1995)—30 percent lack of marketability.

    b. *Estate of Anthony Frank, Sr.*, 69 TCM 2255 (1995)—30 percent lack of marketability.

    c. *Estate of Joseph H. Lauder*, 68 TCM 985 (1994)—40 percent lack of marketability.

    d. *Estate of Jung v. Comm'r*, 101 T.C. 412 (1993)—35 percent lack of marketability.

    e. *Estate of William F. Luton*, 68 TCM 1044 (1994)—35 percent lack of marketability.

Examples of court cases awarding discounts for minority interests include:

    a. *Estate of Anthony Frank, Sr.*, 69 TCM 2255 (1995)—20 percent minority interest discount.

    b. *Estate of Ray A. Ford*, 66 TCM 1507 (1993), aff'd 53 F.3d 924 (8th Cir. 1995)—20 percent minority interest discount.

21. See, e.g., *Moore v. Commissioner*, 62 T.C.M. 1128 (1991).

22. See, e.g., *Estate of Youle v. Commissioner*, 56 T.C. Memo (CCH) 1594 (1989).

Powers of Attorney, Health Care Directives, and Living Wills

How to Prepare for Possible Disability

"It's always something."

—Roseanne Roseannadanna (Gilda Radner)

Good estate planning includes planning for possible disability. This may mean the aftermath of an accident, heart attack, or stroke; the ongoing struggle with Alzheimer's disease; or a gradual decline in general health due to advanced age or chronic illness. As the average life expectancy of Americans continues to climb due to advances in modern medical technology, many of us will find ourselves confronted with the task of caring for loved ones who are no longer able to manage their own finances or even their own health care decisions. All states have laws that provide for powers of attorney and health care directives. This chapter will review the legal documents available and the ramifications of the choices to be made in using them.

FINANCIAL POWER OF ATTORNEY

All states recognize by law the right of an individual to select someone to serve as his or her agent or representative in financial matters. The financial power of attorney or power of attorney for finances is a legal instrument by which you appoint an individual of your own choosing to act for you in handling your personal financial affairs. Under the terms of the power of attorney document, you are the principal, and the individual acting on your behalf is your *attorney-in-fact* or your agent. You may give your attorney-in-fact full authority to act for you in all circumstances, or you may limit the authority he or she has to act only in certain situations, only with respect to certain assets, or only for a limited period of time. Your attorney-in-fact may be authorized to pay your bills, deposit checks, pay loan installments, mortgage your house, purchase personal items, vote stock, sell real estate, file tax returns, hire professional advisors, manage your company, collect rents, or carry out any other business matters that you would normally carry out on your own. If you are named as the attorney-in-fact under a family member's power of attorney, you may, for example, deposit your mother's social security check into her bank account while she is in the hospital, attend the closing on your residence and sign on your husband's behalf while he is out of town at an emergency business meeting, or cash your daughter's college loan checks while she is studying abroad in Europe.

If you execute a *general* durable financial power of attorney, your attorney-in-fact can begin acting on your behalf immediately and in *all* business matters. "General" means that there are no limits on the scope of the power granted. By executing a general durable power of attorney, you are not stating that you are incompetent to manage your own affairs or that you no longer to wish to do so. Rather, you are merely making it possible for someone else to act for you whether or not you are able to act for yourself, and whether it is your actual incapacity or merely your inability to be present to carry out the transaction yourself. This is why is it important to choose someone you trust to serve as your attorney-in-fact and to discuss the power of attorney and your specific desires with that individual.

If you believe that your attorney-in-fact is not acting in accordance with your instructions, or if you wish to name someone else to act for you, you may always revoke your power of attorney. Unless you revoke it, or unless you expressly state in the document a time when your attorney-in-fact's authority ends, the general durable power of attorney will remain effective, even if you later become incompetent. This effectiveness, even in the event of subsequent incapacity, is what makes your power "durable."

Some powers of attorney are only effective upon the future incompetency of the person executing the power. This type of power may be called a conditional or a "springing" power of attorney. Your document's effectiveness may be conditioned upon your becoming seriously ill, physically incapacitated, or mentally incompetent. At such time, your attorney-in-fact's power and authority will "spring" into being, and he or she then will have the immediate power to act on your behalf with respect to all of your financial matters without needing further written authorization from you.

If you do not wish to give your attorney-in-fact full authority to act on your behalf, you may execute a limited or a special power of attorney. You may give your attorney-in-fact the power to sell only one piece of your property, transact business with respect to only one bank account, or only pay your monthly bills. In addition, you may limit the time period in which your attorney-in-fact may act for you. You may direct that your attorney-in-fact have the power to sell your house only on a set closing date or pay your utility bills only during the six months you are visiting relatives in Australia.

Your general durable power of attorney will automatically terminate upon your death. It also will terminate upon the death of your attorney-in-fact if you have not named in your document a successor attorney-in-fact. You may name a successor attorney-in-fact to act on your behalf in the event the first attorney-in-fact named is not able to act due to his or her own mental incapacity, inaccessibility, or death. In addition, you may choose two or more individuals to act together as your attorneys-in-fact. If you appoint two or more individuals, you may require that they reach unanimous consensus before taking any action.

A general durable power of attorney has special uses and advantages in an estate planning context. Under the terms of a standard revocable living trust, an individual trustor usually serves as trustee of his or her own trust until such time as he or she is incapacitated and can therefore no longer serve as trustee. In this case, the trustor typically has already named in the trust document one or more individuals to serve as successor trustee. In most cases, a successor trustee acts in the same way as an attorney-in-fact under a general durable power of attorney. However, the power of the successor trustee is limited to the assets in the trust. Government benefits, pensions, or other retirement assets, which are usually paid directly to the trustor, may not be trust property. Thus, the incapacitated trustor will need a general durable power of attorney to name someone to receive and transfer these payments to his or her trust. Naturally, the attorney-in-fact may be the same individual as the individual serving as successor trustee, but both documents must be executed before that individual may act in both capacities.

A power of attorney may be executed in conjunction with a *standby revocable trust*. A standby revocable trust contains provisions similar to those of a standard revocable living trust. However, the trustor usually does not transfer many, if any, assets to the standby revocable trust at the time the trust document is executed. Rather, it is intended that the trust will be funded by transfers made by the trustor's designated attorney-in-fact once the trustor has become incapacitated. Thus, this trust is "standing by" to receive the trustor's assets and provide a vehicle for their management once the trustor is no longer able to manage them. The roles of the attorney-in-fact and the general durable power of attorney document are obviously essential to carrying out this special needs (or disability) planning option.

In addition to using a general durable power of attorney to begin or continue funding a revocable living trust after your incapacity, some states' laws permit you to authorize your attorney-in-fact under a general durable power of attorney to make gifts to family members or their trusts, to friends, or to charitable organizations. In this way, your attorney-in-fact may either continue your annual giving program even after you have become incapacitated or initiate an estate plan on your behalf to reduce the amount of estate tax your estate will have to pay. In addition, your attorney-in-fact may be given the authority to disclaim property on your behalf. Thus, if you receive a sizable bequest from your spouse or another family member while you are incapacitated, and a disclaimer of that property would not deprive you of needed income or property but would result in better estate tax consequences for your estate, your attorney-in-fact may choose to disclaim the bequest.

There are many reasons to include a general durable power of attorney in your estate plan and to encourage older family members to do the same. For one thing, it is a fairly simple and inexpensive legal document. With proper drafting by an experienced attorney, even a simple power of attorney may be used to handle many different types of transactions from the very basic (purchasing clothing with checks from the principal's personal bank account) to the very complex (sale of the principal's company).

From an estate planning perspective, however, there are some drawbacks to the power of attorney, but these may be avoided by the use of a revocable living trust with provisions to apply upon the incapacity of the trustor. Not all states have expressly recognized a power given to the attorney-in-fact to make gifts. Those states that do permit the attorney-in-fact to make gifts for his or her principal generally do not have uniform laws. Because the power of attorney laws in general are not uniform from state to state, not only may the attorney-in-fact have difficulties in giving property located in different states, he or she may even have problems managing or selling real estate belonging to the principal if such real estate is located outside the principal's state of residence. If the principal owns real estate in several states, he or she may need to execute powers of attorney for each of those states.

Probate costs that could be reduced by the use of a revocable living trust obviously are not reduced if a power of attorney is used instead of a trust. In addition, if a springing power of attorney is used, there are medical and legal costs associated with establishing the incapacity of the principal. However, not all of these drawbacks are applicable in every state, and for most individuals, none are so great as to outweigh the benefits of having the peace of mind that comes from knowing that you have the power to handle your spouse's or your elderly parents' affairs for them when they can no longer do so, and that the person of your choice can do the same for you if ever necessary.

GUARDIANS AND CONSERVATORS

A general durable power of attorney is like any legal document in that it must be executed by a person with mental capacity. What happens when a family member is already mentally incapacitated and has not engaged in prior planning to protect his or her affairs or to make his or her wishes known? All states have laws that permit a family member or friend to go to court and ask for permission to act on the behalf of an incapacitated individual.

A *guardianship* is a relationship created by state law by which the law grants one person—the guardian—the right, authority, and duty to care for another person, the ward.[1] If a guardian is appointed to handle only financial matters, he or she is the guardian of the property or conservator of the ward. This is a partial guardianship or *conservatorship,* which may be granted in many states. Since such a guardianship is limited, the ward will still have the ability to make some personal decisions, such as where he or she will live and what medical treatment he or she will receive. A full guardianship is a guardianship of both the person and property of the ward. If a full guardianship is granted, the ward is totally deprived of all of his or her rights with respect to personal affairs, including issues of custody, institutionalization, medical care, and property management or disposition. In fact, the ward actually loses most of his or her civil rights and liberties, including the right to vote, the right to contract, and the right to sue and be sued.[2]

A court has the sole authority to appoint a guardian or conservator. Thus, although the actual legal process does vary from state to state, it is usually necessary to file a court petition seeking the appointment of a guardian or a conservator. Once the petition is filed with the proper court, state law generally requires that the proposed ward and his or her spouse and children receive notification of the petition being filed. A lawyer, who is called a guardian *ad litem,* is appointed by the court to represent the proposed ward throughout the proceeding. Typically, a medical or psychological evaluation of the proposed ward is ordered by the judge. The judge then reaches a conclusion on the issue of incompetency and, if necessary, appoints a guardian or conservator based on the petition of the person requesting the appointment, the testimonies of the guardian *ad litem* and proposed ward, and the evaluating physician's expert opinion and recommendations. Sometimes the testimony of family members is sought and considered with respect to the choice of the individual to serve as guardian or conservator. Courts have traditionally used a two-part test to determine whether or not a proposed ward should be declared incompetent. First, the court determines whether the proposed ward suffers from a condition such as insanity, illness, or "old age," that affects his or her mental capacity.[3] Second, the court decides whether such a condition affects the proposed ward's ability to properly manage his or her own affairs.[4]

Once appointed, a guardian or conservator is not only responsible for managing the affairs of his or her ward, but he or she must also purchase an expensive bond, make regular reports to the court, and act under the direct supervision of the court in all matters.

By its very nature, the guardianship process involves substantial court and medical costs and involves a public legal proceeding. It may also subject the appointed caretaker to court supervision and rather onerous reporting requirements, thus increasing further costs of management and administration. Although a guardianship is necessary if a family member or loved one is no longer mentally competent to handle his or her affairs and proper planning has not been accomplished, it should be reiterated that, in many cases, the burdens of a guardianship or conservatorship may be avoided by the simple execution of a general durable power of attorney beforehand.

In the estate planning context, a guardian has the power to do some things that an attorney-in-fact, acting under a general durable power of attorney, may have difficulty in doing. As mentioned earlier, some states have not uniformly accepted the ability of the attorney-in-fact to make gifts or engage in estate planning on behalf of the principal; in other states, a guardian may do so with the prior approval of the court. Because such transactions have been subject to court scrutiny and have been expressly authorized by the court, there may be less of a chance that the IRS will challenge the transaction or claim that the transfer of property was an improper or excessively broad exercise of the guardian's authority.

ADVANCE MEDICAL DIRECTIVES

As the media today brings our attention time and time again to rapidly rising medical costs, the horrors of terminal illnesses, the tragic reality of elder abuse, and the proliferation of right-to-die groups, it is little wonder that advance medical directives have gained such wide acceptance and popularity throughout the United States. At a time when medical technology permits individuals to live longer in spite of disease or physical debilitation, an increasing number of individuals want to protect their right to refuse such technology—to refuse life-sustaining or death-delaying treatment—even when they are no longer mentally or physically capable of either consenting to or rejecting such treatment on their own behalf.

In the 1990 case, *Cruzan v. Director, Missouri Dept. of Health,* 497 U.S. 261 (1990), the United States Supreme Court recognized an individual's constitutional "right to die" and required physicians to acknowledge and honor the same so long as there is "clear and convincing evidence" of the individual's desires. As a result of the *Cruzan* decision, all states and the District of Columbia have authorized by law an individual's right to use written instructions to set down this "clear and convincing evidence" to be consulted in the event the individual is not able to communicate his or her desires when the issue arises. These written instructions regarding medical treatment are known as *advance medical directives.*

In the aftermath of *Cruzan,* in order to promote public awareness of this right to express your wishes regarding medical treatment in written form, Congress passed the Patient Self-Determination Act.[5] This Act requires that medical institutions serving Medicare and Medicaid patients provide written educational materials describing a patient's health care decision-making rights under state law, including the patient's right to execute a living will or durable power of attorney for health care, both forms of advance medical directives.[6]

LIVING WILLS

Most states and the District of Columbia have statutes that authorize the execution of a living will. A living will is considered a treatment or instruction directive because its purpose is to instruct attending health care providers on the withholding or withdrawing of life-sustaining or death-delaying measures in accordance with the declarant's wishes. The *declarant* is the person who executes the living will, which also may be called a "Directive to Physician or a Declaration of a Desire for a Natural Death" depending upon the state.

Requirements as to form and execution requirements also vary from state to state. A sample living will form is included at the end of this chapter.

Most states require that the declarant be "competent" or "of sound mind" at the time he or she executes a living will.[7] However, some state laws permit certain specifically authorized individuals to draft and execute living wills on the behalf of incompetent adults.[8] Many state statutes provide model living will forms, although not all states require the use of these forms. Some states permit modification of the model form or merely suggest that the model form be used as a guide in drafting. If your state provides a model form, it is best to copy that form and add modifications only as permitted by your state's law.

Generally, state laws require two adults to witness the execution of a living will. Many states prohibit certain persons, who may potentially benefit from the death of the declarant, from serving as witnesses. Such persons would include blood relatives, spouses, creditors, or others with claims or potential claims against the declarant or the declarant's estate, and those persons financially responsible for the declarant's medical treatment. In addition, many states exclude attending physicians, their employees, or the employees of a medical institution in which the declarant is located at the time of execution of the living will from serving as witnesses. Thus, friends, neighbors, co-workers, or professional advisors, particularly those who are familiar with and understand your wishes, are often the most appropriate persons to serve as witnesses for your living will. People who assist in the execution of your living will and your health care providers are usually protected by statute from criminal prosecution or civil liability for their actions as long as they follow the directions contained in your living will.[9] In some states, a living will is not valid until it is delivered to your physician or filed with the appropriate state court or agency. However, in most states, living wills are valid immediately upon execution and remain valid unless expressly revoked, even in the event of future incapacity.

Most states' living will statutes require that a declarant suffer from a terminal condition prior to allowing the health care provider to take instruction from the provisions of that individual's living will. The definition of "terminal condition" will vary from state to state but, in general, an individual is deemed terminally ill if a prognosis of death has been made for him or her. The Uniform Rights of the Terminally Ill Act defines a "terminal condition" as an "incurable and irreversible condition that, without the administration of life-sustaining treatment, will, in the opinion of the attending physician, result in death within a relatively short time."[10] A "Uniform Act" is a law drafted by a committee of specialists representing all the states and made available to any state wanting to adopt it.

The greatest benefit of such legislation is that it ensures uniformity among the laws of different states so that documents executed in one state are valid and enforceable in another. States may adopt a uniform act just as it is drafted or make their own modifications. Or states may choose to draft legislation of their own, using the uniform act as a model. Some states that have not adopted the Uniform Rights to the Terminally Ill Act but have adopted their own living will legislation require that death be "imminent" or set time limits, such as within six months (the definition of "terminal illness" adopted by Medicare), during which death must occur.[11]

Other terms often used to describe patients with serious medical conditions include *critically ill, chronically ill,* and *severely debilitated.* Such patients would probably not be considered "terminally ill" for purposes of the living will. A critically ill patient is "in the midst of an acute life-threatening episode," such as a heart attack or stroke, or considered to be "in imminent danger of such an episode."[12] If a critically ill patient does not receive treatment it is expected that his or her condition will worsen. A chronically ill patient, on the other hand, suffers from "one or more chronic conditions, which may or may not be life-threatening," but which reduce the chance of that patient's recovery from an attack of an acute disease.[13] A patient who has cancer that is in remission may be characterized as chronically ill. Finally, a severely debilitated individual is "medically stable" in spite of serious impairments. However, he or she still is very vulnerable to new physiological stresses, such as the risk of infection, accidents, or complications of treatment.[14]

Some states that authorize the use of living wills permit the withholding or withdrawal of life-sustaining treatment if a patient is permanently unconscious or in a coma or permanent vegetative state. If an individual is in a coma, he or she appears to be asleep. Although the individual's body is still able to perform the functions of breathing, circulation, internal temperature regulation, reflexive muscle activity, and digestion, functions such as memory, thought, emotion, balance, posture, voluntary movement, speech, taste, smell, and hearing are lost.[15] An individual in a persistent vegetative state, unlike one in a coma, appears to be awake and may often appear to follow movement or respond to sound or other stimuli. However, as with the individual in a coma, an individual in a persistent vegetative state has no self-awareness or true awareness of his or her surroundings.[16]

Living will statutes also usually only provide for the withholding or withdrawal of life-sustaining, life-prolonging, or death-delaying medical treatment. Life-sustaining medical treatment includes those drugs, medical devices, and medical procedures or interventions that keep alive an individual who would otherwise die within a foreseeable, if uncertain, time period.[17] Common methods of providing life-sustaining treatment include:

- the performance of cardiopulmonary resuscitation (CPR)
- the use of mechanical ventilation
- the application of renal dialysis
- the provision of nutritional support and hydration
- the administration of antibiotics

Of these five treatments, only antibiotics have the ability to cure the underlying life-threatening condition. With respect to all five treatments, even if the patient gradually regains some normal body function, he or she will most likely remain dependent on the medical technology to prolong his or her life.[18] Regardless of the age of the patient, in cases of acute illness, the use of even the most aggressive of these treatments still, on average, results in high rates of mortality and serious complications.[19]

Of these five treatments, the ongoing use of mechanical ventilation and/or provision of nutritional support and hydration to sustain a family member in a coma or persistent vegetative state present the most difficult dilemmas for health care providers and family members who are charged with carrying out a patient's wishes. Mechanical ventilation is the use of a respirator to inflate and deflate the lungs of a patient whose own breathing is no longer adequate or has stopped entirely due to disease, trauma, or anesthesia. Nutritional support and hydration are artificial means of providing nutrients and fluids to a patient to prevent malnutrition and dehydration, both of which are fatal conditions. Nutritional support and hydration may be provided through tube feeding (enteral) or intravenous feeding (parenteral). Tube feeding delivers nutrients into the digestive tract, and intravenous feeding delivers nutrients directly into the bloodstream through a catheter inserted into a central vein.[20] The most well-known intravenous procedure is the administration of a glucose, water, or saline solution and medication through a tube inserted in a small vein usually located in the patient's arm or hand. This procedure is effective only in the short term and mainly for the provision of hydration, because the veins used will eventually break down and close up altogether if the fats, proteins, and vitamins necessary to sustain life are introduced to the bloodstream in this way.[21] The other intravenous procedure is total parenteral nutrition (TPN) which does provide sufficient nutrients to keep a patient, even an unconscious patient, alive indefinitely. Thus, it is often the withholding or withdrawal of TPN that is the critical step in following the terms of a family member's living will.

Some individuals may believe that the withholding or withdrawal of nutrition or hydration introduces the cause of death, which they believe to be malnutrition or dehydration. However, when faced with this issue, courts uniformly have held that the cause of death in these cases is the underlying condition or illness that prevents the patient from being able to eat and drink naturally.[22] Other individuals may not want to withhold or withdraw food and water because of the emotional stress it places on them as the ultimate decision-makers. However, medical experts agree that intravenous feeding, like any medical procedure, has inherent risks and may actually cause complications that could *add* to the discomfort or pain suffered by the patient. In addition, some studies suggest that the withholding or withdrawal of food and water is not only *not* painful to the patient, but it may actually improve the quality of a dying patient's last hours or days.[23] Clinical studies have observed that terminally ill patients often reduce their intake of food and water and that, for dying patients, dehydration can lessen nausea, abdominal pain, and other side effects as well as the patient's perception of pain.[24] It has also been found that withdrawing feeding without withdrawing fluids, presumably to keep the patient more comfortable, may actually prolong a patient's dying.[25]

Perhaps the most important thing to remember is that, by law, the withholding or withdrawal of nutritional support and/or hydration does not necessitate the withholding or withdrawal of "comfort care," which includes medications that alleviate pain but do not sustain life. Thus, the alleviation of pain is still possible even if life-sustaining measures have been stopped. In addition, spoon-feeding and providing small bits of water or ice are possible alternatives which provide comfort and care after the withdrawal of intravenous tubes.[26] These alternatives would certainly appear to offer more substantial emotional comfort and a greater sense of dignity than impersonal technology that cannot cure but can only maintain.

DURABLE POWER OF ATTORNEY FOR HEALTH CARE

A durable power of attorney for health care or health care proxy is an appointment or proxy directive in addition to an instruction directive. Using a durable power of attorney for health care, you, the principal, can name an individual to serve as your proxy or attorney-in-fact to make all of your health care decisions for you. Thus, it is a much broader and more flexible document than the basic living will, which only authorizes action with respect to life-sustaining treatment. With a durable power of attorney for health care, you can specify what types of medical treatment you want and don't want, or you can give your attorney-in-fact the broad discretion to make these decisions for you as he or she deems best.

Some state laws specifically authorize the use of a separate legal document called a durable power of attorney for health care. A typical state form is included at the end of this chapter. These states will usually provide a model form that should be used. Other states list medical decision-making as a type of power that may be given to an agent or attorney-in-fact under a general law authorizing the delegation of authority to an agent or the use of a general durable power of attorney. In these states, no separate document is used, and a general durable power of attorney covering financial decision-making will cover medical decision-making as well. Finally, some states' general power of attorney statutes do not expressly authorize or prohibit an attorney-in-fact's making medical care decisions for his or her principal. In these states, the authority to make medical decisions is implied from the grant of authority expressed in the general durable power of attorney document. It should be noted, again, that all states and the District of Columbia authorize the use of living wills. In states that authorize the use of separate durable power of attorney for health care documents, these documents will include the standard living will provisions regarding the withholding and withdrawing of life-sustaining or death-delaying treatment.

The basic competency, witness, and revocation requirements that apply from state to state with respect to living wills also apply to durable powers of attorney for health care. As with the witnesses to a general durable power of attorney for finances, with a durable power of attorney for health care, it is a good idea to choose witnesses who are familiar with your desires. More importantly, in choosing your attorney-in-fact for health care, you should select someone who will be able to respond quickly in the event that you are hospitalized (particularly in the event of an emergency hospitalization away from home), who is willing to carry out your wishes, who understands your wishes and the authority he or she is given by the document, and who is willing to stand up to medical care providers who may be hesitant to follow your directive, or to family members (or guardians or conservators) who are opposed to the wishes you have expressed. Traditionally, states have had family consent statutes that authorize medical care providers to consult certain family members in making medical care decisions when a patient is incapable of making an informed consent to treatment. Your execution of an advance directive provides the direction that your medical care providers otherwise would be lacking and would request from family members. Therefore, particularly if you have selected one family member or a non-family member as your attorney-in-fact, it is important to make your physician and family members aware of your decision to execute the document and to provide at least your physician and attorney-in-fact with copies of the document. It also is important to explain or discuss your desires as stated in the document and the authority granted (or limited) by the document with your physician and attorney-in-fact.

Like a general durable power of attorney for finances, the durable power of attorney for health care document usually permits you to name successor attorneys-in-fact and a guardian of your person (should it ever become necessary for a court to appoint such a guardian for you), who should also receive copies of your document. The power of attorney for health care also is "durable" in that its validity is not affected by your later incapacity. A durable power of attorney for health care may also become effective immediately upon execution or not until such time as you are no longer capable of making your own medical decisions (a springing durable power of attorney for health care).

Under a durable power of attorney for health care, your attorney-in-fact may be authorized to do the following:

- Gain access to medical records relating to your mental or physical health, execute releases necessary to gain such access, and discuss the information contained therein with all appropriate parties

- Employ, compensate, and discharge medical care providers, including surgeons, physicians, psychiatrists, psychologists, therapists, and nurses

- Give, withhold, or withdraw consent to medical treatments, including medications, surgery, and tests

- Admit into or request discharge from a hospital, convalescent center, hospice, nursing home, or any other health care facility or institution

- Authorize administration of medications to relieve pain or consent to surgical or other medical procedures intended to alleviate pain, even in the event that life-sustaining treatments are discontinued or withheld

- Grant releases to medical care providers and their employees for complying with the instructions set forth in the power of attorney document

- Refuse any specific treatments, such as blood transfusions, electroconvulsive therapy, or amputation, that you may find unacceptable or feel are inconsistent with your religious beliefs

- Withhold or withdraw life-sustaining or death-delaying treatment in the event you suffer from a terminal condition or are in a coma or persistent vegetative state

Depending upon your state's laws, you may also be able to include in your power of attorney document your own definitions of the terms *terminal illness, terminal condition, life-sustaining treatment* and *death-delaying treatment,* so that treatments are withheld or withdrawn only as you specifically desire. Finally, you may give your attorney-in-fact the authority to make advance funeral arrangements, authorize an autopsy, or make anatomical gifts.

U.S. courts have uniformly approved the use of advance directives, including the durable power of attorney for health care, and, when asked to enforce their terms, have required medical care providers to comply. Concerns about the willingness of medical care providers to comply with these documents and about their enforceability from state to state do persist. However, there can be no doubt that, at the present time, the durable power of attorney for health care provides the most protection of your constitutional right to determine what happens to your body and control your future medical care even when you are no longer able to communicate your desires to family members or medical care providers.

ANATOMICAL GIFTS (BODY AND ORGAN DONATIONS)

In addition to setting down written instructions for the management of your finances and medical treatment in one or more of the forms already discussed, you may wish to leave written instructions regarding the donation of your body or organs. Such written instructions, even in the absence of a specific law authorizing their use, are generally deemed binding and are followed as long as their terms do not violate any of your state's laws on the disposition of bodies. If you do not leave instructions for your funeral, burial, or the donation of your body or organs, your surviving spouse or next of kin will be responsible for the disposition of your body.

All states and the District of Columbia have adopted the Uniform Anatomical Gift Act. Therefore, gifts made and pre-arranged in your state of residence will be valid and immediately enforceable even if you die in another state. Any competent adult may make a valid gift under the Uniform Anatomical Gift Act by merely signing certain forms. Some states permit you to authorize organ donation as part of renewing your driver's license.

Georgia actually reduces the renewal fee by half if you choose to become an organ donor. In other states, you can obtain the proper forms from the Department of Motor Vehicles, a hospital, or your doctor's office. Some states permit you to make body or organ donations by will. However, it is still important to contact your proposed recipient to ensure that you have complied with its requirements and signed the necessary forms. Permissible recipients include hospitals, surgeons, physicians, accredited medical and dental schools, colleges or universities, organ banks or other storage facilities, and any specified individual who needs the donation for therapy or transplantation.[27] A gift may be made for medical or dental research, medical or dental education, the advancement of medical or dental science or therapy, or transplantation.[28]

In making an anatomical gift, you may either (1) donate your entire body to medical research, which usually is done by designating a medical school, college, university, or other research facility as donee; or (2) donate specific organs, tissues, or bones, usually by designating a particular organ bank or storage facility as donee. If you do not designate a donee, some state laws authorize your attending physician to accept your donation and make provision for its proper ultimate disposition. If you wish to give your body to a medical school or other research facility, you should contact that institution to see if it needs your gift and to determine what documentation it requires. Medical schools will not usually accept a gift of a body from which organs have been removed, and some will not accept bodies that are diseased or past a certain age. Thus, it is important to make certain that you know your proposed donee's requirements, complete its paperwork, and have a backup plan in case your gift is not acceptable at the time it is actually made. Planning organ, tissue, or bone donations—for which there is always a great demand—to schools, research facilities, or specific individuals or physicians should be handled in a similar way. Because of the great demand, however, the same attention to detail may not be necessary if you are planning to make your gift to an organ bank or storage facility. Even so, it is always a good idea to explore all of the options and plan ahead, because timing after death is always critical with anatomical gifts.

If you do not make formal plans to make anatomical gifts, but your surviving family members are aware that you wished to do so, the Uniform Act also authorizes your next of kin to make body or organ donations on your behalf after your death.[29] Therefore, you should discuss your wishes with your spouse or other next of kin who will be responsible for your body after your death. The Uniform Act has provisions ensuring that any donation made by a family member is done in accordance with your wishes. Your surviving family members are prohibited by the Uniform Act from making organ donations if they have actual notice that you were opposed to such donations, or from attempting to prevent any donation that you have instructed to be made after your death. However, under the Uniform Act, anyone who acts in good faith in carrying out your gifts or making gifts on your behalf is protected from civil liability or criminal prosecution under the Uniform Act.

Although state laws—guardianship laws, family consent statutes, and anatomical gift acts—will provide some protection for you if you become unable to care for yourself due to a disability, there is no substitute for taking advantage of the legal means provided for immediate disability planning. You can expressly state your wishes, authorize and limit the authority of another to act for you in financial and medical matters, and plan for gifts before and after death through the use of very simple documents—the general durable power of attorney for finances, the living will, the durable power of attorney for health care, and the anatomical gift form. Disability strikes the young as well as the old, so it is never too early to plan for yourself and encourage your loved ones to do the same.

(Georgia Statutory Form)

Living Will made this _____ day of _____, 199___.

I, _____, being of sound mind, willfully and voluntarily make known my desire that my life shall not be prolonged under the circumstances set forth below and do declare:

1. If at any time I should (check each option desired):

(   ) have a terminal condition,

(   ) become in a coma with no reasonable expectation of regaining consciousness, or

(   ) become in a persistent vegetative state with no reasonable expectation of regaining significant cognitive function,

as defined in and established in accordance with the procedures set forth in Paragraphs (2), (9), and (13) of Code Section 31-32-2 of the Official Code of Georgia Annotated, I direct that the application of life-sustaining procedures to my body be withheld or withdrawn and that I be permitted to die;

I intend the term "life-sustaining procedures" to include withholding or withdrawing (check the option desired):

(   ) nourishment (food) and hydration (water);

(   ) nourishment but not hydration;

(   ) neither nourishment nor hydration; or

(   ) hydration but not nourishment.

2. In the absence of my ability to give directions regarding the use of such life-sustaining procedures, it is my intention that this living will shall be honored by my family and physician(s) as the final expression of my legal right to refuse medical or surgical treatment and accept the consequences from such refusal;

3. I understand that I may revoke this living will at any time;

4. I understand the full import of this living will, and I am at least 18 years of age and am emotionally and mentally competent to make this living will; and

5. If I am female and I have been diagnosed as pregnant, this living will shall have no force and effect unless the fetus is not viable and I indicate by initialing after this sentence that I want this living will to be carried out.   _____ Initial

Signed: _____

_____(city), _____County, Georgia.

WITNESS ATTESTATION

I hereby witness this living will and attest that:

1. The declarant is personally known to me and I believe the declarant to be at least 18 years of age and of sound mind;

2. I am at least 18 years of age;

3. To the best of my knowledge, at the time of the execution of this living will, I:

   a. Am not related to the declarant by blood or marriage;

   b. Would not be entitled to any portion of the declarant's estate by any will or by operation of law under the rules of descent and distribution of this state;

   c. Am not the attending physician of declarant or an employee of the attending physician or an employee of the hospital or skilled nursing facility in which declarant is a patient;

   d. Am not directly financially responsible for the declarant's medical care; and

   e. Have no present claim against any portion of the estate of the declarant.

4. Declarant has signed this document in my presence as above-instructed, on the date above first shown.

Witness: Address:

_____   _____

_____   _____

_____   _____

Additional witness required when living will is signed in a hospital or skilled nursing facility:

I hereby witness this living will and attest that I believe the declarant to be of sound mind and to have made this living will willingly and voluntarily.

_____

Medical director of skilled nursing facility or staff physician not participating in care of the patient or chief of the hospital medical staff or staff physician not participating in the care of the patient.

SAMPLE DECLARATION OF A DESIRE FOR A NATURAL DEATH

I, _____, being of sound mind, desire that, as specified below, my life not be prolonged by extraordinary means or by artificial nutrition or hydration if my condition is determined to be terminal and incurable or if I am diagnosed as being in a persistent vegetative state. I am aware and understand that this writing authorizes a physician to withhold or discontinue extraordinary means or artificial nutrition or hydration, in accordance with my specifications set forth below:

(Initial any of the following, as desired):

_____ If my condition is determined to be terminal and incurable, I authorize the following:

    _____ My physician may withhold or discontinue extraordinary means only.

    _____ In addition to withholding or discontinuing extraordinary means if such means are necessary, my physician may withhold or discontinue either artificial nutrition or hydration, or both.

_____ If my physician determines that I am in a persistent vegetative state, I authorize the following:

    _____ My physician may withhold or discontinue extraordinary means only.

    _____ In addition to withholding or discontinuing extraordinary means if such means are necessary, my physician may withhold or discontinue either artificial nutrition or hydration, or both.

This the _____ day of _____, 19_____.

Signed: _____

I hereby state that the declarant, _____, being of sound mind, signed the above declaration in my presence and that I am not related to the declarant by blood or marriage and that I do not know or have a reasonable expectation that I would be entitled to any portion of the estate of the declarant under any existing will or codicil of the declarant, or as an heir under the Intestate Succession Act if the declarant died on this date without a will. I also state that I am not the declarant's attending physician or an employee of the declarant's attending physician, or an employee of a health facility in which the declarant is a patient or an employee of a nursing home or any group care home where the declarant resides. I further state that I do not now have any claim against the declarant.

Witness _____

Witness _____

CERTIFICATE

STATE OF NORTH CAROLINA

COUNTY OF MECKLENBURG

I, _____, a Notary Public for Mecklenburg County, North Carolina, hereby certify that _____, the declarant, appeared before me and swore to me and to the witnesses in my presence that this instrument is her Declaration Of A Desire For A Natural Death, and that she willingly and voluntarily made and executed it as her free act and deed for the purposes expressed in it.

I, further certify that _____ and _____, witnesses, appeared before me and swore that they witnessed_____, declarant, believing her to be of sound mind; and also swore at the time they witnessed the declaration (i) they were not related within the third degree to the declarant or to the declarant's spouse, and (ii) they did not know nor have a reasonable expectation that they would be entitled to any portion of the estate of declarant upon declarant's death under any will of the declarant or codicil thereto then existing or under the Intestate Succession Act as it provided at that time, and (iii) they were not a physician attending the declarant, nor an employee of an attending physician, nor an employee of a health facility in which the declarant was a patient, nor an employee of a nursing home or any group care home in which the declarant resided, and (iv) they did not have a claim against the declarant. I further certify that I am satisfied as to the genuineness and due execution of the declaration.

This _____ day of _____, 1996.
(SEAL)

Notary Public _____

County of _____

My Commission Expires: _____

DURABLE POWER OF ATTORNEY FOR HEALTH CARE

(Georgia Statutory Form)

NOTICE: THE PURPOSE OF THIS POWER OF ATTORNEY IS TO GIVE THE PERSON YOU DESIGNATE (YOUR AGENT) BROAD POWERS TO MAKE HEALTH CARE DECISIONS FOR YOU, INCLUDING THE POWER TO REQUIRE, CONSENT TO, OR WITHDRAW ANY TYPE OF PERSONAL CARE OR MEDICAL TREATMENT FOR ANY PHYSICAL OR MENTAL CONDITION AND TO ADMIT YOU TO OR DISCHARGE YOU FROM ANY HOSPITAL, HOME, OR OTHER INSTITUTION; BUT NOT INCLUDING PSYCHOSURGERY, STERILIZATION, OR INVOLUNTARY HOSPITALIZATION OR TREATMENT COVERED BY TITLE 37 OF THE OFFICIAL CODE OF GEORGIA ANNOTATED. THIS FORM DOES NOT IMPOSE A DUTY ON YOUR AGENT TO EXERCISE GRANTED POWERS; BUT, WHEN A POWER IS EXERCISED, YOUR AGENT WILL HAVE TO USE DUE CARE TO ACT FOR YOUR BENEFIT AND IN ACCORDANCE WITH THIS FORM. A COURT CAN TAKE AWAY THE POWERS OF YOUR AGENT IF IT FINDS THE AGENT IS NOT ACTING PROPERLY. YOU MAY NAME COAGENTS AND SUCCESSOR AGENTS UNDER THIS FORM, BUT YOU MAY NOT NAME A HEALTH CARE PROVIDER WHO MAY BE DIRECTLY OR INDIRECTLY INVOLVED IN RENDERING HEALTH CARE TO YOU UNDER THIS POWER. UNLESS YOU EXPRESSLY LIMIT THE DURATION OF THIS POWER IN THE MANNER PROVIDED BELOW OR UNTIL YOU REVOKE THIS POWER OR A COURT ACTING ON YOUR BEHALF TERMINATES IT, YOUR AGENT MAY EXERCISE THE POWERS GIVEN IN THIS POWER THROUGHOUT YOUR LIFETIME, EVEN AFTER YOU BECOME DISABLED, INCAPACITATED, OR INCOMPETENT. THE POWERS YOU GIVE YOUR AGENT, YOUR RIGHT TO REVOKE THOSE POWERS, AND THE PENALTIES FOR VIOLATING THE LAW ARE EXPLAINED MORE FULLY IN CODE SECTIONS 31-36-6, 31-36-9, AND 31-36-10 OF THE GEORGIA "DURABLE POWER OF ATTORNEY FOR HEALTH CARE ACT" OF WHICH THIS FORM IS A PART. THAT ACT EXPRESSLY PERMITS THE USE OF ANY DIFFERENT FORM OF POWER OF ATTORNEY YOU MAY DESIRE. IF THERE IS ANYTHING ABOUT THIS FORM THAT YOU DO NOT UNDERSTAND, YOU SHOULD ASK A LAWYER TO EXPLAIN IT TO YOU.

DURABLE POWER OF ATTORNEY made this _____ day of _____, 199_____.

1. I, _____, residing at _____, hereby appoint my spouse, _____, residing at _____, as my

attorney in fact (my agent) to act for me and in my name in any way I could act in person to make any and all decisions for me concerning my personal care, medical treatment, hospitalization, and health care and to require, withhold, or withdraw any type of medical treatment or procedure, even though my death may ensue. My agent shall have the same access to my medical records that I have, including the right to disclose the contents to others. My agent shall also have full power to make a disposition of any part or all of my body for medical purposes, authorize an autopsy of my body, and direct the disposition of my remains.

THE ABOVE GRANT OF POWER IS INTENDED TO BE AS BROAD AS POSSIBLE SO THAT YOUR AGENT WILL HAVE AUTHORITY TO MAKE ANY DECISION YOU COULD MAKE TO OBTAIN OR TERMINATE ANY TYPE OF HEALTH CARE, INCLUDING WITHDRAWAL OF NOURISHMENT AND FLUIDS AND OTHER LIFE-SUSTAINING OR DEATH-DELAYING MEASURES, IF YOUR AGENT BELIEVES SUCH ACTION WOULD BE CONSISTENT WITH YOUR INTENT AND DESIRES. IF YOU WISH TO LIMIT THE SCOPE OF YOUR AGENT'S POWERS OR PRESCRIBE SPECIAL RULES TO LIMIT THE POWER TO MAKE AN ANATOMICAL GIFT, AUTHORIZE AUTOPSY, OR DISPOSE OF REMAINS, YOU MAY DO SO IN THE FOLLOWING PARAGRAPHS.

2. The powers granted above shall not include the following powers or shall be subject to the following rules or limitations (here you may include any specific limitations you deem appropriate, such as your own definition of when life-sustaining or death-delaying measures should be withheld; a direction to continue nourishment and fluids or other life-sustaining or death-delaying treatment in all events; or instructions to refuse any specific types of treatment that are inconsistent with your religious beliefs or unacceptable to you for any other reason, such as blood transfusion, electroconvulsive therapy, or amputation): _____

_____

THE SUBJECT OF LIFE-SUSTAINING OR DEATH-DELAYING TREATMENT IS OF PARTICULAR IMPORTANCE. FOR YOUR CONVENIENCE IN DEALING WITH THAT SUBJECT, SOME GENERAL STATEMENTS CONCERNING THE WITHHOLDING OR REMOVAL OF LIFE-SUSTAINING OR DEATH-DELAYING TREATMENT ARE SET FORTH BELOW. IF YOU AGREE WITH ONE OF THESE STATEMENTS, YOU MAY INITIAL THAT STATEMENT, BUT DO NOT INITIAL MORE THAN ONE:

I do not want my life to be prolonged nor do I want life-sustaining or death-delaying treatment to be provided or continued if my agent believes the burdens of the treatment outweigh the expected benefits. I want my agent to consider the relief of suffering, the expense involved, and the quality as well as the possible extension of my life in making decisions concerning life-sustaining or death-delaying treatment.

Initialed _____

I want my life to be prolonged and I want life-sustaining or death-delaying treatment to be provided or continued unless I am in a coma, including a persistent vegetative state, which my attending physician believes to be irreversible, in accordance with reasonable medical standards at the time of reference. If and when I have suffered such an irreversible coma, I want life-sustaining or death-delaying treatment to be withheld or discontinued.

Initialed _____

I want my life to be prolonged to the greatest extent possible without regard to my condition, the chances I have for recovery, or the cost of the procedures.

Initialed _____

THIS POWER OF ATTORNEY MAY BE AMENDED OR REVOKED BY YOU AT ANY TIME AND IN ANY MANNER WHILE YOU ARE ABLE TO DO SO. IN THE ABSENCE OF AN AMENDMENT OR REVOCATION, THE AUTHORITY GRANTED IN THIS POWER OF ATTORNEY WILL BECOME EFFECTIVE AT THE TIME THIS POWER OF ATTORNEY IS SIGNED AND WILL CONTINUE UNTIL YOUR DEATH AND WILL CONTINUE BEYOND YOUR DEATH IF ANATOMICAL GIFT, AUTOPSY, OR DISPOSITION OF REMAINS IS AUTHORIZED.

IF YOU WISH TO NAME SUCCESSOR AGENTS, INSERT THE NAMES AND ADDRESSES OF SUCH SUCCESSORS IN THE FOLLOWING PARAGRAPH:

3. If any agent named by me shall die, become legally disabled, incapacitated, or incompetent, or resign, refuse to act, or be unavailable, I name the following (each to act successively in the order named) as successors to such agent:

Initialed _____

IF YOU WISH TO NAME A GUARDIAN OF YOUR PERSON IN THE EVENT A COURT DECIDES THAT ONE SHOULD BE APPOINTED, YOU MAY, BUT ARE NOT REQUIRED TO, DO SO BY INSERTING THE NAME OF SUCH GUARDIAN IN THE FOLLOWING PARAGRAPH. THE

COURT WILL APPOINT THE PERSON NOMINATED BY YOU IF THE COURT FINDS THAT SUCH APPOINTMENT WILL SERVE YOUR BEST INTERESTS AND WELFARE. YOU MAY, BUT ARE NOT REQUIRED TO, NOMINATE AS YOUR GUARDIAN THE SAME PERSON NAMED IN THIS FORM AS YOUR AGENT.

4. If a guardian of my person is to be appointed, I nominate the person or persons who are named in paragraphs 1 and 3 of this Durable Power of Attorney for Health Care, in the order therein named, to serve as such guardian.

Initialed _____

5. I am fully informed as to all the contents of this form and understand the full import of this grant of powers to my agent.

Signed _____

The principal has had an opportunity to read the above form and has signed the above form in our presence. We, the undersigned, each being over 18 years of age, witness the principal's signature at the request and in the presence of the principal, and in the presence of each other, on the date and year above set out.

WITNESSES: ADDRESSES:

_____   _____

                                   _____

_____   _____

                                   _____

Additional witnesses are required when a health care agency is signed in a hospital or skilled nursing facility: I hereby witness this health care agency and attest that I believe the principal to be of sound mind and to have made this health care agency willingly and voluntarily.

Witness: _____
(Attending Physician)

Address: _____

_____

YOU MAY, BUT ARE NOT REQUIRED TO, REQUEST YOUR AGENT AND SUCCESSOR AGENTS TO PROVIDE SPECIMEN SIGNATURES BELOW. IF YOU INCLUDE SPECIMEN SIGNATURES IN THIS POWER OF ATTORNEY, YOU MUST COMPLETE THE CERTIFICATION OPPOSITE THE SIGNATURES OF THE AGENTS.

Specimen signatures of agent and successor(s)	I certify that the signature of my agent and successor(s) is correct
_____	_____
(Principal)	(Agent)
_____	_____
(Principal)	(Successor Agent)
_____	_____
(Principal)	(Successor Agent)

NOTES

1. The Center for Social Gerontology, "Guardianship and Alternative Legal Interventions: A Compendium for Training and Practice," (Ann Arbor 1986) cited in *Taste, Smell, and the Elderly: Physiological Influences on Nutrition*, U.S. Government Printing Office, Washington, D.C. (1992).

2. *Taste, Smell, and the Elderly: Physiological Influences on Nutrition*, U. S. Government Printing Office, Washington, D.C. (1992).

3. *Id.* at 19.

4. *Id.*

5. Omnibus Budget Reconciliation Act of 1990 (P.L. 101-964).

6. *Consumers' Guide for Planning Ahead: The Health Care Power of Attorney and the Living Will*, U.S. Government Printing Office, Washington, D.C. (1992) (hereinafter *Consumers' Guide*).

7. *Id.* at 4.

8. *Id.*

9. No civil action has been brought against a physician for following the wishes of a patient with respect to withholding or withdrawing life-sustaining treatment. However, cases alleging battery, violation of constitutional and federal civil rights, breach of fiduciary duty, intentional infliction of emotional distress, and conspiracy have been brought against medical care providers for failing to comply with the wishes of patients. See Francis F. Collin, Jr., "Planning and Drafting Durable Powers of Attorney for Health Care," University of Miami Law Center, Philip E. Heckerling Institute on Estate Planning, Vol. 22A (1988).

10. Uniform Rights of the Terminally Ill Act, Section 1(9).

11. *Consumers' Guide* at 7.

12. *Life-Sustaining Technologies and the Elderly*, Summary, Office of Technology Assessment, Congress of the United States, Washington, D.C. (1987).

13. *Life-Sustaining Technologies and the Elderly*, Summary, at 13.

14. *Id.*

15. Collin, *supra* at 4-42.

16. See *Cruzan v. Director, Missouri Dept. of Health*, 497 U.S. 261, 267 n. 1 (1990).

17. *Life-Sustaining Technologies and the Elderly*, Summary, at 9.

18. *Id.*

19. *Id.* at 30.

20. *Life-Sustaining Technologies and the Elderly*, Summary at 9.

21. *Life-Sustaining Technologies and the Elderly*, Office of Technology Assessment, Congress of the United States, U.S. Government Printing Office, Washington, D.C. (1987). See also, *In Re Hier*, 464 N.E.2d 959, 961-962 (Mass.App. 1984).

22. Collin, *supra* at 4-46.

23. *Life-Sustaining Technologies and the Elderly* at 290.

24. *Id.*

25. *Id.*

26. *Id.*

27. See O.C.G.A. § 44-5-144.

28. *Id.*

29. The Uniform Anatomical Gift Act authorizes the following individuals, listed in the order of priority, to make anatomical gifts on behalf of a decedent after death: (1) the spouse; (2) an adult son or daughter; (3) either parent; (4) an adult brother or sister; (5) the guardian of the person at the time of death; (6) any other person authorized or under an obligation to dispose of the body. See *Medicolegal Forms*, Office of the General Counsel, American Medical Association (1973).

Estate Planning for the Multinational or Non-U.S. Citizen

What to Do if You Are Not a U.S. Citizen

> *Give me your tired, your poor,*
> *Your huddled masses yearning to breathe free,*
> *The wretched refuse of your teeming shore,*
> *Send these, the homeless, tempest-tost to me:*
> *I lift my lamp beside the golden door.*
>
> —Emma Lazarus
> *The New Colossus: Inscription for the Statue of Liberty*

Up to now in the book, we have been discussing rules that apply to citizens of the United States who are married to citizens of the United States. If you or your husband is a citizen of another country, different rules apply. This chapter will review the rules that apply to non-U.S. citizens who live in the United States and to U.S. citizens who live abroad. We will also discuss some special considerations for those who own property in foreign jurisdictions. (Estate taxation of non-resident aliens is beyond the scope of this chapter.)

ARE YOU A U.S. CITIZEN?

A person's citizenship is an objective, factual matter, although it is not always easily determined. For example, many people believe that an individual can be a citizen of only one country at a time. In fact, a person may be a citizen of more than one country at a time without even realizing it. For example, all people born in the United States are U.S. citizens. Hence, if Pierre and Gigi, from France, are traveling in the United States when Gigi gives birth to their son, François, then François would be a citizen of both the United States and France.

Likewise, a U.S. citizen can lose his or her U.S. citizenship if he or she voluntarily

- becomes a citizen of a foreign jurisdiction after having attained the age of 18;

- takes an oath of allegiance to a foreign jurisdiction after having attained the age of 18;

- formally renounces U.S. citizenship before a foreign service officer abroad;

- formally renounces U.S. citizenship during wartime (subject to approval by the attorney general of the United States);

- serves in the armed services of a foreign jurisdiction as a commissioned or non-commissioned officer if such armed forces are engaged in hostilities with the United States;

- assumes public office of a foreign jurisdiction's government after having attained the age of 18 if such individual has acquired the nationality of that foreign jurisdiction or if an oath of allegiance is required for the office;

- is convicted of treason.[1]

ARE YOU A RESIDENT ALIEN?

The term *resident alien* refers to an individual who is a lawful, permanent resident of the United States at any time during the calendar year or is "substantially present" in the United States.[2]

Example: Maria, who has resided in the United States for two years, has a "green card." She is a resident alien.

"Substantially present" means being physically present in the United States for at least 31 days during any calendar year and for a total of 183 or more days during such calendar year or during a three-year period consisting of such calendar year and the two preceding calendar years.[3] There are some exceptions to the substantial presence test. One applies to an alien who is in the United States less than the requisite number of days during the year and who has a tax home in and closer connection to a foreign country. The other applies to "exempt individuals," such as foreign-government-related individuals.[4]

WHO CARES?

U.S. citizens, no matter where they reside or are domiciled, and resident aliens are subject to federal estate taxes in the same manner and at the same rates as resident U.S. citizens. All of their property, wherever located, is includable in their gross estates.[5] Similarly, all gifts made by U.S. citizens and resident aliens are subject to U.S. federal gift tax, no matter where the property is located or where the gift is completed (unless the gift avoids taxation by virtue of, for example, the $10,000 present interest gift exclusion).[6]

ESTATE TAXATION OF RESIDENT ALIENS

All of the estate tax rules discussed in Chapter 4 relating to U.S. citizens also apply to resident aliens.[7] The estate of a resident alien is taxed on the same assets and allowed the same deductions as the estate of a U.S. citizen. The deductions include funeral and administration expenses and claims against the estate (including claims for certain taxes), losses, casualty or thefts occurring during estate administration, and charitable deductions. The marital deduction is also allowed, provided that (1) the surviving spouse is a U.S. citizen, or (2) the property passes to the surviving spouse by means of something called a "qualified domestic trust."[8]

In 1981, Congress changed the estate tax laws to permit an unlimited amount of property to be transferred between spouses free of estate or gift taxes at the time of transfer (the unlimited marital deduction). Such property is taxed only when the surviving spouse dies. Obviously, if the spouse consumes the property, it is never taxed.

In 1988, Congress again changed the marital deduction rules, this time with respect to transfers to non-U.S. citizen spouses. In the 1988 tax law, unless property passing to a non-U.S. citizen spouse (whether or not a U.S. resident), passes by means of a *qualified domestic trust* (QDOT, pronounced "Q-dot"), no marital deduction is allowed.[9] In 1989, amendments to the 1988 tax law provided that the marital deduction would be allowed for property passing to a non-citizen spouse if the spouse becomes a U.S. citizen prior to the date the estate tax return of the decedent is filed, provided that the non-citizen spouse is a U.S. resident on the date of the decedent's death and at all times thereafter prior to becoming a U.S. citizen.[10]

The law also provides that property passing from a decedent to a non-U.S. citizen spouse under a will or outside of the probate estate (for example, life insurance or an IRA or pension or profit sharing plan assets) is treated as passing to a QDOT if such property is irrevocably assigned to a QDOT before the estate tax return is filed.[11] This means that the decedent's executor (or surviving spouse) could create a QDOT after the decedent's death and put the property into it to qualify it for the marital deduction.

In passing the 1988 law, Congress was concerned that a non-U.S. citizen who received property without it being taxed in the decedent's estate because of the marital deduction would then return home to his or her country of origin, and the United States would never get its transfer tax on the assets. The QDOT, which permits the marital deduction in the first decedent's estate, is designed to ensure that this cannot happen.

QDOTS

In order for a trust to be a QDOT, the following requirements must be met:

1. At least one trustee must be an individual U.S. citizen or a U.S. corporation (for example, a bank).

2. The trust instrument must provide that the U.S. trustee has the right to withhold estate tax imposed on any distributions of principal from the trust.

3. The trust must comply with treasury regulations promulgated to ensure the collection of estate tax imposed on the trust.

4. The executor or the decedent must make an irrevocable election to treat the trust as a QDOT.[12]

The QDOT must also meet the other requirements of the marital deduction discussed in Chapter 5. If the trust meets the requirements of the marital deduction provisions of the Internal Revenue Code but does not qualify as a QDOT, then a reformation proceeding (a petition to reform the trust filed in the appropriate state court) may be begun prior to the due date for filing the estate tax return. If the trust is successfully reformed by the appropriate state court, then the trust will qualify as a QDOT at the conclusion of the reformation period.

All trust distributions of income to a non-U.S. citizen spouse are exempt from estate tax, and estate-tax-free distributions of principal are also permitted in the case of hardship.[13] Deferred estate tax occurs upon distributions from the QDOT to the surviving spouse during the lifetime of the surviving spouse (i.e., distributions of principal), upon the death of the surviving spouse, or upon the trust ceasing to qualify as a QDOT.[14]

With respect to distributions made because of hardship, if the spouse has other funds that are readily available to him or her, then the distribution will not be considered to be made on account of hardship. Hardship can relate to the spouse's health, maintenance, or support.

Example: Helmut and Jane had been married for 25 years when Jane died of cancer. Helmut never became a U.S. citizen, although he resided in the United States with Jane after their marriage. Jane established a QDOT in her will for Helmut's benefit. After Jane's death, Helmut contracted a rare blood disease for which there was no known cure. Helmut's physician suggested that he try an experimental course of treatment which Helmut's insurance company refused to pay for. Helmut, who made a reasonable salary, but could not afford the treatment suggested by his physician without insurance coverage, may receive a distribution from Jane's QDOT without having to pay immediate estate tax on it.

The QDOT regulations also provide that, if the fair market value of the assets of the QDOT at the time of the death of the first spouse exceed $2 million, then at least one trustee of the QDOT must be a "bank," or the trustee must furnish a bond (an expensive insurance policy) to the IRS in the amount of 65 percent of the value of the assets in the QDOT.[15] If the value of the assets in the QDOT does not exceed $2 million on the date of death of the first spouse, then the QDOT must either satisfy the bond or the bank requirement, or the trust instrument must expressly provide that no more than 35 percent of the trust assets, determined on an annual basis, may be invested in real property located outside the United States.[16]

An annuity payable to the surviving spouse will meet the QDOT requirements if the surviving spouse either pays the deferred estate tax annually on the "corpus portion" of each annuity payment or agrees to transfer or roll over the corpus portion of each annuity payment to a QDOT within 60 days of receipt of it.[17]

If more than one QDOT is established with respect to any decedent, then that decedent's estate tax return must designate a person (called the designated filer) responsible for filing the deferred estate tax returns required. The designated filer must be a U.S. bank or U.S. citizen. If the filer is an individual, he or she must have a home in the United States. The designated filer must also file certain informational returns.[18]

CREDITS

A resident alien is basically entitled to the same credits for purposes of determining his or her estate tax as a U.S. citizen. Specifically, the unified credit (the $600,000 exemption), the state death tax credit, the credit for foreign death taxes paid, and the credit for tax on prior transfers are all available. With respect to resident aliens, the foreign death tax credit is especially important. Because it was not covered in Chapter 4, we will examine it closely here.

The United States has entered into estate tax treaties with Australia, Austria, Denmark, Finland, France, Germany, Greece, Ireland, Italy, Japan, The Netherlands, Norway, South Africa, Sweden, Switzerland, and the United Kingdom, and gift tax treaties with Australia, Austria, Denmark, France, Germany, Japan, Sweden, and the United Kingdom. The Internal Revenue Code provides that, if the United States has an estate tax treaty with a country, then the foreign death tax credit is the greater of the amount provided in the treaty and the amount provided in the Internal Revenue Code.[19] If two or more jurisdictions are involved, and two or more foreign death tax credits are allowed under a treaty with another county and the Internal Revenue Code, the aggregate amount is credited. (There is a limitation, of course, equal to the maximum amount of the federal estate tax imposed with respect to the property.)

The foreign tax credit is allowed for any estate, inheritance, or succession tax actually paid with respect to property situated in a foreign country and included in a decedent's estate for federal estate tax purposes. No interest or penalties due with a foreign tax qualifies for the credit. If any recovery of a foreign death tax for which a credit is claimed occurs, the person recovering the amount must notify the IRS so that the tax can be redetermined. Also, the credit is limited to foreign death taxes actually paid and for which the credit is claimed within four years of filing the federal estate tax return.

Finally, the foreign death tax credit is not available to the estates of all resident aliens. If the U.S. president determines that the foreign country of which a resident alien is a citizen does not give U.S. citizens a reciprocal foreign death tax credit, and that it is in the U.S. public interest to allow the foreign death tax credit of such country only if it is reciprocal, the president may proclaim that no foreign death tax credit will be allowed to the citizens of that country until their country reciprocates.[20]

GIFT TAXATION OF NON-RESIDENT CITIZENS AND RESIDENT ALIENS

As previously discussed, U.S. citizens are subject to gift tax on transfers of property whether the property is in trust or otherwise, whether the gift is direct or indirect, and whether the property is real, personal, tangible, or intangible. The estate and gift tax rates are now unified. If a U.S. citizen transfers property in excess of $10,000 per donee per year, then he or she begins to use up the $600,000 exemption amount. Once the exemption amount is used, then gift tax must be paid. Spouses may choose to split the gift, whereby liability is joint and several between them. This is an elective right to which both spouses must consent, but it is *not* available unless each spouse is a U.S. citizen or resident.[21]

As with the estate tax rules, U.S. law provides for an unlimited marital gift tax deduction between spouses when both are U.S. citizens. However, no marital deduction from the gift tax is allowed for a lifetime gift from a U.S. citizen or resident to a non-U.S. citizen spouse. There is no good reason to distinguish between a transfer of assets by gift and at death, but nonetheless, that is the case.[22] The Internal Revenue Code does provide, however, for an increase to $100,000 of the annual gift tax exclusion to a non-U.S. citizen spouse.[23]

Example: Harry is married to Masaka, a non-U.S. citizen. Masaka is not happy with the idea of having a U.S. citizen trustee serve with her as a co-trustee on Harry's QDOT. Harry may transfer $100,000 to Masaka outright and free of trust every year, thereby transferring a significant amount of property to her while he is alive in order to avoid having to transfer it at death via a QDOT trust in his will.

ANNUAL EXCLUSION GIFTS

Resident aliens may both give and receive the $10,000 per donee per year present interest gift exclusion. These gifts need not even be reported to the IRS. Remember, the exclusion applies only to present interest gifts. Future interest gifts such as reversions in property, remainders in property, and other interests which are limited to commence in use, possession, or enjoyment at some future time are not counted as part of the exclusion.

CHARITABLE GIFT TAX DEDUCTION

The charitable gift and estate tax deduction, which is unlimited, is not restricted to gifts for use in the United States or to domestic charities. Therefore, a gift to a foreign charitable organization that meets the charitable purpose test of the Internal Revenue Code for use outside the United States is deductible for charitable gift tax purposes. Furthermore, the charitable gift tax deduction is unlimited.

Example: Isabella contributes $100,000 to the Animal Defense Fund of Madrid, Spain, a charitable organization. Her gift qualifies for the unlimited charitable gift tax deduction.[24] (Note, however, that this does not necessarily mean the gift qualifies for the charitable income tax deduction.) If Isabella makes the gift by bequest in her will, it will also qualify for the estate tax charitable deduction.

GENERATION-SKIPPING TRANSFER TAX

Resident aliens are subject to generation-skipping tax in the same manner as U.S. citizens. The purpose of the generation-skipping transfer tax is generally to ensure that Congress gets to tax transfers at each generation's death. There is a $1 million exemption for each transferor. In other words, Mom may transfer the first $1 million to her grandchildren, generation-skipping tax exempt, and so may Dad.

In order to understand the generation-skipping transfer tax, several statutory terms and definitions must be mastered. For starters, the terms *transferor* and *generation* are critical to the understanding of the tax. The transferor is either the decedent (if the transfer is at death) or the donor (if the transfer is during life). Generally, a generation is defined along family lines. Mom and Dad are assigned to one generation, Son and Daughter to the next generation, and Grandson and Granddaughter to the third generation. If Mom and Dad skip Son and Daughter and go directly to Grandson and Granddaughter, then a generation-skipping transfer has been made. If the transfer is to non-family members, then ages are assigned to determine whether or not a generation-skipping transfer has been made. Generally, if the person is 37½ years or more younger than the transferor, then a generation-skipping transfer has been made.

There are three types of generation-skipping transfers: (1) taxable terminations, (2) taxable distributions, and (3) direct skips.[25] A taxable termination occurs upon the termination of an interest in a trust if, after the termination, all interests in the trust are held by skip persons[26] (those more than one generation below the person who established the trust).

Example: Betty Ann creates a trust paying income to her daughter for life and, upon her daughter's death, to her daughter's children equally. A taxable termination occurs at the daughter's death, because an interest in a trust has terminated and, at that point, no one but skip persons (Betty Ann's grandchildren) has an interest in the trust.

A taxable distribution occurs when there is a distribution of principal or income from a trust to a skip person. The amount of the generation-skipping transfer tax paid from the trust with respect to the taxable distribution is also treated as a taxable distribution.[27]

Example: Kim creates a trust providing for payments to her children and grandchildren at the trustee's discretion. If the trustee makes a distribution to Kim's grandson, then a taxable distribution occurs (provided that Kim has already used her $1 million exemption and, if she has not, the distribution will use part of it).

A direct skip occurs when property is transferred directly to a skip person. A gift by a grandparent to a grandchild is a direct skip. Each transferor, again, receives a $1 million exemption, and a married couple may elect to treat generation-skipping transfers as being made one-half by each spouse.[28]

Example: Rebecca transfers $1,500,000 to a trust for her grandchildren. Isaac, Rebecca's husband, agrees to let Rebecca use $500,000 of his $1 million exemption on the transfer. Rebecca pays no generation-skipping tax (although she will pay gift tax), and the trust is generation-skipping tax exempt if the election is made.

To compute the generation-skipping transfer tax, the taxable amount is multiplied by a flat 55 percent rate.[29]

U.S. CITIZENS WITH PROPERTY IN OTHER JURISDICTIONS

Estate planning is much simpler when all of a person's property is located in one jurisdiction, the same one where her estate will be administered. Ideally, this would be the same jurisdiction as her domicile. In most cases, such centralization minimizes taxes of the relevant jurisdictions. However, this is not always feasible, it will sometimes be necessary to determine whether an individual should have one will or a separate will for each jurisdiction where property is located.

Separate wills are commonly used because they eliminate the interrelationship of an estate's administration between jurisdictions. With multiple wills, each foreign jurisdiction need only be aware of the property located in *that* jurisdiction, which provides greater confidentiality. Multiple wills also permit speedier probate, because the will being probated is a will that complies with the rules of the foreign country. If a foreign will is desirable, it is essential to consult with legal counsel in each jurisdiction where a foreign will is to be executed.

If you fall into the category of having property in a foreign country, consider the following guidelines when signing your foreign will:

- For a person with multinational interests, it is usually preferable to omit any reference to the residence or domicile of the person signing the will. This is because the foreign jurisdiction may then require copies of the domestic will.

- In multiple will situations, the language of revocation in one will must not inadvertently revoke wills (and codicils thereto) in other jurisdictions.

- The preamble or one of the early provisions of the will should clearly define the property to which the will pertains.

Example: I, Claudette Clifford, declare the following to be my last will and testament (to be known as my "French Will," applicable only to my real property, situated at the time of my death, in the country of France, or any political subdivision thereof, which I may own or to which I shall be entitled at the time of my death, and over which I may have a power of appointment, all property being hereinafter referred to as my "French estate"). This will may not be revoked unless the revocation clause of another will specifically refers to this will and revokes it."

- The will should define terms such as *child, children,* and *issue.* It should indicate whether these terms apply only to natural born or also to adopted children.

- If a cash bequest is made, specify the currency of payment to avoid problems with changes in the rate of exchange.

- The residuary clause in the will (the part that begins "All the rest, residue, and remainder of my property") should be limited to property in the foreign country.

- The will should specify how death taxes are to be paid. Otherwise, the estate plan may be disrupted. Are death taxes to be paid out of the foreign property or out of property located, for example, in the United States?

- Also consider having the will authorize the executor to abandon property in the foreign location if such property is small. It sometimes costs more to transfer title and pay taxes than property is worth.

- If the term *minority* is used, indicate which law applies (the law of the foreign jurisdiction or the law of a state in the United States).

- If multiple wills are used, the executor in the home country should have the authority to remove the executor in the foreign jurisdiction. This gives the "home" executor indirect control over the foreign executor.

- Appointment of a U.S. citizen as an executor of a foreign estate may cause the estate (i.e., the foreign property) to be subject to United States' income tax as a domestic estate.[30] Therefore, this election should be made only after consultation with legal counsel with respect to the tax effects. Appointment of a U.S. citizen as executor can also cause a foreign estate to be subject to a 30 percent tax on U.S.-source capital gains.[31]

- There should probably be a clause waiving bond. Otherwise, the jurisdiction where the will is probated may require this unnecessary expense.

- The will should provide a way for the executor (or the trustee) to resign and name successors.

- The foreign will should eliminate unnecessary expenses of administration, such as the expense of a judicial accounting, if permitted by the foreign jurisdiction.

- The will should indicate where it should be offered for primary probate. The governing law of the will should be designated (which would presumably be the law of the jurisdiction where probate is directed).

- The will should include a simultaneous death clause indicating the order of deaths in the event of a common disaster.[32]

NOTES

1. 8 U.S.C.A. § 1481(a) (West 1970 & Supp. 1994).

2. I.R.C. § 7701(b) defines both resident and non-resident aliens.

3. I.R.C. § 7701(b)(3)(A).

4. I.R.C. §§ 7701(b)(3)(B), 7701(b)(5)(A)(iii).

5. I.R.C. §§ 2001, 2031-2046.

6. I.R.C. §§ 2001, 2031-2046 and I.R.C. §§ 2501(a)(1), 2503(b).

7. The term *resident alien* for estate and gift tax purposes is not defined.

8. I.R.C. §§ 2056A, 2053.

9. I.R.C. § 2056(d)(2).

10. I.R.C. § 2056(d)(4).

11. I.R.C. § 2056(d)(2)(B).

12. I.R.C. § 2056A(a)(1)(A),(B).

13. I.R.C. § 2056A(b)(3)(B).

14. Prop. Treas. Reg. § 20.2056A-5(a), (b).

15. Prop. Treas. Reg. § 20.2056A-2(d)(1)(i).

16. Prop. Treas. Reg. § 20.2056A-2(d)(1)(ii).

17. Treas. Reg. § 20.2056A-4(c).

18. Treas. Reg. § 20.2056A-9.

19. Treas. Reg. § 20.2014-4(a).

20. I.R.C. § 2014(h).

21. I.R.C. § 2513(a)(2).

22. I.R.C. § 2523(i)(1).

23. I.R.C. § 2523(i)(2).

24. I.R.C. § 2522.

25. I.R.C. § 2611(a).

26. I.R.C. § 2612(a).

27. I.R.C. § 2612(b).

28. I.R.C. § 2652(a)(2).

29. I.R.C. §§ 2641, 2642.

30. A bill was introduced in the U.S. House of Representatives on February 16, 1995, which provides a two-prong test for determining whether an estate or trust is a domestic estate or trust for U.S. tax purposes. H.R. 981, 104th Congress, 1st Sess., § 208 (1995). An estate or trust would be domestic if: (1) A U.S. court is able to exercise primary supervision over the administration of the entire estate or trust, and (2) a U.S. fiduciary has authority to control all major decisions concerning the trust or estate. A foreign estate or trust would be any estate or trust that is not domestic.

31. See footnote 30.

32. All provisions suggested for foreign wills are from Lawrence, Robert C., III, *International Tax and Estate Planning,* pp. 8-12–8-27 (Practicing Law Institute, 1996).

Special Needs and Government Entitlements

Medicaid, Social Security, and Other Government Benefits

I thank God for my handicaps, for through them,
I have found myself, my work, and my God.

—Helen Keller

Federal and state governments provide medical care and income for certain persons who are indigent or disabled or both. These benefits include Medicaid, supplemental security income (SSI), and social security disability income. In order to qualify for SSI or Medicaid, an individual generally cannot have more than a certain level of assets, nor more than a stipulated amount of income on an annual basis. One of the challenges in estate planning is to prevent inheritances or amounts received in tort claim judgment cases (which have rendered individuals disabled) from cutting off these governmental benefits.

Also, some individuals (or their children) wish to intentionally impoverish themselves in order to qualify for Medicaid. It should be pointed out that Medicaid is a program for indigent people, and attempting to get Medicaid when one has adequate resources for self-care is a clear abuse of congressional intent. The Medicaid application requires an affirmative statement that the applicant understands that anyone "who dishonestly obtains or attempts to obtain assistance to which he is not entitled . . . is guilty of a crime and can be prosecuted under (state) law." A copy of the Georgia Department of Human Resources application for medical assistance is included at the end of this chapter. Remember, care provided by Medicaid may be inferior to some private-pay care. Anyone considering intentionally impoverishing himself or herself in order to qualify for Medicaid should first visit some Medicaid facilities to see what type of care is provided and then visit private-pay facilities to compare the two. In an attempt to curb this type of abuse, Congress has enacted legislation to prevent it. In this chapter, we will look at this legislation and what it does to put a damper on the once-prevalent technique of transferring assets to children, parents, or trusts to qualify for Medicaid.

Legitimate concerns include providing for disabled children after their parents are gone and supplementing care of indigent parents without cutting off governmental aid. The parents of disabled children do not usually want to leave assets directly to those children for two primary reasons:

1. The children, if they have mental disabilities, may not be able to manage their own assets.

2. The inheritance would cut off any benefits the government might be providing. The same could be said of many aging, indigent parents.

Good estate planning can protect these children and parents and the benefits to which they are entitled. In addition, for a person who has been disabled through another's negligence and has received a tort claim settlement or judgment as a result of a lawsuit, structuring settlement assets in a way that does not cut off governmental benefits is vitally important. In this chapter, we will discuss in detail how to do this.

THE CURRENT STATE OF AFFAIRS

It will likely come as no surprise to you that the number of chronically ill Americans 65 years of age and older is increasing rapidly—in fact, at the rate of 783 Americans per day.[1] Longer life is accompanied by increases in the prevalence of chronic illness and disability. In other words, people are living longer, but they have chronic health problems our health care system can manage but not cure. The general attitude of our government is that caring for the elderly should be left to families, charitable organizations, and the private sector. Only the most vulnerable should be cared for by the government itself.

Generally, older people in our society want to be independent, retain their homes, and pass an inheritance on to their children and grandchildren.[2] The adult children of these elders want good care for their parents (without bankrupting the family), they want their parents spared the indignities of poverty, but they do not want to personally be their parents' nurses or caregivers.[3] In addition, these children would prefer not to be required to contribute to their parents' care, and, of course, they would like to inherit from their parents. To achieve these ends, many middle-aged children of aging parents want their parents to qualify for publicly provided nursing home benefits. The public attitude, as evidenced by the 1993 Omnibus Budget Reconciliation Act (hereinafter called "the 1993 Act"), is that public funds should be a means of last resort for the payment of the costs of end-of-life care. The goals of our elders who need long-term care are therefore difficult or impossible to achieve.

MEDICAID TRUSTS

At one time, there was no policy in this country (except in isolated court decisions) preventing a person from transferring assets to a trust in a way that would allow that person to get on Medicaid, at least to the extent that their rights to benefits from the trust were limited or subject to trustee discretion.[4] In 1985, such trusts were determined to be contrary to public policy.[5] Despite the legislation enacted, however, these trusts continued to be drafted by attorneys. Appropriately drafted, these trusts continued to effectively protect the trust corpus from consideration by state Medicaid agencies as an asset owned by the disabled person. In order to achieve this protection, only a portion of the trust was generally available to the person establishing it.

The 1993 Act rendered ineffective some trusts that had formerly permitted limited interests to be distributed to those establishing them without disqualifying such persons from receiving Medicaid benefits.[6] Generally, under the 1993 Act, if an individual has disposed of assets (not in trust) for less than fair market value within 36 months of applying for Medicaid, that person is ineligible for medical assistance for all or part of that time.[7] If assets are transferred to a trust, then the individual is ineligible for 60 months. This means that, in reality, medical benefits after such a transfer are determined under a special formula.[8]

The formula for determining available medical assistance in the event of a transfer within 36 or 60 months (depending on whether or not the transfer was made to a trust) can be expressed as follows:

Total value disposed of ÷ monthly institutional cost = period of ineligibility (which is unlimited) if Medicaid is applied for prior to the expiration of the 36 or 60 month look-back period.[9]

Example: Janice transfers $75,000 to her children and one year later applies for institutional care the average cost of which (in that state) is $3,000 per month. Janice is disqualified for Medicaid for a period of 25 months ($75,000 ÷ 3 = 25).

Medicaid law considers transfers of a person's assets to a trust by his or her spouse or any other person (for example, a court-appointed guardian) as if they were made by that person himself or herself. The purpose for which the trust is established does not matter. Nor does it matter whether the trustees have exercised discretion under the trust or whether there are restrictions on when or whether distributions may be made from the trust or on the use of distributions from the trust.[10]

In the case of an irrevocable trust, if there are *any* circumstances under which payment from the trust could be made to or for the benefit of the person who establishes it, whatever payment could be made to such person is considered an available resource for Medicaid purposes. If payment may be made only to another person (other than the person establishing the trust), this is considered a transfer of assets subject to the 36 and 60 month look-back rules.

Since the 1993 Act, however, three types of trusts have emerged that may be funded with a trust beneficiary's assets that are not deemed to be assets of an individual for public benefit assistance purposes. These trusts are discussed in the following three sections.

INCOME ASSIGNMENT TRUSTS

One type of trust that will not interfere with the creator's eligibility for Medicaid is the income assignment trust. The income assignment trust is an irrevocable trust created by court order and funded with the beneficiary's own income sources. It is restricted in the amounts that the trustee may distribute to (or for the benefit of) the beneficiary. Under the 1993 Act, property in an income assignment trust in excess of the state income cap (the most income a person may receive and still be eligible for Medicaid in a particular state) is not considered legally available to the trust beneficiary to disqualify him or her from Medicaid entitlements. In effect, the concept of asset ownership (what the trust beneficiary, who is also the grantor in fact of the trust, owns) does not apply if certain conditions are present:

1. The trust is composed only of pension, social security, and other income of the individual.

2. The state will receive all amounts remaining in the trust upon the death of the individual up to an amount equal to the total medical assistance paid on behalf of the individual under the state plan.

3. The state makes medical assistance available to such individual who is in a medical institution for a period of not less than 30 consecutive days but does not make such assistance available to the individual for nursing facility services.[11]

It should be emphasized that this type of trust is legally involuntarily funded, because it is created by court order for mentally incapacitated persons, for example. (Although, if mentally aware, the individual would desire this imposition.) The court, in establishing such a trust, will generally limit the trustees to distributing less income to the beneficiary than the applicable state income limit for Medicaid eligibility. The excess income received by the trust, not being available to such a person, would not cut off Medicaid eligibility because the state recovers the trust balance to the extent of its contribution when the trust beneficiary dies. Furthermore, because the assignment of income into the trust was legally involuntary on the part of the beneficiary, the 60-month look-back period does not apply. The court, not the beneficiary, made the transfer. The theory is that the state has an interest in seeing that an incapacitated person's property and affairs are properly administered. The incapacitated person is passive and legally viewed as incapable of consenting to the transfer.[12]

TRUSTS FOR DISABLED PERSONS ESTABLISHED WITH CHARITABLE ORGANIZATIONS

Trusts for a disabled person that are established and managed by charitable organizations may be funded from that individual's own assets without disqualifying the individual from receiving state medical assistance.[13] If the individual is over age 65, however, he or she may be subject to the 60-month look-back rule.[14] These trusts, sometimes called "pooled account trusts," must meet the following conditions:

- The trust must be established and managed by a not-for-profit organization.

- A separate account must be maintained for each beneficiary, although the trust may pool these accounts for purposes of investment and management.

- These trusts must be established solely for the benefit of the individuals who are disabled, as defined by Medicaid, by the parent, grandparent, or legal guardian of the individual, by the individual, or by a court.

- To the extent that amounts remaining in the beneficiary's account upon the death of the beneficiary are not retained by the trust, the trust must pay the state an amount equal to the total amount of medical assistance paid on behalf of the beneficiary under the state plan from the amounts remaining in the account.[15]

It should be noted that, prior to the 1993 Act, there were several types of trusts that could be established by individuals without rendering them ineligible for Medicaid. For example, in some states a parent could make a gift to a child (or someone else, for that matter), and the person to whom the property was given could create a discretionary trust (a trust where the trustee could make distributions of income or corpus in his or her own discretion) to provide for care the state aid did not cover. Under the 1993 Act, if assets of an individual are used to fund a trust benefiting the individual or his or her spouse, the trust corpus will be deemed available to the trust's creator-beneficiary or his or her spouse. Now anyone acting upon the request of such individual (such as the child to whom the assets were transferred) and using that individual's own assets to fund the trust is deemed to be that individual (the creator), who is, in effect, creating the trust for himself or herself.[16]

TRUSTS FOR DISABLED PERSONS NOT YET 65

A trust may be created for an individual under age 65 with such person's own assets without disqualifying that person from Medicaid eligibility if the state will receive all amounts remaining in the trust upon the death of such individual up to an amount equal to the total Medicaid assistance paid on behalf of the individual under a state plan.[17] Thus, for example, a parent, grandparent, legal guardian, or a court may take funds paid on a tort claim judgment (or any other assets, such as inheritance) and use those funds to establish such a trust. Although the 1993 Act that established these trusts is silent on this point, the Director of the Medicaid Bureau for the Health Care Financing Administration has said that, as long as the trust is established before an individual is age 65, the trust should be exempt for as long as the individual is alive.

Example: At age 26, John, a student working on his Ph.D. in nuclear physics and being courted by top companies worldwide, was scuba diving when his oxygen tank malfunctioned, causing John, who was pulled to safety by his diving buddy, to suffer brain damage. As a result of the accident, John now has the mental capability of a small child. A $5 million judgment was obtained against the oxygen tank manufacturer. John's parents, who have two other children, placed the $5 million in a trust providing that the state would receive whatever funds it had advanced for John's care at his death. John may be on public assistance for life. According to the terms of the trust, at John's death, the state receives from the trust what it has expended for his care. The rest of the trust, if any, goes to John's estate.

TRUSTS CREATED FOR CHILDREN WITH SPECIAL NEEDS AND ELDERLY PARENTS BY OTHERS

As we have seen, the 1993 Act severely curtailed the effectiveness of trusts created by individuals for themselves and trusts created by their spouses and children for them using the individual's own assets. However, while the 1993 Act, in effect, voided these trusts by causing the assets or income (or both) to be deemed available assets to the person establishing the trust or such person's spouse where benefits from such trust would be available to them, the 1993 Act did not eliminate the effectiveness of trusts created by persons other than the beneficiaries of the trust. This means that the door is still open for parents to create trusts for their children with special needs that do not have the effect of cutting off Medicaid or SSI (or other governmental benefits) and trusts created by children for their elderly parents. The idea is that basic maintenance can be provided through a governmental program such as Medicaid, SSI, or social security disability income, with the trust providing the "extras."

These trusts must be carefully drafted. If assets are given outright to a child or elderly parent, then those assets are legally available and must be consumed before public funds are restored. Similarly, if assets are placed in a trust that *requires* or allows a child or elderly parent to be supported out of the trust, then the value of the trust will be counted as a resource available for the support and maintenance of the beneficiary, and public funds will be cut off until the trust resources are consumed. Therefore, it is extremely important that trusts for children with special needs and elderly parents are properly drafted so they do not cut off governmental benefits.

The type of trusts that will be effective in this respect are called *discretionary trusts* or *supplemental care trusts.* When discretionary and supplemental care trusts are drafted for the benefit of others (to whom the one establishing the trust owes no duty of support), then chances are good that they will be available for discretionary or supplemental care benefits for the beneficiary without cutting off governmental benefits. In this respect, it is crucial to render the trust income and corpus legally unavailable to the beneficiary, while at the same time, ensuring that the trustee may use it to provide for the beneficiary's care other than support.

DISCRETIONARY TRUST TERMS

Whether trust income and assets are available to the beneficiaries (and thereby to the beneficiary's creditors, including governmental entities providing benefits) depends on the terms of the trust. For the most part, the language in the trust instrument will be interpreted by the courts if a question arises. The courts will look to the intent of the person establishing the trust to see if that person intended for trust resources to support the beneficiary or simply to be available if the trustee should determine that assets should be distributed to the beneficiary. Sometimes evidence from outside the document is considered if the document itself is vague.[18] If the person establishing the trust has a duty under law to support the beneficiary, then this will also be considered by the courts.[19]

Obviously, Medicaid and Social Security regulations provide guidelines for what assets are available to an individual requesting public assistance.[20] The courts also provide interpretation of the meaning of asset availability. Court cases illustrate that a state may not characterize as available to a trust beneficiary phantom assets and income that cannot be used to meet an individual's basic needs.[21] For example, the North Dakota Supreme Court struck down a state regulation that treated all trusts as available to the trusts' beneficiaries. In the North Dakota case, the mother of a developmentally disabled adult created a trust that was to pay for her son's special needs not otherwise provided for by any public agency. She had no duty of support toward her adult son. Her intent, which was to provide only for what the state did not provide, could not be negated by the state regulation. The North Dakota Supreme Court also said that the trust did not violate federal or state public policy.[22] Hence, the trust did not cut off any governmental aid for the adult son.

In a New York case, a trust included the language, "It is not my intention to provide for support for my sister, but rather, to give her supplemental help." The court said that this language sufficiently expressed the intent that other resources available, including state aid, were to be considered by the trustee. Therefore, the court held that the trust did not cut off the sister's aid.[23]

In an Illinois case, a trust providing for "comfortable living expenses not otherwise furnished by the state" for a sibling was held not to cut off state aid.[24]

This principle of availability has prevented states from attributing sources of income or resources to an applicant for public assistance if the resources are merely tangential. The standard is "actual availability." Actual availability limits what the states may consider in determining assets and income available to an individual applying for benefits.[25]

WHAT'S LEFT?

To summarize, the 1993 Act does not affect trusts created by parents for children, or children for parents, or by siblings for one another, or by persons for unrelated friends where:

- the person establishing the trust has no duty to support the one for whose benefit the trust is established (parents have support duties toward minor children, but not adult children);

- the intent of the trust is not to support the beneficiary, but to provide for "extras";

- the person establishing the trust uses his or her own assets (and not the beneficiary's assets) to fund it.

PERMISSIBLE TRUST PROVISIONS AFTER THE 1993 ACT

Through working with parents of children with special needs over the years, attorneys have developed provisions for trusts for such children. Examples of provisions which may be put in these trusts without cutting off governmental aid include the following:

DISCRETIONARY DISTRIBUTIONS OF PRINCIPAL AND INCOME

The trustee may be allowed to distribute the net income and the principal of the trust to the beneficiary, or use it for the beneficiary's benefit, as the trustee, in his, her, or its sole, absolute, and uncontrolled discretion, determines.

NO REIMBURSEMENT TO FEDERAL OR STATE GOVERNMENTS

The trustee may be authorized to spend principal or income for the needs of the beneficiary not otherwise provided for by federal, state, or local governmental financial assistance and benefits, or by the providers of such services. Such needs include spending money, health services not otherwise provided, private rehabilitative training, housing, supplementary educational aid, radios, record players, television sets, bicycles, sports equipment, recreation, camping, vacations, automobiles, automobile maintenance, and transportation. The trustee is under no obligation to spend principal or income for such needs, but if he, she, or it does decide to do so, in no case shall the trustee pay or reimburse any amounts to the federal, state, or local government.

Education, Medical, and Recreational Trips

The trustee may spend principal or income for the expenses of a person to accompany the beneficiary on trips to providers of medical, dental, or psychological diagnostic work or treatment, for rehabilitative or educational training, or on vacations or recreational outings, and for the travel expenses of relatives of the beneficiary, to visit the beneficiary, or the travel expenses of the beneficiary (and a person to accompany the beneficiary) to visit the beneficiary's relatives.

Coordination with Governmental Benefits

In making distributions, the trustee may take into consideration the amounts the beneficiary is entitled to from any federal, state, or local governmental agency, including, but not limited to, Social Security Administration benefits, Veterans Administration benefits, Medicaid, and Supplemental Security Income benefits. Any distributions to the beneficiary should supplement, rather than supplant, any such benefits which would otherwise be available. If the beneficiary's eligibility for any such benefits or for benefits from any other entitlement programs would be jeopardized by any distributions from the trust, the trustee should withhold distributions. The trustee should assist the beneficiary in obtaining the full benefit of these programs. The trustee should collect, expend, and account separately for all governmental assistance benefits, and should not commingle them with these trust funds.

Governmental Action

In the event that it is determined by a court or other authority of competent jurisdiction that the trust, as it benefits the beneficiary, renders the beneficiary ineligible to receive Social Security benefits, Supplemental Security Income, Medicare or Medicaid, or other similar federal, state, or local government financial assistance and benefits, or if the trustee, in its sole, absolute, and uncontrolled discretion, determines that the trust could be subject to attachment or bankruptcy proceedings by a creditor of the beneficiary or by the federal or state government, then the trustee is authorized (but not required), in its discretion, to terminate the trust. In such event, the trustee distributes the remaining principal and income to a designated person who is deemed to be someone who can voluntarily use the trust assets to care for the beneficiary on an informal basis.

Visitation

The trustee may be required to periodically visit the beneficiary at the beneficiary's residence or the facility where the beneficiary resides. The trustee or the trustee's agent may be required to inspect the living conditions and the medical treatment the beneficiary is receiving (if the beneficiary is under treatment). It may also be prudent for the trustee to make periodic evaluations regarding the beneficiary's status, in terms of:

- Physical, eye, and dental examination by an independent physician, optometrist or ophthalmologist, and dentist;

- Education and training programs;

- Available government programs and benefits;

- Work opportunities and earnings;

- Recreation, leisure time, and social needs;

- Appropriateness of existing residential and program services;

■ Legal rights to which the beneficiary may be entitled, including free public education, rehabilitation, and programs that meet constitutional minimal standards.

Appointment of Advocate

The trustee may appoint or hire an advocate for the beneficiary to represent and advance the beneficiary's interests in daily, community, and national affairs. The duties of such an advocate include, but are not limited to, familiarizing himself or herself with the beneficiary's personal needs, interests, and any rehabilitation, therapy, or work programs in which the beneficiary participates; familiarizing himself or herself with the community resources available to the beneficiary; raising questions and concerns about the beneficiary's programs; maintaining contact with those who provide services to or for the benefit of the beneficiary; and familiarizing himself or herself with networks for the protection of the beneficiary's rights.

Educational or Long-Term Placement Advisor

The trustee may appoint or hire an educational or long-term placement advisor or geriatric care manager. The long-term placement advisor and the trustee would visit long-term placement facilities for the beneficiary, and the long-term placement advisor's decision with respect to the facility wherein the beneficiary is placed may be binding on the trustee.

MEDICAID RECOVERIES BY STATE GOVERNMENTS

Prior to the 1993 Act, states were not required to recover amounts paid for medical assistance on behalf of an individual when that individual died. However, under the 1993 Act, states are now required to seek recovery from an individual's estate for medical assistance payments made on behalf of that individual.[26] An individual's estate includes all real and personal property and other assets included in the individual's estate under state probate law. It may also include (at the option of the state) legal title or interests the individual had in assets at the time of death. This may include assets conveyed to a survivor, heir, or heir of the deceased person through joint tenancy, living trust, or "other arrangement."[27]

These mandatory state recovery provisions apply to individuals required to spend all but a minimal amount of their resources for institutional care. They also apply to the estate of individuals who received medical assistance when they were at least 55 years old.[28] However, in the latter case, the state may seek recovery only for medical assistance for nursing facility services, home and community-based services, and related hospital and prescription drug services.[29]

Finally, a state must seek recovery from an individual's estate for nursing facility and long-term care services if the individual received or is entitled to receive benefits under a long-term care insurance policy under which assets or resources are disregarded. A state is not required to seek recovery in this situation if, as of 14 May 1993, the state plan had an amendment disregarding payments under such a long-term care insurance policy.[30]

SAMPLE MEDICAID APPLICATION

Georgia Department of Human Resources
APPLICATION FOR MEDICAL ASSISTANCE

We will consider this application without regard to color, sex, age, handicap, religion, national origin, or political belief.

Applicant's Name _____

Applicant's Husband or Wife's Name _____

Applicant's Responsible Individual (if minor) _____

Does applicant plan to enter a Medical Care Facility?   ☐ Yes   ☐ No   Date Entering _____
If Yes, list name, address, telephone number.

Is applicant currently in a Medical Care Facility?   ☐ Yes   ☐ No   Date Entered _____
If Yes, list name, address, telephone number.

Facility Name _____

Address _____

_____

Telephone _____

If No, list home address, telephone number.

Address _____

_____

Telephone _____

PLEASE ANSWER THE FOLLOWING QUESTIONS	APPLICANT	HUSBAND OR WIFE (if applicable)
1. Birthdate (Month / Day / Year) and Age		
2. Sex (M or F)		
3. Social Security Number		

Is this person now receiving, or has this person ever received, food stamps, AFDC (Welfare),   ☐ Yes   ☐ No
or Medicaid in Georgia? If Yes, when and in what county?

Is this person now receiving, or has this person ever received, Medicaid from the Social Security   ☐ Yes   ☐ No
Administration through the Supplemental Security Income (SSI) program? If Yes, when?

Does this person have any unpaid medical bills for the three months prior to the month of application?   ☐ Yes   ☐ No

When you apply for Medicaid in Georgia, we will automatically determine whether you are eligible for the Qualified Medicare Beneficiaries (QMB) program. You will receive a letter telling you whether or not you qualify for QMB. According to the law, QMB benefits begin the month after your Medicaid eligibility is determined. QMB benefits are not available for the current month or any months prior to the month of the determination of your Medicaid.

Your social security number will be used for computer matching with the records of other government agencies to help us determine your Medicaid eligibility.

RACE / ETHNIC AFFILIATION

We would like you to tell us your racial or ethnic identity although you don't have to. This information is being collected only to be sure that everyone receives assistance on a fair basis. This information will not affect your eligibility.

- ☐ White
- ☐ Black
- ☐ Hispanic
- ☐ Asian or Pacific Islander
- ☐ American Indian or Alaskan Native

PLEASE READ THIS CAREFULLY BEFORE SIGNING

I hereby apply for medical assistance under Title XIX of the Social Security Act. I understand that the Georgia Public Assistance Act provides that any person who dishonestly obtains or attempts to obtain assistance to which he is not entitled or who assists someone else in obtaining assistance dishonestly is guilty of a crime and can be prosecuted under Georgia law.

I further understand that whoever

(1) Knowingly and willfully makes or causes to be made any false statement or representation of a material fact in any application for any benefit or payment under a State plan approved under this title.

(2) At any time knowingly and willfully makes or causes to be made any false statement or representation of a material fact for use in determining rights to such benefit or payment.

(3) Having knowledge of the occurrence of any event affecting (A) his initial or continued right to any such benefit or payment, or (B) the initial or continued right to any such benefit or payment of any other individual in whose behalf he has applied for or is receiving such benefit or payment, conceals or fails to disclose such event with an intent fraudulently to secure such benefit or payment either in a greater amount of quantity than is due or when no such benefit or payment is authorized, or

(4) Having made application to receive any such benefit or payment for the use and benefit of another and having received it, knowingly and willfully converts such benefit or payment or any part thereof to a use other than for the use and benefit of such other person, shall be guilty of a misdemeanor and upon conviction thereof shall be fined not more than $10,000 or imprisoned for not more than one year, or both.

I understand that signing an application for benefits which include medical assistance assigns benefits available form any liable third party to the Georgia Department of Medical Assistance to the extent of the cost of care paid by Georgia Medicaid Program.

ALL OF THE INFORMATION WHICH I HAVE PROVIDED IS TRUE AND COMPLETE TO THE BEST OF MY KNOWLEDGE

_____   _____
Signature of Applicant   Signature of Responsible Individual

_____   _____   _____
Date   Relationship   Date

_____   Address _____
Signature of Witness

       _____
_____
Date

Form268 (Rev. 11-89)

NOTES

1. Kruse, Clifton B. Jr., *Third Party and Self-Created Trusts*, Section of Real Property Probate and Trust Law, American Bar Association, 1995, p. 1. The author wishes to express her gratitude to Mr. Kruse for his help and assistance in the preparation of this chapter of the book.

2. Kruse, at p. 3 and 4.

3. Kruse, at p. 4.

4. Scott and Fratcher, *The Law of Trusts*, Section 155, 4th ed. (1987), p. 167.

5. 42 U.S.C. § 1396a(k).

6. See House–Senate Conference Committee Bill, § 13611(b), "Transfers of Assets; Treatment of Certain Trusts," amending 42 U.S.C. 1396p.

7. Section 13611, House–Senate Conference Committee Bill, subparagraph (1)(C)(i).

8. *Id.* at subparagraph (1)(B)(i); (1)(B)(i)(ii)(I).

9. *Id.* at subparagraph (1)(E)(i)(I) and (II).

10. 42 U.S.C. 1396p.

11. *Miller v. Ibarra*, 746 F. Supp. 19 (D. Colo. 1990).

12. See *Zybach v. Nebraska Department of Social Services*, 411 N.W. 2d 627 (Neb. 1987); *Lee v. State Department of Public Health and Welfare*, 480 S.W. 2d 305 (Mo. App. 1972).

13. Section 13611, House–Senate Conference Committee Bill, subparagraph (3)(B)(4)(C).

14. There is some authority that funding a pooled account trust subjects the grantor to a non-exempt transfer of assets penalty of 36 months. See Department of Health and Human Services, State Medicaid Manual, Part 3, Eligibility, Transmittal Letter 64 (Nov. 1994) § 3258.10B, p. 3-3-109.19.

15. Section 13611, House–Senate Conference Committee Bill, subparagraph (3)(B)(4)(C).

16. Section 3259 of the *State Medicaid Manual*.

17. 42 U.S.C. 1396p(d)(4)(A).

18. See *Snyder v. Department of Public Welfare*, 556 A.2d 31 (Pa. Comm. 1989); *Department of Mental Health v. Phillips*, 500 N.E. 2d 29 (Ill. 1986).

19. See, for example, *Garrand v. Garrand*, 615 P.2d 422 (Utah 1980) and *Coverston v. Kellogg*, 357 N.W. 2d 705 (Mich. App. 1984).

20. Title XIX of the Social Security Act. See 42 U.S.C. 1396–1396p (West 1982).

21. *Whaley v. Schweiker*, 663 F.2d 871 (9th Cir., 1981).

22. *Hecker v. Stark County Social Service Board*, 1994 W.L. 709003 (N.D.).

23. *In Application of Penn Yan Manor, Matter of Ross*, 409 N.Y.S. 2d 201 (Sur. Yates Co. 1978).

24. *Department of Mental Health v. Phillips*, 500 N.E. 2d 29 (Ill. 1986).

25. *State of Washington v. Bowen*, 815 F.2d 549 (9th Circuit, 1987).

26. 42 U.S.C. § 1396p(b)(1).

27. 42 U.S.C. § 1396p(b)(4).

28. There has been some question raised as to whether this should be 65.

29. 42 U.S.C. § 1396p(b)(1)(B).

30. 42 U.S.C. § 1396p(b)(1)(C).

Including Charity in Your Estate Plan

Charitable Giving Techniques
Frequently Used in Estate Planning

A generous person will be enriched, and
one who gives water will get water.

—Proverbs 11:25
NRSV Bible

Most of us make gifts to charitable organizations during our lifetime. You may send $1,000 to your alma mater in honor of your twenty-fifth class reunion, add $100 to your church's organ fund, or give $500 to your local symphony during its annual phone-a-thon. You also may be considering naming your favorite charity, such as your college, a local arts organization, or a medical research institute, to receive a bequest at the time of your death.

You give because it makes you feel good. You give to charitable organizations whose work or mission you strongly support. You give because you believe it will improve your community for your family's future. What you may not realize is that when you give to charity, you may be eligible for substantial tax benefits and savings that can prove advantageous not only in the year of the gift (when you may get income tax deductions or capital gains tax savings) but also in the long run when your gift may substantially reduce your estate taxes.

CURRENT GIFTS

The IRS permits you to claim a current charitable contribution of cash as an itemized deduction on your individual income tax return in the year in which you make the gift.[1] However, your income tax deduction may be limited depending upon the amount of your adjusted gross income (AGI).

Your gross income is simply the total amount of income you earn in any one year from your job, investments, property, and/or alimony.[2] Your AGI is equal to your gross income minus certain deductions for business, losses from the sale of property, and depreciation—the typical itemized deductions you claim on your annual income tax return.[3] The maximum allowable charitable income tax deduction for a gift of cash in any one year is equal to 50 percent of your AGI. This 50 percent deduction also is only available if your gift of cash is made to a 50-percent-type charitable organization. Examples of 50-percent-type organizations include churches, educational organizations or institutions, medical institutions, and certain publicly supported charitable organizations.[4] As a general rule, most organizations to which you would make a donation (a church, a museum, a university, a university's athletic program, the United Way, the American Cancer Society, or the Salvation Army) are 50-percent-type organizations. If your combined cash charitable contributions in one tax year are greater than 50 percent of your AGI, the IRS permits you to carry over the excess deduction for five years until it is used up (the 50 percent limitation will also apply in all following years).

Tangible Personal Property

Gifts of tangible personal property and appreciated assets (stocks, bonds, or mutual funds) may also be given to charity, but such gifts are subject to different rules. Tangible personal property is the legal term for property that is used in your home (furniture, artwork, cars), on your person (jewelry, furs), or in your business (typewriters, computers, desks). Rare books, art, antiques, coin and stamp collections, precious stones and gems, as well as equipment (such as computer equipment) are all types of tangible personal property commonly donated to charitable organizations. Special tax rules relate to charitable contributions of tangible personal property.

In the year of your gift, you may claim an income tax deduction for the fair market value of a gift of tangible personal property made outright to a charitable organization if the property can be used directly by the charity for its charitable activities. If you contribute tangible personal property unrelated to the charitable purpose of the charitable organization and such property must be sold in order to be used by the charitable organization, your income tax deduction is limited to your basis in the property rather than the fair market value of the property donated.[5] Your basis in property is the price you paid for it. If you received property as a gift, your basis is the price paid by the person who gave it to you.

Example: Susan owns a Louis XVIII armoire, which she purchased 10 years ago at an auction. She paid $10,000 for the armoire. Now its fair market value is $25,000. If Susan sold her armoire for its fair market value, she would realize a gain of $15,000 ($25,000 – $10,000 = $15,000). If Susan gave her armoire to the American Cancer Society, which would presumably have to sell it in order to use it to further the Society's charitable mission, Susan could claim a charitable deduction on her income tax return for her basis of $10,000. If Susan gave her armoire to a museum, which could use it directly as part of a display of period furniture, she could deduct its full fair market value.

Determining whether the use of donated tangible personal property is related to your donee's charitable mission is not always a simple task. For example, if a painting donated to an educational institution is displayed in the institution's library for study by art students, the painting is being used for educational purposes, so such use is not an unrelated use. However, if the educational institution sells the painting and uses the sale proceeds for educational purposes (i.e., to purchase science laboratory equipment), such use of the painting is an unrelated use.[6] Other uses of donated tangible personal property approved as related uses by the IRS include the display of porcelain art donated to a retirement home,[7] the display in a state office building of wildlife etchings donated to the state,[8] and the display of a donated stamp collection in a university's art gallery for study by students.[9]

If you are considering making charitable contributions of tangible personal property, you should refer to IRS Publication 561 (Determining the Value of Donated Property), and IRS Publication 526 (Charitable Contributions), and IRS Form 8283 (Noncash Charitable Contributions) for assistance in valuing your income tax charitable deduction and related issues. To request copies of these publications, call the IRS Forms Distribution Center at 1 (800) 829-3676. All noncash gifts in excess of $500 must be reported on IRS Form 8283. For a gift of an appreciated asset with a value in excess of $5,000, a qualified appraisal of the asset by a professional appraiser is required.

Gifts of Appreciated Property

Gifts of appreciated property—particularly, gifts of highly appreciated common stock—are the most common noncash gifts given to charity because of the potential for double tax savings. If you give appreciated property to a charitable organization, not only are you entitled to an income tax deduction for the full fair market value of the property, but you will also not be taxed on the appreciation of the property.

Example: Beth purchased $1,000 of stock in The Home Depot, Inc., seven years ago. Today, Beth's investment is worth $10,000. Beth would like to make a donation of $10,000 to her favorite charity this year. If she gives her stock to charity, she may claim an income tax deduction for the full $10,000 this year. If Beth in January 1997 is in the 31 percent federal income tax bracket and the 6 percent state income tax bracket (and the top federal [28 percent] and state [6 percent] capital gains tax brackets), her gift of stock will save her $3,700 in income tax in the year of the gift *and* will enable her to avoid $3,060 in federal and state capital gains tax that she would have paid if she had sold the stock instead of giving it to charity.

As with gifts of cash, however, the income tax charitable deduction for gifts of appreciated property may be subject to certain limitations. As previously explained, in any one tax year, the maximum allowable deduction for charitable contributions is 50 percent of your AGI. This 50 percent limitation applies to gifts of cash.[10] This percentage limitation is even more restrictive, however, for gifts of long-term capital gain property, such as appreciated stock owned by the donor for more than one year. A long-term capital gain is the gain in value of any property you own for more than one year (18 months in some cases under the Taxpayer Relief Act of 1997). A short-term capital gain is the gain in value of any property you own for one year or less.

The income tax charitable deduction related to a gift of long-term capital gain property, even when the gift is made to a 50-percent-type charitable organization, is limited to 30 percent of your AGI in the year of the gift.[11] In addition, if you make a gift of long-term capital gain property to a private foundation rather than a 50-percent-type public charity, your income tax charitable deduction will be further limited to the lesser of (1) 20 percent of your AGI in the year of your gift of appreciated property, or (2) 30 percent of your AGI for gifts of cash.[12] (Private foundations will be discussed later in this chapter.) If you make gifts in excess of these percentage limitations, you may carry over the excess for up to five years so that you may get the benefit of the full deduction.[13]

Bargain Sales

If you would like to donate property to a charitable organization but feel that you cannot afford to part with the entire value of the property, you may want to consider making a charitable contribution of the property through a bargain sale. If you make a bargain sale of property to a charitable organization, you sell your property to that charity at a substantial discount in fair market price.

When you make a bargain sale to a qualified charitable organization, the excess of the property's fair market value over the sale price paid by the charitable organization constitutes your charitable contribution to the purchasing organization. The price you receive from the charitable organization is treated by the IRS for tax purposes as part gift and part sale.[14] Your basis (cost) in the property is allocated between the percentage "sold" and the percentage given to the charitable organization.

Example: Donald owns a piece of real estate worth $500,000. Donald purchased this property for $100,000 (therefore, his basis in the property is $100,000). Donald would like to sell this real estate to the Community Foundation for $250,000. This transaction will be a gift of $250,000 (the difference between the sales price paid by the charity and the full fair market value of the property) and a sale of $250,000 (the amount actually paid by the charity to Donald). Donald may claim a $250,000 charitable contribution deduction for his gift and must report capital gain on the sale part. The basis is split equally between the sale portion and gift portion, making Donald's capital gain $200,000.

Some transactions that appear to be outright contributions of property to a charitable organization may in fact be bargain sales even though the donor receives no cash from the charitable organization. If you donate property subject to an indebtedness, such as mortgaged real estate, to a charity, the transaction is treated as a bargain sale, and the amount of the indebtedness is regarded as the amount you "receive" as payment from the charity in return for your gift.[15] Because you are deemed to have received value in exchange for your gift (release from the mortgage or other indebtedness), you may also be treated as having taxable gain for income tax purposes.

DEFERRED GIVING

A charitable bequest is the most common form of deferred giving. A charitable bequest is a deferred gift because, although you have included a charitable gift in your present will, the gift will not actually be made to the charitable beneficiary until after your death. A bequest may be of cash, marketable securities, tangible personal property, or a percentage of the residue of your estate. At your death, your estate will be entitled to an estate tax charitable deduction for the full fair market value of your bequest.

A number of different charitable trusts can be used to create a combination of current and deferred gifts to benefit yourself, your husband, children, grandchildren, or other family members as well as one or more charitable organizations. These trusts are called split-interest trusts by the IRS, because the income and remainder interests in the trusts are split between charitable and noncharitable beneficiaries. You can create a split-interest trust under the terms of your will (a testamentary split-interest trust), but typically an individual will choose to create a split-interest trust that becomes immediately operational during her lifetime. If you create a testamentary split-interest trust, your estate will be entitled to an estate tax charitable deduction for the value of the charitable gift but not the value of the gift to the noncharitable beneficiary.

Charitable Remainder Trusts

A charitable remainder trust is a split-interest trust that provides for payments to be made to one or more individuals for a certain period of time, and then for the remainder to pass to one or more charitable organizations selected by the individual who creates the trust. If you create a charitable remainder trust, you and/or your husband may be the income beneficiary or beneficiaries. You may also name your children (or anyone else) as the trust's income beneficiaries. The income beneficiaries have the right only to trust income.

They do not own the trust property, and the value of the trust property is not included in their estates for tax purposes.

In addition to selecting the income beneficiaries of your charitable remainder trust, you must also decide how long the income beneficiary or beneficiaries will receive payments from the trust. An income beneficiary may receive payments for his or her lifetime or for a set number of years (not to exceed twenty).[16] Typically, a donor who creates a charitable remainder trust will name herself and her spouse as income beneficiaries for their lifetimes.

If you create a charitable remainder annuity trust, the income beneficiary (or beneficiaries) will receive a fixed sum from the trust.[17] This fixed sum is the annuity. If you create a charitable remainder unitrust, the income beneficiary (or beneficiaries) will receive a fixed percentage of the value of the trust property valued each year.[18] The fixed percentage paid is the unitrust amount. Annuity or unitrust amount payments may be made monthly, quarterly, semi-annually, or annually. Your trust *must* be either a charitable remainder annuity trust or a charitable remainder unitrust in order to qualify for income, gift, and estate tax charitable deductions.

The income passing to the income beneficiary may be subject to gift taxation if the income beneficiary is someone other than yourself or your spouse. If the income beneficiary of your charitable remainder trust is your child, the payments from the trust are treated as taxable gifts from you to your child. If the total value of the payments made to your child exceeds $10,000 (indexed), then you will be required to file a gift tax return. You may use some or all of your exemption amount (discussed in Chapter 4), however, to offset this tax so that you do not actually have to pay any gift tax.

At the end of the income term, the remaining trust property will pass to the charitable beneficiary or beneficiaries you have selected. Your charitable income tax deduction in the year you create the trust is the value of this remainder interest passing to charity. This value is calculated from IRS tables estimating the life expectancy of the life income beneficiary (or beneficiaries), the interest rate applicable at the time the trust is created, and the amount of property expected to ultimately pass to the charity. Therefore, the older the life income beneficiaries are at the time the trust is created, and the fewer life income beneficiaries there are, the more trust property will pass to charity, and the greater the income tax deduction for you. As with current gifts, income tax deductions for gifts to charitable trusts are subject to annual percentage limitations. However, you may carry over any excess for up to five years after you make the gift to the trust.

In addition to income tax deductions, there are other tax advantages to establishing a charitable remainder trust. The charitable remainder trust itself, like a charitable organization, is exempt from taxation.[19] Therefore, if you transfer highly appreciated property (such as stock) to the trust, the trustee may sell that property without having to pay immediate capital gains tax on the appreciation. The trustee may then invest the entire amount of the sales proceeds to generate income for the income beneficiary or beneficiaries. In addition, at the death of the survivor of husband and wife income beneficiaries, the property held in the trust passes to the charitable remainder beneficiary, therefore escaping estate taxation due to the unlimited marital and charitable estate tax deductions.[20] Note, however, that if you create a testamentary charitable remainder trust and name someone other than your husband as beneficiary, your estate will have to pay an estate tax on this noncharitable portion.

Example: Rachel owns appreciated real estate worth $500,000. She purchased this real estate several years ago for $50,000. Rachel and her husband are approaching retirement and she would now prefer to own an income-producing asset. If Rachel sells the real estate in January 1997, she will have to pay $153,000 in capital gains tax (at the 28 percent federal and 6 percent state tax rates) and will therefore have only $347,000 to invest to produce income. However, if Rachel transfers the real estate to a charitable remainder trust, the trustee (who may be Rachel) may sell the real estate without having to pay any immediate capital gains tax. The trustee will have the entire $500,000 to invest to generate income for Rachel and her husband for their lifetimes. At the death of the survivor of Rachel and her husband, the remaining trust property will pass to the charities of Rachel's choice and will not be subject to estate taxation in either her estate or the estate of her husband.

You may be concerned that your children will feel "disinherited" when the property in your charitable remainder trust goes to a charity at your death. If this is a concern, you may choose to couple the creation of a charitable remainder trust with the creation of an irrevocable life insurance trust (discussed in Chapter 5), the beneficiaries of which are your children and/or grandchildren. In the context of gifts to charity, the irrevocable life insurance trust is used as a "wealth replacement" vehicle. By using both trusts, you may make a substantial gift to charity at your death *and* potentially increase the amount of inheritance you leave your children, because both the charitable remainder trust and the irrevocable life insurance trust may escape any taxation in your estate.

Example: Margaret, age 63, creates a charitable remainder trust and funds it with $1 million of undeveloped real estate. Margaret names herself as the sole unitrust amount recipient of her trust. As the unitrust amount recipient, each year she is to receive 8 percent of the value of the trust property, valued annually, in quarterly installments. Margaret names Women's College as the remainder beneficiary of her trust. In the year she creates the charitable remainder trust, Margaret receives an income tax deduction equal to the value of the remainder interest that will pass to Women's College at her death. If the IRS "rate of the month" applicable at the time she creates the trust is 6.4 percent, the value of Margaret's income tax charitable deduction will be $307,510.

Margaret uses a portion of her quarterly unitrust payments to pay premiums on a $1 million permanent variable universal life insurance policy on her life. The annual premiums on this type of life insurance policy for a 63-year old woman in good health (preferred, non-smoker) are equal to $29,389. Margaret establishes an irrevocable life insurance trust to own the policy. Margaret names her three children as the trustees of the life insurance trust. The trust is both the owner and the beneficiary of the policy so that the insurance proceeds paid to the trust are not included in her estate for tax purposes. Margaret may transfer up to $30,000 ($10,000 per each child who is named as a trust beneficiary) to the insurance trust annually to pay premiums without incurring any gift tax on such a transfer. At Margaret's death, the remainder of her charitable remainder trust passes to Women's College, and her estate owes no tax on this transfer. The $1 million proceeds of the policy pass to her three children pursuant to the terms of the trust. Again, her estate owes no tax on this transfer. Margaret has successfully moved $1 million to charity and $1 million to her family and paid no estate taxes on these transfers.

A good asset to give outright to charity at your death or to use in funding a charitable remainder trust is your qualified retirement plan or individual retirement account (IRA). These assets are typically included in your taxable estate, and distributions from your qualified plan or IRA after your death are taxable as ordinary income to your heirs.

Charitable Lead Trusts

Charitable lead trusts are the reverse of charitable remainder trusts. The charity is given the "lead" interest in the trust, which is either an annuity amount (charitable lead annuity trust) or a unitrust amount (charitable lead unitrust), to be paid annually for a certain number of years. The remainder of a charitable lead trust comes back to the trustor/donor or passes to members of her family or other designated noncharitable beneficiaries.[21] The trust may be established for a specified number of years or for the life of one or more individuals living at the time the trust is created. Unlike the charitable remainder trust, there is no minimum or maximum charitable payment for either the charitable lead annuity trust or the charitable lead unitrust.[22] If the income earned by the charitable lead trust is not sufficient to pay the charity its annuity or unitrust amount, however, the trustee may invade the corpus of the trust to make the full payment.

The year you create a charitable lead trust, you may be entitled to an income tax charitable deduction equal to the value of the charitable income interest, which is calculated under the IRS Treasury Tables.[23] However, in order to obtain this income tax deduction, you must be treated as the owner of the trust for income tax purposes. Thus, after the first year, you will be taxed on all of the income earned by the trust but will not get additional charitable deductions for the annual amounts paid to charity. It also is important to note that the charitable lead trust, unlike the charitable remainder trust, is a fully taxable trust. Therefore, the trustee of a charitable lead trust, unlike the trustee of a charitable remainder trust, may not sell appreciated assets owned by the trust without incurring a capital gains tax on the sale.

Lead trusts may be created during life or in your will (testamentary lead trusts). Perhaps the most famous testamentary charitable lead trust ever is the one created under the last will and testament of Jacqueline Bouvier Kennedy Onassis. In May 1994, when Jackie died of cancer, the whole country mourned. Throughout her life, she had been a role model for the American people. Intelligent, glamorous, kind, and generous, Jackie loved her family, was loyal to her friends, and devoted to the United States of America.

Following her death, Jackie's last will and testament became a matter of public record, giving us another a glimpse of the former first lady's unselfishness and concern for the American people. More important, perhaps Jackie's will was a model of effective estate tax planning. Jackie Onassis was fortunate to have an extremely large estate to plan—$200 million, according to *Fortune* magazine. Had she left her entire estate to her two children,

Caroline and John, Jr., her executor would have first had to turn over 55 percent ($110 million) to the IRS. Jackie, however, chose not to do that.

Jackie left family homes and certain personal effects to specified individuals. She left her home in Newport, Rhode Island (Hammersmith Farm), to her stepbrother, Hugh D. Auchincloss, Jr., and her home in Martha's Vineyard (and all other real estate) to her children. In her will, she named the persons she wished to receive her personal effects as well as those of her first husband, John Fitzgerald Kennedy. She also left cash bequests to her children and some of her close friends. She exercised a general power of appointment over a testamentary trust given to her under the last will and testament of John F. Kennedy and appointed the trust property of her late husband equally to their two children.

In order to make these bequests and devises, Jackie's estate had to pay a 55 percent estate tax on the value of the homes, the cash gifts, and the tax dollars themselves. Tax had to be paid on the tax dollars because the estate tax is a tax-inclusive tax. Thus, for example, if half of Jackie's estate (approximately $100 million) was allocated to the payment of estate taxes and the making of the gifts mentioned above, Jackie's executor would have taken the $100 million, disbursed $45 million in gifts of cash and assets to her family and friends, and then paid the remaining $55 million to the IRS. Assuming a total estate of $200 million, there would still be another $100 million to distribute after these initial distributions and tax payments.

As to the remainder of her estate (approximately $100 million), Jackie provided for two interests—charity and her grandchildren. First, she established a testamentary charitable lead trust to provide a stream of income to a private foundation she created. This foundation, the C&J Foundation, was established by Jackie to promote cultural and social betterment of humankind and to alleviate human suffering. At the end of a term of 24 years, the trust terminates and the remaining trust property is distributed to Jackie's grandchildren then living.

Jackie's charitable lead trust provided for an 8 percent annual annuity to be paid to the C&J Foundation. This means that 8 percent of the initial fair market value of the assets going into the trust is paid to the Foundation every year for 24 years. Projections calculated on special charitable giving software indicate that the C&J Foundation, based on these facts, would receive a total of $185,676,123 over the 24-year period. In exchange for this generous bequest to charity, the federal government allowed Jackie's estate to claim a substantial estate tax charitable deduction. In fact, in Jackie's case, based on the assumption that $100 million would be available to pay the estate taxes and fund the lead trust, the estate tax would be only $3,293,686 ($96,706,314 going to the lead trust) versus the estate tax of $55 million paid on the other $100 million (going to family and friends). At the termination of Jackie's charitable lead annuity trust, her grandchildren will receive the balance of the trust after the payment to the federal government of another type of tax, the generation-skipping transfer tax.

The beauty of Jackie's estate plan is that it allows a significant part of her estate to be used by a charitable organization for a number of years by deferring taxes on the dollars given for a long period of time. The longer the charitable organization may use the dollars (and the more dollars the charitable organization gets to use), the more tax is deferred or, if children are the only remainder beneficiaries, the more tax is eliminated altogether. This particular tax benefit may only be accomplished through the use of a charitable lead trust.

OTHER CHARITABLE GIVING TECHNIQUES

There are several other techniques that can be used to combine charitable giving with income and transfer tax savings. Although not as common as charitable remainder trusts or as well-publicized as Jacqueline Kennedy Onassis's charitable lead trust, these techniques should be considered for any individual who wishes to include current or deferred charitable giving in his or her estate plan.

Gift of a Remainder Interest in Residence or Farm

Generally, you are allowed an income tax deduction for a gift of a remainder interest in a personal residence or farm. If you give a remainder interest to charity, you retain only the use of the personal residence or farm for your lifetime or a term of years selected by you.[24] The value of your income tax charitable deduction for this gift is the value of the remainder interest calculated using the IRS Treasury Tables. After you give the remainder interest in your personal residence or farm to a charitable organization, a portion of any subsequent additions or improvements you make to the residence or farm are deductible as additional contributions for the use of the charitable organization.[25] At your death or at the end of the term of years, the residence or farm passes to the designated charitable remainder beneficiary.

The term *personal residence* means any residence you own, even if it is not your principal residence. Thus, the term includes vacation homes as well as stock in a co-op apartment if the unit the stock represents is used by you as a personal residence.[26] The term *farm* means any land used for raising livestock or the production of crops.[27] The IRS has ruled that the gift of a remainder interest in a personal residence or farm does not have to cover the entire property.[28] For example, if you own a residence encompassing 100 acres, you may give a remainder interest in 50 of the acres to charity while retaining all interest in the other 50 acres. In addition, your gift does not have to be of your entire interest in the property.[29] You may give 50 percent of the remainder interest in your residence to a charitable organization and 50 percent to an individual. The charitable organization and individual then will own the residence as tenants in common.

The gift of a remainder interest in a personal residence or farm must be outright. No deduction is allowed if the remainder interest in the personal residence or farm is contained in a trust.[30] However, in one case, the IRS did allow a deduction for a remainder interest given through a revocable living trust.[31] Presumably the IRS permitted this deduction because the individual who creates a revocable living trust is treated as the owner of all property in the trust for purposes of income taxation.

Example: Sarah owns a vacation home on an island off the coast of Georgia. She decides to give a remainder interest in her home to a nature conservatory. She executes a deed that names herself as the owner of the property for life, remainder to the nature conservatory. In the year in which she records this deed, Sarah is entitled to an income tax charitable deduction for the value of the remainder interest in her vacation home which she has given to charity. The home is not taxed in her estate.

Charitable Gift Annuities

A gift annuity agreement is typically a simple contract signed by you and the charitable organization at the time the gift is made. When you enter into a gift annuity agreement, you transfer cash, securities, real estate, or other property to a charity in exchange for the charity's promise to pay you or a beneficiary you designate an annuity for life or for a term of years. As previously explained, an annuity is merely a fixed-dollar amount, chosen at the time the donation is made, that does not increase or decrease during the payment term. Payments may be made by the charity monthly, quarterly, semi-annually, or annually. The annuity rate the charity pays depends on your age or the age of your named beneficiary. The *annuitant* is the person named to receive the annuity, whether it is you, your spouse, or another family member. On the death of all of the annuitants, the remaining assets from which the annuity was generated passes to the charitable organization.

The American Council on Gift Annuities recommends maximum annuity rates that are almost universally observed by charitable organizations issuing gift annuities. The Council's rates are reviewed every three years and changed periodically to reflect current interest rates and mortality tables. (The Council's current annuity rates were established as of March 1997.) Generally, the annuity rate recommended by the Council results in an annuity that has a value of approximately 40 to 60 percent of the amount paid or transferred by the donor to the charity.

The gift annuity offers more security than a charitable remainder trust if the charity issuing the annuity is financially secure. The gift annuity is a legal obligation of the issuing charitable organization. Even if the assets you contributed to the charity are exhausted in annuity payments, the charitable organization is still responsible for the entire amount owed to you under the gift annuity agreement. Because of this contractual liability, however, some charitable organizations are reluctant to enter into gift annuity agreements, and others reinsure their annuity commitments with commercial insurance companies.

You are entitled to income, gift, and estate tax charitable deductions for the portion of your gift that qualifies as a charitable gift. Like a bargain sale, a gift annuity transaction is treated as part gift and part sale. When you transfer property in exchange for a gift annuity, you receive an income tax deduction for the difference between the value of the cash or property transferred and the present value of the annuity to be received by the annuitant.[32] The charitable income tax deduction is based on the age(s) of the annuitant(s), the number of annuitants, the value of the gift, the frequency of annuity payments, and the IRS "rate of the month."

If you transfer appreciated property to a charity in return for an annuity, the portion of the gain attributable to the annuity (the sale portion in the bargain sale transaction) is taxed to you. If you are the annuitant, however, the gain is taxed in installments spread over your entire lifetime. The portion of your basis attributable to the annuity in each annuity payment is first recaptured tax-free. The installment part of the capital gain is taxed as capital gain. The remainder of the annuity payment is then taxed to you as ordinary income.

Example: Katherine (age 81) transfers $10,000 of General Motors stock that she purchased for $2,000 (her basis) to a charity in exchange for a 9.1 percent annuity for her life. (American Council on Gift Annuities recommends 9.1 percent as the rate for donors aged 81.) The annuity payments are to be made quarterly to Katherine. What will her charitable income tax deduction be? How will the $910 per year annuity be taxed to her?

Katherine will be able to deduct $5,604.15 as a charitable income tax deduction in the year of her gift. This deduction may be claimed up to the contribution ceiling of 30 percent of her AGI. (Remember, for appreciated securities held long term, the contribution ceiling is 30 percent.) If Katherine is not able to use the entire deduction in the year of the gift, she will get the benefit of the five-year carry-over period for the excess.

Katherine will be taxed annually on her $910 annuity as follows:

Ordinary income	$386.75
Capital gain income	$418.55
Tax-free return of basis	$104.70
Total	$910.00

A deferred gift annuity is similar to an immediate payment gift annuity except that the annuity payments begin at a future date determined by the donor rather than at the time of the gift. The deferred gift annuity may be a good giving technique if all of the following are true:

1. You wish to support your favorite charitable organization now.

2. You could benefit from a large income tax deduction in the current year.

3. You do not need current income.

4. You want to create a guaranteed income for yourself and your spouse at retirement.

When you contribute cash or property to a charitable organization in exchange for a deferred gift annuity, the amount of the original gift is invested and allowed to compound over time. This allows the charitable organization to pay a higher rate of return than would otherwise be the case for a person of the same age who transferred cash or property to the charity in exchange for an immediate payment gift annuity. In addition, your charitable income tax deduction is higher than for an immediate payment gift annuity because the annuity payments are deferred.

Pooled Income Funds

A pooled income fund is a trust established by the charitable organization itself. The charitable organization invites donors to make contributions to its pooled income fund. The pooled income fund (or trust) operates much like a mutual fund, paying income for life to the donor, or to the donor and the donor's designated secondary beneficiary, and paying the remainder to the charitable organization at the death of all beneficiaries. On the death of each beneficiary, the value of the units in the trust owned by that beneficiary are severed from the fund and transferred to the charitable organization.

In the last several years, many charitable organizations have established pooled income funds. Some charitable organizations have marketed their funds with great success. Others have not marketed them at all, so donors to these organizations may not even know that a pooled income fund is a giving option. Some charitable organizations have two or three pooled income funds, each with a different investment philosophy. For example, a charitable organization might have a growth fund (where assets are invested toward achieving growth, with little emphasis on current income, which could yield a larger income tax deduction for the donor); a balanced fund (where assets are invested in a mix of growth-oriented and high-income assets, providing reasonable income with some emphasis on capital appreciation); and/or an income fund (where assets are invested for maximum income, with little emphasis on growth). Thus, when you contribute to a pooled income fund, you may be able to choose which type of investment philosophy you believe is most desirable.

When you transfer property to a pooled income fund, it is commingled and invested with the contributions of other donors. You may transfer cash or securities to a pooled income fund and receive an income tax charitable deduction for your contribution in the year in which it is made. Appreciated property, again, makes a good contribution choice because the sale of the property by the fund will avoid capital gains taxation. Because you are transferring the remainder interest in the property contributed to the fund to the charitable organization, your contribution is irrevocable. You can make additional contributions to the fund and receive an income tax charitable deduction each year you make an additional gift.

Your income tax charitable deduction is based on the return of the fund (or, if the fund is less than three years old, a rate calculated with reference to the floating IRS rates). Thus, the growth fund, assuming it would generate the least income, would generate the highest income tax deduction for you. In addition, the age of the beneficiary or beneficiaries on the date of the gift, the value of the gift, and the life expectancy of the beneficiary or beneficiaries are all considered in the calculation of your deduction.

The pooled income fund offers many benefits if you do not have the financial means to make a substantial donation to your favorite charitable organization but would like to make a meaningful contribution to the charitable organization's work. By donating to a pooled income fund, you obtain:

- the opportunity to make a meaningful gift to charity.

- the ability to receive income for life.

- the means to avoid capital gains taxation on appreciated long-term capital gain property.

- a partial income tax deduction in the year of your gift.

In addition, unlike establishing a charitable remainder or lead trust, no legal fees are incurred in making this type of gift.

Example: Ellen and her husband Joe contribute $20,000 to the pooled income fund established by their local community foundation. Their contribution is pooled with the contributions of other donors for investment purposes. Therefore, the size of the amount invested to generate income for Ellen and Joe is actually larger than their $20,000 contribution. If the total fund value is $2 million, then Ellen and Joe will be entitled to 1 percent of the fund's annual income. At the death of the survivor of Ellen and Joe, their original contribution and any appreciation in its value will pass to the community foundation.

PRIVATE FOUNDATIONS

You can choose to create your own charity to achieve your charitable goals and maintain control over assets contributed for charitable purposes. You may establish a private foundation during your lifetime or under the terms of your will. A *private foundation* is defined by the IRS as any charitable organization except:

- organizations such as educational institutions, hospitals, churches, governmental entities, and publicly supported public charities.

- publicly supported organizations financially supported by membership fees and contributions from the general public.

- organizations created to support other existing charitable organizations.

- organizations operated exclusively to test for public safety.[33]

These charitable organizations are *public charities*. Your church, your local art museum, your local community foundation, the United Way, and the Boys and Girls Clubs of America are all examples of public charities.

A private foundation may be established as either a trust or a corporation. To get tax-exempt status for your foundation from the time of its formation, you must file IRS Form 1023 (Application for Recognition of Exemption under Section 501(c)(3) of the Internal Revenue Code) with the IRS within 15 months of the date of formation. If an organization has tax-exempt status, it does not have to pay income or capital gains taxes, and contributions to it are tax-deductible by donors. In some states, private foundations must also file a separate state application for exemption. Whether or not your foundation has to file for state exemption, it will be subject to state oversight or supervision to some extent. This power of supervision is typically vested in a state's attorney general, who is given the authority by statute to enforce the foundation's governing instrument (i.e., its trust agreement, if a trust, or its articles of incorporation and bylaws, if a corporation) on behalf of its beneficiaries (i.e., the general public).

In the year of your contribution to the foundation, you will receive an income tax charitable deduction equal to the full fair market value of all cash contributed.[34] If you contribute capital gain property, your deduction will be limited to your basis in the property (unless you made your contribution prior to June 30, 1998, and unless your contribution was of marketable securities.)[35] This deduction is not limited if you contribute property to a public charity (see the earlier discussion of percentage limitations under gifts of cash). Your deduction is further limited to 30 percent of your AGI (with the five-year carry-over period for excess contributions) if you contribute cash. If the property contributed is capital gain property, your deduction will be limited to 20 percent of your AGI (with the five-year carry-over period for excess contributions).[36] These limitations are 50 percent and 30 percent, respectively, if you give to a public charity rather than a private foundation. However, like a public charity, if your private foundation sells the capital gain property, it will not pay a capital gains tax on the sale. If you leave property to your private foundation in your will, your estate will be entitled to an estate tax charitable deduction for the full value of the property contributed.

In order to curb abuses (or perceived abuses) in the operation of private foundations, Congress included a complex and comprehensive set of operating restrictions applicable to private foundations in the Tax Reform Act of 1969.[37] These restrictions do not apply to public charities. Failure to comply with these restrictions will cause the imposition of excise taxes on the offending foundation. In addition, the individual foundation manager (who could be you) may also be penalized for noncompliance. Finally, if a foundation's noncompliance is egregious, the foundation may be stripped of its tax-exempt status. Notwithstanding these restrictions and possible penalties, the potential benefits of creating a private foundation may convince you that this is truly the best vehicle for carrying out your charitable giving plan.

You may find the private foundation to be an attractive charitable giving vehicle if you want to make a substantial gift to charity and do not need to receive income from the donated property for the rest of your life. In addition, the charity or charities selected as beneficiaries of your private foundation can begin receiving funds immediately rather than having to wait until your death. Finally, the creation of a private foundation gives you the chance to make a lasting contribution to your community. A private foundation will not terminate upon your death and can stand as a lasting legacy in your memory. A private foundation is run by trustees. You and your spouse can serve as trustees and receive reasonable compensation for serving the foundation in such capacity. As trustees, you will control the investment and management of the foundation's funds and the ultimate distribution of such funds for charitable purposes selected by you. Younger family members can be trained to select grant recipients, evaluate the success of past grants, and manage the foundation's assets. You may eventually choose to name your children or other family members as trustees. They also will be able to pay themselves reasonable salaries from the foundation and will have sole decision-making authority with respect to the grants your foundation makes after your death.

Through the federal, state, and municipal tax systems, we are all present donors to the largest public charity in the country—the government. Yet many of us disapprove of government inefficiencies and the way our tax dollars are spent. Through passage of legislation providing for income, gift, and estate tax deductions for property given to charity, Congress has recognized the efficiency of allowing private sector charitable organizations to satisfy the educational, charitable, medical, and religious needs of American communities. In giving to charity, one is also rewarded with the personal satisfaction of directly participating in community improvement. In estate planning—as in life—when you give, you (and your family) will receive.

NOTES

1. I.R.C.§ 170(a)(1).

2. See I.R.C. § 61(a).

3. See I.R.C. § 62(a).

4. See I.R.C. § 170(b)(1).

5. According to Treasury Regulation § 1.170-4(b)(3)(ii), the burden is on the donor to determine and prove whether or not the donated tangible personal property will be put to an unrelated use by the charitable donee. A donor may treat the donated property as not being put to an unrelated use by the charitable donee if (1) the donor establishes that the tangible personal property is not in fact put to an unrelated use, or (2) at the time the tangible personal property contribution is made or is treated as having been made, it is reasonable to anticipate that the property will not be put to an unrelated use by the charitable donee.

6. I.R.C. § 170(e)(1).

7. Private Letter Ruling 8143029; See also Private Letter Ruling 8247062.

8. Private Letter Ruling 8301056.

9. Private Letter Ruling 8208059.

10. See I.R.C. § 170(b)(1).

11. I.R.C. § 170(b)(1)(C).

12. I.R.C. § 170(b)(1)(D).

13. I.R.C. § 170(d).

14. I.R.C. § 1011(b).

15. Treas. Reg. § 1.1011-2(a)(3).

16. See I.R.C. § 664(d)(1)(A),(2)(A).

17. I.R.C. § 664(d)(1).

18. I.R.C. § 664(d)(2).

19. I.R.C. § 664(c).

20. I.R.C. § 2055.

21. I.R.C. § 2522(c)(2) and § 2055(e)(2).

22. I.R.C. § 664(d)(1)(A) and (2)(A).

23. Treas. Reg. § 20.2031-7; § 25.2512-5; § 20.2055-2(f)(2)(v) and § 25.2522(c)-3(d)(2)(v), as revised by Internal Revenue Notices 89-24 and 89-60.

24. I.R.C.§§ 170(f)(3)(B)(I), 2522(c)(2) and 2055(e)(2).

25. See Private Letter Ruling 8529014.

26. Treas. Reg. § 1.170A-7(b)(3).

27. Treas. Reg. § 1.170A-7(c)(4).

28. See Private Letter Ruling 8202137 (approving the gift of a remainder interest in 77 acres of a residence with a total of 174 acres. The acreage given to the charitable organization in this case did contain the donor's dwelling and improvements, while the rest of the property not given was pasture and woodland).

29. Revenue Ruling 87-37, 1987-19 I.R.B. 5, *revoking* Revenue Ruling 76-544, 1976-2 C.B. 288. In Revenue Ruling 87-37, the IRS approved a deduction where a donor gave 90 percent of the remainder interest in his personal residence to a charitable organization and the other 10 percent to an individual to hold as tenants in common.

30. Treas. Reg. § 2055-2(e)(2)(ii) and (iii); Treas. Reg. § 1.170A-7(b)(3); and (4) Treas. Reg. § 25.2522(c)-3(c)(2)(ii) and (iii). See also Revenue Ruling 76-357, 1976-2 C.B. 285.

31. Private Letter Ruling 8225158.

32. See I.R.C. § 170, § 1011 and § 72.

33. I.R.C. § 501(c)(3).

34. I.R.C. § 170(e)(5).

35. I.R.C. § 170(e)(1)(B)(ii).

36. I.R.C. § 170(b)(1)(D).

37. See I.R.C. §§ 4940-4945.

Asset Protection

How to Protect Assets from Lawsuits

*I believe that in our constant search for security, we can
never gain any peace of mind until we secure our own soul.*

—Margaret Chase Smith

Several years ago, one of my clients who is a doctor called me and said, "I've been practicing medicine for twenty years and I have a net worth of about three and a half million dollars. Every day I have to worry about somebody suing me for malpractice. If you can't tell me how to protect the assets I've accumulated up to this point in time, I am going to quit practicing immediately, because it's just not worth the risk."

This woman was a doctor in a small town that desperately needed her services. I started thinking about her situation and about other clients who had expressed similar concerns (albeit in less urgent terms). Then and there, I knew I had to learn more about asset protection techniques. I called a friend of mine who is a creditors' rights attorney and got on the fast track to learning what to do for my doctor client and others similarly situated.

Asset protection is indeed a part of estate planning. We worry about Uncle Sam taking our estates, but we also worry about unknown creditors who may appear in the future (anyone who drives a car is at risk.) This chapter will examine various asset protection techniques and when to use them. It will not address methods for persons who have known or easily anticipated creditors to shelter assets from their creditors. (That's the bailiwick of creditors' rights attorneys.) Rather, this chapter focuses on techniques that may be used by the woman (for herself or for her husband) who has no pending or threatened lawsuits against her when she has the means to pay her debts (i.e., she is solvent). For example, a doctor or lawyer worried about future malpractice claims might profit from these techniques.

FRAUDULENT CONVEYANCES

Many asset protection techniques involve transferring assets. If a transfer is considered a "fraudulent conveyance" under applicable state or federal law, a creditor may set it aside. If the individual has filed for bankruptcy, then the bankruptcy trustee may set it aside. What, then, is a fraudulent conveyance?

Subject to the applicable statute of limitations (a law mandating that a legal action be taken within a certain period of time), if a transfer is made with actual intent to hinder, delay, or defraud creditors, it is voidable (may be set aside).[1] Because debtors seldom testify that they had an actual intent to hinder, delay, or defraud creditors, the law has established certain "badges of fraud" which are used to prove such intent. The existence of one or more of these badges of fraud will be considered in determining the transferor's intent. *Badges of fraud* include transfers to relatives, transfers to partners of the individual, transfers to partnerships in which the individual is a partner, and transfers to corporations in which the individual is a director, officer, or person in control. All of these are referred to as transfers to "insiders."[2] Other examples of badges of fraud include:

- a transfer with the transferor retaining possession or control of the transferred property.

- the concealment of a transfer (for example, failure to properly record a deed or failure to revise the transferor's financial statement to show that a transfer was made).

- a transfer made after the transferor has been sued or threatened with suit.

- the transfer of substantially all of the transferor's assets.

- absconding assets, removing assets from the court's jurisdiction, or hiding assets (specifically excluding an asset from a financial statement, for example).

- a transfer for an inadequate consideration.

- a transfer that renders the transferor insolvent.

- a transfer occurring shortly before or shortly after a substantial debt is incurred.

All of these badges of fraud may be considered by a court in determining whether a debtor had actual intent to delay or hinder creditors.[3]

In addition to actual fraud, many state laws (as well as the Federal Bankruptcy Code) provide that a transfer is voidable by existing creditors or a bankruptcy trustee without regard to the intent of the transferor if the transfer is made without equivalent consideration and the transferor is insolvent at that time (or becomes insolvent as a result of the transfer). This is known as constructive fraud.[4]

Insolvency means the sum of your debts is greater than all of your assets. *Debt* means a liability on a claim. Every debt or claim against a debtor that can be enforced in the courts is taken into consideration.

Example: Sam has assets of $1 million and a lawsuit pending against him for $2 million. Whether Sam is insolvent depends on the valuation of the $2 million claim. This will involve an assessment of the likelihood of success of the plaintiff suing Sam, whether or not Sam would have a right of contribution against someone else who may be jointly liable with him, and any other relevant factors. If, after considering all of these factors, the valuation of the $2 million lawsuit is deemed to be only $500,000, then Sam would not be insolvent.

Assets are measured at their fair value (for mortgaged property, the equity in the property). If you are planning to make transfers for creditor protection purposes, it will be important to maintain evidence of your solvency as these transfers are made.

Let's go to the second prong of the test. What does a transfer without receiving a reasonably equivalent (or fair market) value mean? The United States Supreme Court has held that *any price negotiated* is reasonably equivalent, as a matter of law, absent collusion.[5] It would be hard to argue in any court that contributions to charities involved "reasonably equivalent value" received by the debtor, even though the debtor receives intangibles (such as her name on the building or invitations to VIP events sponsored by the charity).

If a fraudulent transfer is found, state law remedies include the avoidance of the transfer to the extent necessary to satisfy the creditor's claim. If the court so orders, the creditor may recover a judgment for the lesser of the asset transferred or the claim. State courts may also grant injunctions against further disposition of assets and appoint a receiver to take charge of assets transferred.[6] A trustee in bankruptcy is not limited to the amount of the creditor's claim but can avoid the transfer in its entirety for the benefit of the bankruptcy estate if he or she utilizes the fraudulent transfer provisions of the Bankruptcy Code.[7]

The techniques discussed in the remainder of this chapter assume that an individual is solvent after any transfer and that there is no actual intent to hinder, delay, or defraud creditors. Remember, there are two categories of creditors:

1. creditors who have only those remedies provided them by state law

2. creditors in a federal bankruptcy proceeding

TRUSTS

Whether a trust works for asset protection purposes depends on several factors, including who the trustor or settlor (person establishing the trust) is, what the terms of the trust are (what directions did the trustor give to the trustee in the document?), who the beneficiaries of the trust are, and whether the trust is revocable or irrevocable.

If you establish a trust and transfer your assets to it and you are even a permissible beneficiary of the trust, the general rule is that your creditors (including a bankruptcy trustee) can reach the property to the maximum extent the trustee could distribute it for your benefit.[8] Some states, however, vary from this general rule.

Example: Eleanor establishes a trust, naming her brother, Carl, as the trustee, and transfers assets to it. The trust is irrevocable, and Eleanor retains an interest in the trust income for her lifetime, remainder to Jim and Robert, her sons. The general rule is that Eleanor's creditors or bankruptcy trustee can reach her entire life income interest in the trust.

What if Eleanor's trust had been revocable and totally for the benefit of Jim and Robert? In other words, the only thing she retained was the right to revoke the trust and get the trust property back. On this point, states differ. Under some state laws, creditors cannot compel the trustor or settlor (who established the trust) to revoke a trust for their benefit, but other states permit it. Federal bankruptcy law provides that, for bankruptcy purposes, the property of the debtor does not include any power that the debtor may exercise solely for the benefit of an entity other than the debtor.[9] By negative implication, then, powers exercisable for the benefit of the debtor are included in the bankruptcy estate, which means that a bankruptcy trustee should be able to exercise any power any trustee could exercise for the debtor's benefit for the benefit of the debtor's creditors.[10]

If Eleanor transferred assets to her brother, Carl, as trustee of an irrevocable trust, and she named her sons Jim and Robert as the only beneficiaries, *then* she has made a transfer that is *not* subject to her creditors. What if, however, Eleanor, not Carl, were the trustee of this trust, and years later Eleanor went bankrupt? Could Eleanor continue to be the trustee of this trust for her sons? What if Eleanor had been taking a fee for serving as trustee each year? Eleanor's bankruptcy estate has the same rights that Eleanor had as trustee, including her right to trustee fees.[11] This does not mean that her bankruptcy trustee could actually *serve* as successor trustee, however, because under the trust contract, the trustee's services are based on personal skills and trust confidence in which the identity of the person chosen is critical to the contract. The bankruptcy trustee cannot assume a contract if it would result in a material change in the identity of the performing party and the identity of that person was an essential element of the contract.[12] Therefore, Eleanor's bankruptcy trustee should not be able to replace her as the trustee of the trust for her sons.

If a trust is used to "creditor-proof" assets for the benefit, for example, of family members, it is important to observe all trust formalities and to keep assets in the trust carefully segregated from your own property. If you establish such a trust, although you could be the trustee, it is somewhat risky, because one of the badges of fraud discussed previously is retaining control over transferred property, and serving as trustee may constitute such control. If possible, name an independent trustee.

SPOUSAL GIFTS

If either you or your husband is more at risk than the other, the most common technique for protecting assets from future creditors of the exposed spouse is to simply transfer assets to the non-exposed spouse. If this is done, it is best if the transferred property *and income therefrom* is kept completely separate from the spouse who transferred it. An outright transfer to a spouse would protect the assets from the creditors of the transferor spouse but subject them to the creditors of the transferee spouse. For this reason, property is often transferred by one spouse to a trust for the other spouse.

What if both spouses are exposed?

Example: Paul and Robin are both doctors—Paul a gynecologist and Robin an orthopedic surgeon. Paul establishes a trust for Robin, transferring $500,000 of his assets into it and naming Robin as the trustee and Robin and their children as the beneficiaries. Simultaneously, Robin transfers $500,000 of her assets to a trust of which Paul is the trustee and Paul and their children are the beneficiaries. Paul and Robin will both be treated as having established the trusts for their own benefit, and the trusts will not achieve the desired protection from creditors.[13] This arrangement would also be a problem for estate planning purposes because trusts established by two persons for each other are interrelated, with the arrangement leaving both of them in approximately the same positions as they would have been in had they not created the trusts. Each trustor will be treated, for federal estate tax purposes, as the owner of the trust of which he or she is the beneficiary.[14]

Any time trusts are used as asset protection techniques, the gift tax consequences should be kept in mind. Unless the spouse is the sole beneficiary for the spouse's life, and the trust is one of the marital trusts discussed in Chapter 5, then the trustor will either have to use some of her exemption amount to get the property into the trust or make sure that it qualifies for the $10,000 (indexed) per donee per year annual exclusion (or pay gift tax if her exemption is fully used). To qualify gifts to a trust for the annual exclusion where the beneficiaries do not have a right to get current income from the trust, the same kind of withdrawal rights discussed in connection with the insurance trust (discussed in Chapter 5) are used. Annual exclusion gifts to a trust are good asset protection techniques because they are relatively small, and they are commonly used, well-recognized means of estate planning.

An individual making gifts to a trust for asset protection purposes must remember that, in addition to gift tax consequences, the assets will no longer be available to her or her husband. Transfers of property such as art, Chinese porcelain, or raw land not currently being used would be good candidates for transfer, as long as the transferor no longer continues to use the assets after the transfer. Remember that continuing to use assets after a transfer may be considered a fraudulent conveyance and constitutes continuing concealment.

OFFSHORE TRUSTS

Perhaps the ultimate asset protection technique is the offshore trust in which assets are physically removed from the United States and transferred to another jurisdiction. A foreign bank or trust company is usually named as trustee of the trust for the benefit of the individual who has established it. The trustee will have discretion with respect to whether or not to distribute funds. If the individual establishing the foreign trust is later sued in the United States, and the creditor or bankruptcy trustee wants to recover trust assets, then he or she will have to bring the suit again in the foreign jurisdiction. This, of course, involves going through the motions twice, which is itself a deterrent. Even if a judgment is obtained in a foreign jurisdiction, the courts in that jurisdiction may protect the assets in the foreign trust under local law.

Entire books have been written about the pros and cons of various offshore jurisdictions. We will not attempt to go into that much detail here, but some of the more popular offshore jurisdictions include the Cayman Islands, the Cook Islands, the Channel Islands, Liechtenstein, Jersey and Guernsey, and Bermuda.

In order to ensure that a foreign trust is going to be effective as an asset protection technique, the assets of the trust must be capable of being physically held in a foreign jurisdiction. Assets such as Krugerrands, jewelry, and foreign securities are examples of such assets. Stock certificates in U.S. corporations that are taken to a foreign bank are not examples of such assets because a U.S. court could order a U.S. corporation to reissue the stock in favor of a judgment creditor.

Example: Marietta, who has her own securities firm, holds warrants in several U.S. corporations. Marietta establishes a trust in the Cayman Islands and transfers her warrants to the Royal Bank of Cayman Islands as trustee. Five years later, Marietta is involved in a lawsuit and a judgment is rendered against her. Her judgment creditor can petition a court to order the U.S. company to reissue the warrants in favor of the creditor, despite the fact that the Royal Bank holds the warrants.

In a foreign trust, the trustor (or settlor) cannot have any authority to distribute assets from the trust or to cause distributions to be made, or a bankruptcy court can order her to distribute and hold her in contempt if she doesn't.[15]

Foreign trusts typically contain clauses that say, in the event of war, natural catastrophe, or a lawsuit against the trustor, the trustee must turn the assets over to an emergency trustee in another jurisdiction, who is automatically appointed in such event. The emergency trustee transfers the assets to a third jurisdiction, which may be unknown to the original trustee and to the trustor. In this situation, it is very difficult for a creditor to find the assets. In fact, one of the theories behind establishing offshore trusts to begin with is that a creditor, knowing it will be very difficult to ever get his or her hands on the assets, may decide to settle on terms most favorable to the debtor rather than even try.

For income tax purposes, a foreign trust will be treated as owned by the one who establishes it.[16] This means all income of the trust will be taxed every year to the trustor, even if no income is distributed. Furthermore, for estate tax purposes, if the trust can be used to satisfy the trustor's debts, then it will be included in the trustor's estate for estate tax purposes.[17]

FAMILY PARTNERSHIP

Family partnerships are popular asset protection techniques as well as estate planning techniques. (Using such a partnership as an estate planning technique was discussed in Chapter 6.) The technique works well for asset protection because, under the terms of the partnership agreement, no one may become a limited partner without the consent of the general partners. The most a creditor can get is something called a "charging order," a right to get from the partnership whatever would otherwise have been distributed to the limited partner against whom a judgment has been rendered. Whether anything at all is distributed to the limited partner is dependent upon the general partner who may decide not to distribute anything. Because a limited partner has no ability to *demand* distributions from the partnership, neither would a limited partner's creditors. However, a creditor who stands in the shoes of the limited partner, although he or she doesn't become a limited partner, must pay tax on the limited partner's share of the income that is not distributed. This makes the interest obtained by the creditor quite burdensome.[18]

In general, a bankruptcy trustee has greater remedies available than a creditor exercising rights under state law. A bankruptcy trustee may attempt to withdraw from the partnership and receive a fair value of the partnership interest if the partnership agreement does not prohibit this. However, most partnership agreements would likely have a provision that a withdrawing partner does not receive any value in his or her share until dissolution.

It is important to remember that a general partner of a partnership has a high fiduciary duty under the law to all the partners. If the general partner withholds distributions attributable to a partnership interest held by a bankruptcy trustee and makes distributions to other partners, or if the general partner unnecessarily withholds all distributions, this may be considered a breach of the general partner's fiduciary duty. If a breach of fiduciary duty has occurred, a bankruptcy trustee holding the rights of a limited partner may be able to compel a dissolution of the partnership.[19]

What if the creditor is the creditor of a general partner, not a limited partner? Either a creditor or judgment creditor may seek a judicial dissolution once the specified term of the partnership ends or the partnership's purpose is achieved.[20] If the general partner goes bankrupt and is faced with a trustee in bankruptcy, then the trustee may, in fact, be able to get to the general partner's share of assets in the partnership. In fact, under some state laws, the filing of bankruptcy by a general partner dissolves the partnership.[21] Several courts have held, however, that the bankruptcy of a general partner does not dissolve the partnership. In some circumstances, the bankruptcy trustee may assume the general partner's rights and obligations under the partnership agreement, including the right to manage the partnership.[22]

If a parent acts as general partner of a family partnership and makes an assignment for the benefit of creditors or files a voluntary bankruptcy petition, the Revised Uniform Limited Partnership Act (the law in every state) provides that partnership will be deemed to have been dissolved, unless otherwise provided in the agreement or unless all partners consent in writing. If the general partner is a corporation controlled by the parent and the bankruptcy trustee seizes the stock of the corporate general partner, then the trustee could gain control of the partnership assets.[23] Therefore, it is best, if possible, that an exposed parent *not* serve as general partner or hold a controlling interest in a corporate general partner.

Recently, most states have enacted laws establishing entities called *limited liability companies*. The advantage of a limited liability company general partner is that no member of the limited liability company is personally liable for the partnership's debts. (With an individual general partner, the individual general partner *is* liable for the partnership's debts.) A parent should not own a controlling interest in the limited liability company general partner any more than he or she should in a corporate general partner.

INVESTMENT IN EXEMPT ASSETS

Some property is, by state law, exempt from creditors in a nonbankruptcy context. In addition, the Bankruptcy Code (federal law) provides its own set of exemptions. Federal bankruptcy law exempts:

- up to $15,000 of residential property
- an automobile of up to $2,400
- up to $8,000 in household furnishings
- up to $1,000 of jewelry
- up to $1,500 of debtor's tools of trade
- any unmatured life insurance contract
- prescribed health aids
- the right to receive social security and other public assistance benefits.[24]

Generally, the debtor may choose between the property listed as exempt under the Bankruptcy Code and property exempt under nonbankruptcy federal law and applicable state law.

One technique used for protecting assets from creditors is to take full advantage of exemptions available under state and federal law. This means converting nonexempt assets to exempt assets. As with other techniques discussed in this chapter, the conversion must be done in such a way that it is not deemed to be a fraudulent conveyance. If the acquisition of exempt property or repayment of debt encumbering exempt property is desirable, there are a number of assets that might be considered.

Your Home

Each state has its own homestead exemption law. To the extent that a homestead exemption applies, the only claims to which the homestead would be subject outside of bankruptcy would be federal statutory liens such as federal income tax liens,[25] claims for property taxes, and claims by secured creditors who lent money for the purchase of the home. You should consult with an attorney in your state to find out what your state law is concerning the homestead exemption. Georgia has a very small homestead exemption ($5,000), whereas the homestead exemption in Texas and Florida is unlimited.

Life Insurance

Under the laws of some states, life insurance policy proceeds and cash surrender values are exempt from attachment by the insured's creditors (again, assuming no fraudulent transfer exists).[26] In some states, however, cash surrender values of policies may not be exempt to the same extent as death proceeds.

If you live in a state where there is little or no protection of life insurance death proceeds, it may be desirable for you or your husband to transfer life insurance to an irrevocable trust for the benefit of the other spouse and children. This can almost always be justified because it is a valid estate planning technique (discussed in Chapter 5). Not only does such a trust protect the cash proceeds from creditors when the insurance pays off, but it keeps the proceeds from being subject to estate tax in either spouse's estate.

Some states even exempt life insurance proceeds from the beneficiary's creditors as well as the insured's creditors. If you have received life insurance proceeds as a result of another person's death, it is a good idea, if you live in such a state, to keep the property segregated and identifiable as exempt property. If you purchase something else with the insurance (such as a house), be sure that the purchase is clearly traceable to the exempt life insurance. Under some state laws, annuities are exempt.[27] Again, check with estate planning counsel in your state.

Qualified Employee Benefit Plans

Qualified employee benefit plans include profit sharing plans, 401(k) plans, and pension plans. Individual retirement accounts (IRAS) are not included as qualified employee benefit plans subject to the Employee Retirement Income Security Act (ERISA) of 1974. The provisions of ERISA prohibit alienation and assignment of plan benefits. Therefore, creditors may not reach benefits of ERISA-qualified employee benefit plans under state law mechanisms such as garnishment and levy.[28]

The U.S. Supreme Court has held that a debtor's interest in an ERISA-qualified pension plan is excluded from the bankruptcy estate (even in a federal bankruptcy proceeding). In other words, such assets are exempt from creditor's claims.[29] The Supreme Court's holding applies only to ERISA-qualified plans and not to plans established by governmental entities and churches. In non-ERISA-qualified plans (such as IRAS), a debtor's interest is generally includable in her bankruptcy estate because ERISA provisions are inapplicable.[30] Please remember that the IRS is, more or less, a super-creditor. The fact that a debtor's interest in an ERISA-qualified plan is excluded from her bankruptcy estate does not mean it is exempt from liens for unpaid taxes.[31]

Be aware that at least one court has held that, once a debtor withdrew all the funds in a pension plan after a bankruptcy petition was filed and used the money personally (for personal investments and not as pension plan investments), the funds had come into the unrestricted possession of the debtor and no longer constituted exempt pension assets.[32]

IRAS are not governed by ERISA. In general, they are trusts established for the benefit of the one creating the trust and are, therefore, subject to creditors as discussed earlier in this chapter. However, under the laws of certain states, they are exempt. Even though they may be exempt from state judgment creditors, this does not mean that a federal exemption for the IRA exists.[33]

SPOUSAL LIABILITY PLANNING

Spouses should take care to act in a manner that does not cause one spouse to become liable for the other spouse's debts. For example, if your husband incurs liability, do not sign notes or other evidences of obligation. Do not authorize your husband to act as your agent in contracting the debt (if you are concerned about this area, that is), and do not allow him to purport to act on your behalf. Your husband's creditors should agree not to look to your property to satisfy his debts, and you should be careful to conduct your affairs in a manner that would not suggest you have any intent of becoming liable on his debts.

Example: Peter wants to start a new business. Because Marie, his wife, is wealthy and Peter is not, he asks Marie to advance funds to the business. Marie's accountant takes tax deductions related to the business on a joint tax return, and Marie signs the payroll and business checks. Marie has conducted herself in a manner that indicates she is assenting to liability on debts of Peter's business.

In some jurisdictions, a type of marital property called *tenancy by the entirety* is not subject to the debts of either spouse. Only a few states recognize this type of property, but if you live in one of those states, it can be a very valuable type of ownership for asset protection purposes.

If you file a joint federal income tax return with your husband, you are each fully liable for the tax. This means that, if your husband does not pay the tax, you are liable for all of it and must pay all of it out of your separate property. For this reason, if asset protection is an issue, you may consider filing a separate return, or if either you or your husband happens to be involved in a risky business, you might consider filing separate income tax returns.

UNATTRACTIVE ASSETS

Some assets you might own could be unattractive to anyone outside an immediate family group. Even though a creditor may get a judgment, the very unattractiveness of the assets that the creditor could seize would cause the creditor to settle quickly and favorably with the debtor. We have already discussed why the family limited partnership and offshore trusts are helpful in this regard. Other assets that might fit into this category include property encumbered by burdensome restrictions (such as zoning or easements) and hazardous waste real estate.

Planning with remainder interests can also be helpful in this regard. For example, suppose Judy transfers her house to a qualified personal residence trust (discussed in Chapter 6). Judy's children have a remainder interest, and Judy has the right to live in her house for 10 years. Judy's creditors can only get the right to live in the house for 10 years—and they may not want to live in Judy's house! The creditor or bankruptcy trustee should not be able to sell the house and apply the value of the income interest to their claims.[34]

EXPECTANCY PLANNING

Perhaps you and your husband are not concerned about asset protection, but you have a child about whom you are concerned. If you leave property by will directly to your child, then that property will be subject to his or her creditors. Consider, instead, leaving it to a trust for the child's benefit.

Generally, if your child has no enforceable rights to distributions from the trust and no control over distributions, the trust will effectively protect assets from his or her creditors.[35] For example, appropriate terms for such a trust might be that the trustee has discretion to distribute the trust property to your son and his children at the complete discretion of the trustee. In this situation, it is not at all sure that your son would ever receive anything, so his creditor can't get anything.

Even in bankruptcy, neither a creditor of a beneficiary who did not establish the trust nor a bankruptcy trustee can reach any part of the trust in which the beneficiary has an interest except to the extent of the beneficiary's interest. This can give great protection to a child who either currently has creditors or may have creditors in the future. If the trust includes something called a "spendthrift provision" (a provision stating that, if the beneficiary files bankruptcy or has judgments rendered against him or her, then the assets in the trust are not available to satisfy such claims), the creditors generally cannot reach anything that the beneficiary cannot assign, unless and until trust assets are actually distributed to the beneficiary.[36] This is true even if the beneficiary has a definite interest in the trust. Spendthrift provisions, however, are generally not effective protection against the United States or any state, against dependents who have a claim for alimony or child support, or against furnishers of necessities to the beneficiary.[37] If you are establishing a trust for your child, be aware that, if you give the child a withdrawal right (as discussed in connection with insurance trusts in Chapter 5), your child's bankruptcy trustee can exercise the withdrawal right on behalf of the creditors.[38]

The area of asset protection is very complicated and fraught with pitfalls. If you have concerns in this area, find an expert in your state. (See Chapter 2 for pointers on how to find the right attorney.) Remember that laws vary significantly from state to state, so you should consult competent counsel in your area.

NOTES

1. 11 U.S.C.A. § 548(a)(1).

2. Uniform Faraudulent Transfers Act § 1(7)(i) and § 5(b).

3. Uniform Fraudulent Transfers Act § 4(b).

4. 11 U.S.C.A. § 548(2).

5. *BFP v. Resolution Trust Corporation*, 114 S. Ct. 1757 (1994).

6. Uniform Fraudulent Conveyance Act.

7. 11 U.S.C.A. § 101(15), (41).

8. IIA Austin W. Scott and William F. Fratcher, *The Law of Trusts* § 156 (4th ed. 1987) ("Scott").

9. 11 U.S.C.A. § 541(b).

10. 11 U.S.C.A. § 541(a)-(b).

11. 4 *Collier on Bankruptcy* § 541.13 (15th ed. 1988).

12. *2 Collier on Bankruptcy* § 365.05.

13. *U.S. v. Grace*, 395 U.S. 316, 324 (1969).

14. Scott § 156.3.

15. *Brune v. Fraidin*, 149 F.2d 325, 328 (4th Cir. 1945).

16. I.R.C. § 679.

17. *Outwin v. Comm'r*, 76 T.C. 153, 168 and 5 (1981).

18. Revised Uniform Limited Partnership Act § 702.

19. 11 U.S.C.A. § 323 and § 541.

20. Uniform Partnership Act § 32(2)(a).

21. U.P.A. § 31(5).

22. See *Weaver v. Nizny*, 175 B.R. 934, 937-38 (Bankr. S.D. Ohio 1994).

23. *In re Cardinal Indus. Inc.*, 116 B.R. 964, 982 (Bankr. S.D. Ohio 1990).

24. 11 U.S.C.A. § 522(d).

25. *U.S. v. Heffron*, 158 F.2d 657, 659 (9th Cir., 1947).

26. e.g., Tex. Ins. Code Ann. art. 21.22 § 1 (Vernon Supp. 1994).

27. e.g., Fla. Stat. Ann. § 222.14 (West Supp. 1991).

28. See *Mackey v. Lanier Collection Agency & Serv., Inc.*, 486 U.S. 825, 836-38 (1988).

29. *Patterson v. Shumate*, 504 U.S. 753 (1992).

30. *Bernstein v. Greenpoint Sav. Bank*, 149 B.R. 760, 765-66 (Bankr. E.D. N.Y. 1993).

31. 11 U.S.C.A. § 522(c)(2)(B).

32. *Velis v. Kardanis*, 949 F.2d 78, 82 (3d Cir. 1991).

33. *Deming v. I.R.S.*, Bankr. L. Rep. (CCH) ¶76,083 at 84, 199-200 (Bankr. E.D. Pa. July 13, 1994).

34. See *Geddes v. Livingston*, 804 F.2d 1219, 1222-23 (11th Cir. 1986).

35. Restatement (Second) of Trusts § 155(1).

36. Scott § 152.5.

37. Restatement (Second) of Trusts § 157(a), (b), (c), and (d).

38. 11 U.S.C.A. § 541(a).

Retirement Plan Assets

Integrating IRAs, 401(k)s, Pensions, and Profit Sharing Plans into the Overall Estate Plan

National surveys confirm that retirement is one of the most troubling passages in adult life for Americans.

—Gail Sheehy
New Passages

We're about to enter the most complicated area in all of estate planning. The coordination of qualified retirement plan and individual retirement account (IRA) benefits with the rest of the estate plan in order to reduce both income and estate taxes involves patience, persistence, stamina, and perseverance. If you have large amounts of money in pension plans, profit sharing plans (including 401[k] plans), or IRAs (or other qualified retirement plans), this chapter will be extremely important. This chapter covers only qualified retirement plans (plans governed by the Employee Retirement Income Security Act, or ERISA) and IRAs. Other types of retirement plans—such as incentive stock options, non-qualified stock options, and any other nonqualified plan—are not discussed here.

The challenge in estate planning for retirement assets is that these assets are subject to income taxes as well as estate taxes. Anything left in a retirement plan at death will be drained by income taxes, because income taxes have not yet been paid. The estate taxes (if the total estate is more than $600,000) must also be paid. In fact, estate taxes are actually paid first. Fortunately, a deduction for income tax purposes is available for the estate tax paid that is attributable to the asset.[1]

Example: Henrietta died with a $2 million estate, and all of it was in an IRA. The estate tax on this asset is $588,000. The income tax on this asset (which was payable to her estate, because Henrietta had forgotten to name a beneficiary) would be calculated as follows:

$2,000,000

– $ 588,000 (estate taxes)

= $1,412,000

× .396 (Henrietta's estate's federal income tax bracket)

= $ 559,152

After taxes, Henrietta's estate will have only $852,848 to pass to its beneficiaries.

Remember, retirement plan assets (including IRAS) are non-probate assets. This means that they do not pass according to your will (or according to the state intestacy statute if you don't have a will). These assets pass according to beneficiary designations that you complete. When you establish a retirement plan account, whether with your employer, a bank, or a brokerage firm, that employer, bank, or brokerage firm will ask you to name a beneficiary. If you fail to name a beneficiary, then one is named for you (a default beneficiary). With some employers, the default beneficiary might be your spouse. With others, it might be your estate. It is extremely important that you learn the rules and designate beneficiaries in a tax-efficient way. For some retirement plan techniques, beneficiary designation forms should be specially drafted for you by your estate planning attorney. (More about this later.)

One reason this area is so complex is that different sets of rules apply depending on the circumstances. For example, one set of rules applies if distributions to a beneficiary from a retirement plan asset are made before the participant's so-called *required beginning date* (or RBD, which is April 1 of the year following the year in which the plan participant reached age 70½). Another set of rules applies if the participant dies on or after the RBD. Furthermore, one set of rules applies if there is a *designated beneficiary* (or DB, defined later in the chapter). Another set applies if there is no DB.

Because one of the goals of planning well with respect to retirement plan assets is to defer income tax on such assets as long as possible, let's begin with a discussion of how to name a beneficiary to defer income taxes for as long as possible (i.e., to allow the beneficiary to leave the assets in the tax-free retirement plan environment for the longest period of time). In order to achieve this goal, elections made by the participant and his or her spouse are extremely important.

MINIMUM DISTRIBUTION RULES

The minimum distribution rules in the Internal Revenue Code[2] are designed to ensure that individuals saving for retirement do not get the benefit of a tax-free retirement plan environment for too long a period. Congress didn't want to deprive the Treasury of its tax dollars indefinitely. Therefore, strict penalties apply if assets are left in retirement plans too long. The penalty applies if an individual fails to begin taking distributions out of the retirement plan by his or her RBD.[3] To satisfy the minimum distribution rules, payments, once begun, must be in the form of an annuity over the lifetime of the participant or the lifetime of the participant's DB (if the DB is not the spouse, such person will be treated as if he or she is not more than 10 years younger than the participant.)[4]

If a participant dies before his or her RBD, assets must come out of the plan within five years of the participant's death, unless the participant has a DB.[5] Generally, DBs are individuals and certain (but not all) trusts.

If there is a DB other than a spouse, that DB may receive the retirement assets in annual installments over his or her life or life expectancy, beginning no later than December 31 of the year after the year in which the participant died.[6] If the spouse is the DB, the payments may be made over the spouse's life expectancy, but the beginning date may be deferred until December 31 of the year in which the *participant* would have reached age 70½.[7]

Example: In 1997, Sam died on June 30. He was 60½ years old. He named his wife, Corrine, as the designated beneficiary of his $1 million IRA. Because Corrine is his wife, she may wait until December 31, 2007 (the year in which Sam would have reached 70½), to begin withdrawing funds from the IRA. She may then withdraw them over her life expectancy.

THE BENEFITS OF DEFERRING WITHDRAWALS FROM RETIREMENT PLAN ASSETS

The importance of being able to defer the withdrawal of funds from a retirement plan asset is illustrated by a wonderful example from a book by Natalie B. Choate, *Life and Death Planning For Retirement Benefits*:

Example: Two brothers died, and each left his entire estate, including a $500,000 IRA, to his daughter. Both daughters, Lena and Tina, were 38 years old. Each of the daughters, after taking an around-the-world cruise, buying a new house, and paying the estate taxes on her father's estate, was left with just one asset—the $500,000 IRA. Each daughter decided to regard the inherited IRA as her own retirement nest egg and resolved to: (1) withdraw from the IRA only the minimum amount required by law, (2) invest the after-tax proceeds of the withdrawal, and (3) accumulate the earnings (after taxes) as her retirement fund.

Each daughter kept her resolve, investing both in-plan and out-of-plan assets in 8 percent bonds and paying income taxes on all plan withdrawals and bond interest at the rate of 36 percent. But, there was one difference: Tina's father had named Tina as his DB, so Tina was entitled to withdraw her father's IRA in installments over her 44.4-year life expectancy. Lena's father had named no beneficiary; he never got around to filling out a designation of beneficiary form. Under the terms of the account agreement governing his IRA, because he had not named any beneficiary, his beneficiary was his estate. Lena, the sole beneficiary of the estate, had to withdraw all money from her father's IRA within five years of his death.

After 30 years, Lena now has a $1,500,000 investment portfolio all outside of any IRA. Tina has an investment portfolio of $1,400,000 outside the IRA, and another $1,500,000 still inside the IRA she inherited from her father. Tina has 14.4 years remaining in her life expectancy over which to withdraw the remaining IRA balance. After 30 years, the daughter who used the "installments over life expectancy" payout method has almost twice as much money as the daughter who withdrew benefits under the "five-year rule."[8]

DESIGNATED BENEFICIARIES

What is a designated beneficiary? An individual is a designated beneficiary (DB) and a trust can be a DB if certain technical requirements are met. (These will be discussed later in the chapter.) But estates, charities, corporations, and trusts that do not meet the technical requirements are not DBs, and naming these entities as beneficiaries will mandate withdrawal of all assets in the plan within five years of the participant's death.

If you name "my surviving children" as your DB, then, according to the Treasury Regulations written by the IRS, the payout period is computed using the life expectancy of the beneficiary with the shortest life expectancy (i.e., the oldest child). If you instead divide your retirement assets into separate accounts and name one child as the beneficiary of each account, then each child may withdraw his or her portion over his or her life expectancy. This would be advantageous to all of the younger children. If even one beneficiary is named who is not a DB, then the entire account must be paid out within five years.

Example: Sabrina names her church and her son, Fortenoy, to receive her IRA (equally) at her death. Because her church is not a DB, the 50 percent payable to Fortenoy must come out of the retirement plan within five years of her death. If she had instead separated the retirement asset into two separate accounts, then Fortenoy's half could have come out over his life expectancy instead of within five years of Sabrina's death.

When is a trust a DB so that, if the trust is named as beneficiary, the assets do not have to come out of the retirement plan within five years of the participant's death? The IRS allows you to "look through" a trust and deem payments to be made to the beneficiaries of the trust (and hence paid over the life expectancy of the oldest trust beneficiary) if the trust meets five requirements. These five requirements are:

1. The trust must be valid under state law.

2. The trust must be irrevocable as of the RBD.

3. The trust must have only individuals as beneficiaries (no estates, corporations, or charities).

4. The beneficiaries of the trust must be "identifiable from the trust instrument."

5. A copy of the trust must be provided to the plan administrator.[9]

If a participant dies before the RBD, any trust established by a will by definition will be "irrevocable" (because the will and its trusts become irrevocable at death). Once the participant reaches the RBD, however, this requirement becomes a major challenge.

NAMING A BENEFICIARY ON THE REQUIRED BEGINNING DATE (RBD)

The RBD is significant for beneficiary designation purposes for three reasons:

1. Once a beneficiary is named, the payout period is locked in and cannot thereafter be extended. Although you can change the beneficiary of your retirement plan after your RBD, the change will not give you a greater deferral period while you are alive. If your spouse is the beneficiary, however, he may roll your retirement assets into his IRA if he survives you and start withdrawing over his life expectancy at that time.

2. If you name a trust as the beneficiary, it must meet the requirements previously discussed to get a payout greater than five years. (Note that the trust must be irrevocable on the RBD.)

3. You must decide whether to recalculate your (and your spouse's, if applicable) life expectancy annually, which you are allowed to do.[10]

SPOUSE AS BENEFICIARY

Naming a spouse as beneficiary of your retirement plan assets generally provides the greatest opportunities for tax savings. First, because two people have a greater life expectancy than either of them alone, naming a spouse lengthens the payout period (for tax deferral). Second, naming the spouse ensures a marital deduction (discussed in Chapter 4) for the plan assets, avoiding—or at least deferring—transfer tax. Third, the spouse who receives a lump sum retirement plan distribution may roll the plan assets over into his or her own IRA and leave it there (if desired) until the spouse's RBD. The spouse may then name his or her own beneficiary of the IRA, achieving even further income tax deferral.

Example: Jeannette is age 70. Her husband is age 80. Jeannette's life expectancy is 15 years. The joint life expectancy of Jeannette and her husband is 17.6 years. If Jeannette and her husband were both age 70, their joint life expectancy would be 20.6 years. Naming her husband as beneficiary of her retirement plan asset would increase the payout period, decrease the annual payments, and result in the money staying in the tax-free environment longer.

TRUST AS BENEFICIARY

In order to have a trust deemed a DB, as of the RBD, the requirements previously listed must be met. Remember, one of the advantages of having a trust as a DB is that an extended payout period (i.e., greater than your life expectancy) can be achieved. This means that you cannot use a revocable living trust after your RBD. If you do, upon your death, there will be no DB, and assets will have to come out of the plan "at least as rapidly" as they were being withdrawn before the participant's death. You must, therefore, use an irrevocable trust after your RBD to get maximum income tax deferral. You may *always* change the beneficiary of your plan, even though you have named an irrevocable trust. What you can't change is the payout *period* after the RBD.

Obviously, people are not going to rush in to their estate planning attorneys to have irrevocable trusts created on April 1 of the year following the year in which they turn 70½ (the RBD). Therefore, one approach to having a trust as beneficiary that qualifies as a DB is to have an unfunded (nothing in it other than a token amount) irrevocable trust created prior to the RBD and name that trust as the plan or IRA beneficiary.

Another approach is to use a revocable living trust that becomes irrevocable on the RBD. If this approach is used, your right to withdraw all assets from the trust must be preserved in order to avoid a gift tax problem upon the date that the trust becomes irrevocable.

Example: Sylvia names an irrevocable trust for the life of Jack, her son, as beneficiary of her IRA. The trust currently has only $1 in it (clipped to the last page) and meets the rules listed earlier. Upon her RBD, Sylvia can withdraw from her IRA over her life expectancy plus 10 years. If the IRA is payable to her estate, there is no DB and she must withdraw from her IRA, at her RBD, over her own life expectancy alone. If she dies with no DB, all funds must come out of the IRA "at least as rapidly" as Sylvia was withdrawing prior to death. However, Sylvia dies with a DB (the trust for Jack) after her RBD and before all benefits have been paid to her. At this point, a "flip" occurs. The life-plus-ten-years rule does not apply to distributions after the date of death (when death occurs after the RBD). (See "Naming a Nonspouse Designated Beneficiary" later in this chapter.) At Sylvia's death, the minimum required distributions will be based on the *actual* original joint life expectancy of Sylvia, the participant, and Jack, the only trust beneficiary (a DB), which can slow down payments dramatically.[11] (Note that this is an exception to the "at least as rapidly" rule.)

RECALCULATION OF LIFE EXPECTANCIES

If you name your spouse as the beneficiary of your retirement plan assets, you must decide whether (when you reach your RBD) to recalculate every year the life expectancies of yourself and your spouse. Under the tables that are used (found in the Treasury Regulations[12]) to recalculate life expectancies, your life expectancy (and the life expectancy of your spouse) never reach zero while you are alive. This means that one advantage of recalculating life expectancies is that the plan will never run out of money as long as you (or you and your spouse, if you recalculate both life expectancies) are alive.

The disadvantage of recalculating life expectancies is that the life expectancy of the participant (and spouse, if applicable) will be zero for purposes of calculating the minimum distribution required in the year following the year of death.[13] Therefore, if only the participant is recalculating her life expectancy (for example, if she is a widow), and she then dies, the benefits must be distributed totally by the end of the year following the year of her death.

Example: Linda and Harold are recalculating both life expectancies annually as they withdraw from Harold's qualified retirement plan. If Harold predeceases Linda, his life expectancy is reduced to zero, and Linda must withdraw the remaining benefits over her life expectancy alone. If Linda then subsequently dies, Linda and Harold's children must receive the balance of the benefits in the plan within one year following Linda's death.

Therefore, while it may be advantageous for the participant and the participant's spouse to recalculate life expectancies, it may prove detrimental to their children. The decision is often not an easy one to make.

Consider the following guidelines:

1. If both you and your husband are in excellent health and have good "gene pools," recalculation of both life expectancies probably makes sense. This means that you both expect to live long lives, you would like for the retirement plan assets to stay in the tax-free environment as long as possible, and to be there for the balance of your life expectancies.

2. If both you and your spouse have shorter-than-average life expectancies, for whatever reason, then a payout over your joint life expectancy would probably make the most sense because, if one of you were to die prematurely (which is probable if you both have bad "gene pools" or illnesses that shorten your life expectancies), then, with recalculation, the other one would have a shortened payout period based on the survivor's life expectancy alone.

3. You may recalculate your life expectancy but not your spouse's, or vice versa.[14] In many cases, this may be the best approach. For example, suppose your husband is the participant, and he elects to have his life expectancy but not yours, recalculated. In this way, you and your husband are assured of a minimum payout period equal to your life expectancy even if both of you die prematurely. If your husband outlives the joint life expectancy of both of you, he is assured that he will get benefits as long as he lives. If you survive him, and if the plan permits, then you may withdraw the remaining benefit and roll it into your own IRA, deferring payments until your RBD. Remember, recalculation is permitted only if the spouse is the beneficiary.

NAMING A NONSPOUSE DESIGNATED BENEFICIARY

When determining the joint life expectancies of the participant and a nonspouse DB, distribution is based on the participant's life expectancy plus someone who is no more than 10 years younger than the participant regardless of the DB's actual age. In other words, the DB is deemed to be not more than 10 years younger than the participant every year.

Example: Paul is age 71 in his "first distribution calendar year," and his nonspouse DB is age 47. The DB will be deemed to be age 61. The joint life expectancies of two people age 71 and 61 is 25.3 years. Therefore, 1/25.3 must be paid out to Paul in his first distribution calendar year. If Paul's beneficiary were 65, instead of 47, then the actual joint life expectancy of two people ages 65 and 71 would be used instead of the artificial life expectancy of someone 10 years younger than Paul.

It is important to note that this rule does not apply to distributions after the participant's date of death.[15] At Paul's death, the *real* joint life expectancies of Paul and his DB are used. This means that the DB has an extremely long payout period for what remains in the plan at Paul's death. Note that this is an exception to the "at least as rapidly" rule.[16]

CHANGING BENEFICIARIES AFTER THE REQUIRED BEGINNING DATE

You, as a participant, can change your DB after your RBD if you had a beneficiary on your RBD. However, if you change to a younger DB after the RBD, you cannot lengthen the maximum payout period. Conversely, if you change to an older DB, it will shorten the maximum payout period.

Example: Trudy has named her youngest son, Clyde, as the DB of her retirement plan as of her RBD. Clyde is 35 years younger than Trudy. The minimum required distribution is based on Trudy's life plus 10 years. If Trudy changes her DB to her boyfriend, Robert, who is two years younger than she is, subsequent payouts will be measured by the new shorter life expectancy of Trudy and Robert. If Trudy, however, had originally named Robert and then changed to Clyde, the designation of Clyde after the RBD would have no effect on the minimum distributions.

DISTRIBUTIONS FROM MORE THAN ONE PLAN

If you participate in more than one plan, or if you have, for example, more than one pension or profit sharing plan, the minimum required distribution must be calculated separately for each plan. However, a different rule applies for IRAs. The minimum required distribution must also be calculated separately for each IRA, but the participant may take the entire distribution from just one of the IRAs.[17] This is true even if each IRA has a different DB. This feature provides for planning opportunities.

Example: Lulu has three IRAs and names as beneficiary of each IRA, a different one of her three children. Lulu has different assets in each IRA, causing the IRAs to become unequal in value, even though she is taking exactly the same amount from each IRA to meet her minimum distribution requirement. In order to keep the three IRAs equal in value, so that each child will receive an equal amount at her death, Lulu may take more out of the IRA that has increased most in value during the year.

ESTATE TAX PLANNING FOR RETIREMENT PLAN BENEFITS

Everything we have talked about up to this point in the chapter relates to deferring income tax on retirement plan benefits by allowing plan assets to remain in the plan for as long as possible. However, we must also consider how to avoid estate tax on retirement plan assets.

Example: Suppose that Don has $1 million in an IRA and $300,000 of other assets. His wife, Priscilla, has $100,000 in tangible personal property. Don and Priscilla have wills that create testamentary trusts to receive $600,000 at the death of the first of them to die. Don has named Priscilla as beneficiary of his IRA. If Don were to die first, Priscilla would receive the IRA and presumably, roll it over into her own IRA and thus die with an estate of $1,100,000 (assuming she does not spend down Don's IRA). Only $300,000 of Don's estate would be able to go into his testamentary credit shelter trust. This means that his trust was underfunded, and Don lost $300,000 of his $600,000 exemption. (See Chapter 5 for a more complete discussion.)

At issue in this situation is how to get some of Don's IRA into his credit shelter trust, *but still cause the payout to be made over Priscilla's life expectancy.* In other words, we want to defer income tax on the assets but also protect them from estate tax. This is not going to be easy. Most attorneys will have no earthly idea what you're talking about if you try to talk to them about it. Only an estate planning attorney who has been at it a while might be able to help.

What we want in this situation is for $300,000 of Don's IRA to be paid to the credit shelter trust, and further, we want the credit shelter trust to be deemed a DB, so that payouts from the IRA to the trust can be made over Priscilla's life expectancy (because she will be the oldest trust beneficiary) at Don's death. Priscilla can be the trustee and (as discussed in Chapter 5) can have the right to withdraw for her own health, support, maintenance, and education (although she cannot use the trust to fulfill her support obligations toward her minor children).

Several hurdles will have to be crossed before we can get to this result, the first of which is that the trust must be a designated beneficiary (DB). In order to be a DB, the trust must be irrevocable on Don's required beginning date (RBD, April 1 of the year following the year in which Don turns age 70½). If the trust is created by Don's will, it is by definition revocable until Don dies. This means that the trust will meet the requirements only if Don dies before his RBD. We must assume that Don will live beyond his RBD and, therefore, the trust created in the will won't do the job. What, then, shall we do?

What we must do is create a separate trust (separate from Don's will) that is irrevocable and that will be nominally funded (meaning we will attach, for example, $1 to the last page). Then, at Don's death, whatever amount is necessary to make up the difference between what goes to the credit shelter trust in Don's will and the remaining part of the credit shelter amount can be given to this irrevocable trust. The terms of the IRA trust will be basically the same as the terms of the credit shelter trust in Don's will. For example,

Priscilla will be the trustee and will have the right, as trustee, to withdraw for herself and Don's children for health, support, maintenance, and education (but not for her support *obligations,* which are imposed as her parental obligations by state law). All the beneficiaries are identifiable, and the payout to this trust, after Don's death, will be over the life expectancy of the oldest beneficiary, presumably Priscilla. This satisfies the requirement that the trust be a DB.

The next hurdle will be to determine how, because the IRA is a nonprobate asset (not controlled by Don's will), we can coordinate it with the probate assets and make sure that the right amount of property goes to the IRA trust, which is the DB. Don's attorney should draft a beneficiary designation form saying, basically, that the amount of the IRA going to the irrevocable trust will be that amount needed, after consideration of the amount of Don's probate assets going to the credit shelter trust in his will, to make up the balance of Don's exemption amount. To paraphrase (and not use legalese), the IRA beneficiary form would say something like:

> *I, Don, hereby designate as the primary beneficiary of my IRA the following:*
>
> A. *First, after considering the amount of my probate estate going to the trust in my will, which is designed to receive the maximum amount I can pass to a nonspouse, noncharitable beneficiary without creating an estate tax (hereinafter "exemption amount"), I hereby give to my Irrevocable IRA Trust (previously established by me to be a trust designated beneficiary) that amount of the remaining exemption amount not going to my testamentary trust.*
>
> B. *All the rest, residue, and remainder of my IRA I hereby leave to my wife, Priscilla.*
>
> C. *If my wife, Priscilla, predeceases me, I hereby give, devise, and bequeath my IRA to my three adult children.* (If Don's children are minors, he can leave the full $600,000 amount to the Irrevocable IRA Trust. Payout will be over the life expectancy of the oldest child.)

This is, indeed, a frustrating area because people who need to use their IRAs or qualified plan benefits to help fund the credit shelter trust must, in effect, establish irrevocable trusts during their lifetimes in the event they should die after their RBDs. People who can fully fund their credit shelter trusts with other assets will not have to add this layer of complexity.

Example: Miles has an estate of $2 million. $1 million of which is in an IRA. His wife, Agatha, has an estate of $1 million. Miles will not have to worry about establishing an irrevocable trust. His $1 million not in the IRA can fully fund the credit shelter trust in his will, so he may name Agatha as beneficiary of his IRA.

NOTES

1. I.R.C. § 691(c).

2. I.R.C. § 401(a)(9).

3. I.R.C. § 401(a)(9)(A),(C).

4. I.R.C. § 401(a)(9).

5. I.R.C. § 401(a)(9)(B)(ii).

6. I.R.C. § 401(a)(9)(B)(iii).

7. I.R.C. § 401(a)(9)(B)(iv).

8. Choate, Natalie B., *Life and Death Planning for Retirement Benefits,* Ataxplan, 1996, at p. 12-13.

9. Prop. Reg. § 1.401(a)(9)-1.

10. I.R.C. § 401(a)(9)(D).

11. Prop. Reg. § 1.401(a)(9)-2, Q-3.

12. Treasury Regulations § 1.72-9, Tables V and VI.

13. Prop. Reg. § 1.401(a)(9) - 1, Q&A J-4.

14. Prop. Reg. § 1.401(a)(9) - 1, Q&A E-7(b).

15. Prop. Reg. § 1.401(a)(9)-2, Q-3.

16. I.R.C. § 401(a)(9)(B)(i).

17. IRS Notice 88-38, 1988-1 C.B. 524.

Life Insurance

How Much and What Kind?

Be prepared.

—Girl Scout Motto

Life insurance can be a very useful tool, not only for providing a measure of financial security for your family, but also for solving serious estate planning problems. For most couples, the wages you (and your husband) earn are essential for meeting the basic needs of family members—not only your spouse and children, but also grandchildren and elderly parents. In addition, wages may be a critical source of funds for paying off a home mortgage or debts you may have incurred in starting up your own business. Unless you are independently wealthy, if something should happen to a wage earner in your family (you or your husband), a substitute source of funds will be absolutely necessary to continue meeting these basic financial obligations.

Life insurance proceeds can provide a capital base that if invested, can replace a salary. Insurance proceeds can be used to pay tuition for private school, college, or graduate school; to pay off a mortgage or a car loan; or to supplement the incomes of elderly parents who have substantial medical or nursing care expenses. Proceeds from a life insurance policy are also a quick source of cash that can be used to pay funeral expenses, final medical bills, other outstanding debts, probate fees, income taxes, property taxes, and, if necessary, federal and state death transfer taxes, all of which are due shortly after death.

If you do not have young dependents or large debts, or if your estate is not large enough to be concerned about estate taxes, you may decide that you do not need to purchase life insurance. Remember, however, that—as with all decisions related to estate planning—your short- and long-term needs should be re-evaluated periodically as your needs and the needs of your family change.

Because the life insurance decision-making process is typically an ongoing one that must be re-enacted periodically throughout life, you should start by developing a good working relationship with one or more professionals who can guide you through the process. By maintaining such a relationship over time, you will benefit from the professional's ability to watch, evaluate, and re-evaluate your family's financial progress with you. A good insurance professional will not only tell you *which* products will help you reach your financial goals, but also *why* those products are best suited for you. If you are hesitant to initiate such a contact because you feel you do not know enough to engage in a meaningful discussion about life insurance, this chapter should help you get a grasp of the basics.

WHICH INSURANCE PRODUCT SHOULD I CHOOSE?

The number, variety, and complexity of life insurance products currently available is staggering. The only certainty is that no single product is right for everyone. Just as your needs will vary significantly from your neighbor's, so your own needs will vary significantly over your lifetime. That is why, when beginning the process of purchasing life insurance, it is critical to become familiar with the basic types available.

TERM INSURANCE

The two basic types of life insurance are *permanent* and *term*. Permanent insurance is considered the best product to buy if you need insurance protection for your whole lifetime. Term insurance is considered the best product to buy if you need protection for a specific period of time, such as one year, five years, or ten years. Term insurance is "pure" insurance protection; there is no savings or investment component to term insurance. The beneficiaries of your term policy will receive a benefit from the policy only if you die while the policy is in force. Unlike permanent insurance, term insurance has no value to be withdrawn during your lifetime.

Term insurance is typically the cheapest form of life insurance, particularly for a young purchaser. The premiums are lower for a term policy, because the policy is designed to provide only insurance protection and provides such protection only for a limited period of time. Premiums are obviously lower for younger purchasers (individuals in their 20s, 30s, and 40s), because their risk of dying is lower. If you purchase *level term insurance*, your annual premium will not vary from year to year, because it has been calculated by dividing the total amount of premiums due for the policy by the number of years in the term. If your term insurance does not have level premiums, your premiums may increase as you age. Some term policies guarantee the premium rate for several years, but some guarantee it only for the first year.

Premium payments may also increase if you choose to renew the policy at the end of the term (although there is no guarantee that your term policy will even be renewable at that point in time). A common form of term insurance is *annual renewable term* insurance. This type of insurance is automatically renewable at the end of the term without requiring you to prove your insurability by undergoing a medical examination each time you renew. However, your premium will increase each time you renew the policy, because, as you age, your risk of dying (and the risk that the insurance company will have to pay your beneficiaries at your death) increases over time. Thus, term insurance can gradually go from very affordable to barely affordable.

Who Should Purchase Term Insurance?

Term insurance may be a wise investment for individuals who need a substantial amount of coverage for a specified period of time and have limited financial resources available to make an insurance purchase. For these individuals term insurance may serve a variety of purposes, including:

- Income replacement for a couple primarily dependent upon one spouse's earnings
- Debt protection for a couple with a mortgage on a new home
- Educational funding for a family with children of any age
- Business security for a new company in need of a loan or a line of credit
- Business protection for a company with a few key employees

PERMANENT INSURANCE

Permanent life insurance (also called *straight life* or *ordinary life*) is the product you will want to purchase if you need protection for your entire lifetime. With permanent life insurance, you get the added benefit of a tax-free savings component. This savings component is the policy's *cash value* (also called "cash reserve" or "cash surrender" value). The cash value of a life insurance policy is the amount you would receive as a refund if you canceled your coverage and surrendered the policy to the insurance company. This buildup of cash value in the policy makes it possible for you to do some things you could not do with a term policy, such as:

■ Borrow the amount of the cash value from the insurance company

■ Cancel the policy and receive its accumulated cash value from the insurance company

■ Discontinue the insurance coverage and have the insurance company convert your accumulated cash value into a current or deferred annuity (discussed later in this chapter)

■ Stop making premium payments without reducing the death benefit payable to your beneficiaries but reducing the coverage period from your lifetime to a shorter period

■ Stop making premium payments while reducing the death benefit payable to your beneficiaries but continuing coverage for your entire lifetime

Another benefit of permanent life insurance is that you may choose from several different types of policies. This means that you should be able to find a permanent policy that closely meets your needs.

Traditional Whole Life Insurance

Traditional whole life insurance differs from other types of permanent insurance in that it features a fixed death benefit and fixed premiums. Although you may choose other premium payment schedules, the annual premiums on a traditional whole life insurance policy are typically set at the time the policy is purchased and calculated based on the assumption that they will remain fixed (and will be paid) until your death. Premiums paid during the first years you own this type of policy are generally larger than are necessary to cover the risk that you will die in those early years. The excess is invested by the insurance company and used to build up the cash value of the policy. (Remember, the cash value is the amount that would be paid to you in a lump sum if you chose to cancel and surrender the policy.) The insurance company is required by law to limit its investment of whole life policy premiums to certain types of investments. Because of the limited return of these investments, it is possible that your policy may not have any cash value for the first three to ten years you own it. In addition, your cash value will never be greater than your death benefit from a whole life policy.

Most people are attracted to the cash build-up feature of permanent life insurance products such as traditional whole life insurance because they can borrow against the cash value or cash reserve, thereby getting money out of the policy without losing their insurance coverage. At death, if you have borrowed from the policy and not repaid the loan, the amount borrowed will be deducted from the death benefit payable to your beneficiary.

Traditional whole life insurance is obviously more expensive than term insurance, because you are purchasing a savings vehicle (the cash reserve) as well as insurance coverage. There are "blended" whole life insurance products on the market—part whole life and part term—for which you may be able to pay lower premiums. However, in return for the reduction in premiums, you may also have to give up some of the guaranteed features (such as the guaranteed fixed premiums, the guaranteed minimum cash value, or the guaranteed fixed death benefit) of a traditional whole life insurance policy.

Who Should Purchase Traditional Whole Life Insurance?

This type of insurance may be attractive to individuals more concerned with securing a guaranteed death benefit than with paying low premiums. Older individuals, risk-averse individuals, individuals who are purchasing insurance to pay estate taxes, and individuals with plenty of current income available to pay the higher premiums on a whole life policy are the most common purchasers of traditional whole life insurance. Younger individuals, who have fewer financial resources, may not be able to afford traditional whole life policies. And individuals with plenty of cash to save and invest may find that other savings and investment vehicles, of which there are many, are more cost-effective and attractive than a traditional whole life policy.

Universal Life Insurance

As with traditional whole life insurance, universal life insurance pays a death benefit and has a savings feature. Many universal life policies separate the insurance, expense, and reserve features so that you can tell how much of each premium payment goes to pay company expenses (such as overhead costs), how much is withheld to pay policy proceeds, and how much is allocated to savings.

Your savings component, the cash reserve, is typically invested by the insurance company in fixed-income assets such as treasury bills or short-term corporate bonds. Your rate of return (i.e., the buildup of your cash value) can vary substantially from one company to another, depending upon a company's particular investment preferences and strategies. Rates of return can also fluctuate with changes in interest rates and market conditions.

Unlike other investments that generate currently taxable income, the interest earned on the investment of your cash reserve in a universal life policy is not taxed to you as it is earned and accumulates in your policy. Thus, a universal life insurance policy is a type of tax-deferred investment, or "tax shelter," because it shelters some interest income from taxation until such time as you actually withdraw the interest.

A universal life insurance policy provides more flexibility than a traditional whole life policy. If you own a universal policy, you may change the death benefit or premium (within certain guidelines), make irregular premium payments, or make partial withdrawals from your cash reserve. However, along with this greater flexibility comes less certainty. Unlike a traditional whole life policy, a universal policy does not have fixed premiums or a guaranteed death benefit. In addition, the insurance coverage will continue only as long as you make premium payments or as long as there are sufficient cash reserves to make the payments for you as they come due.

Who Should Purchase Universal Life Insurance?

An individual who has an irregular income stream may wish to purchase a universal life insurance policy, because he or she can either skip premiums (which will then be paid from the built-up cash reserve) or make extra deposits (which will build up or replenish the cash reserve to meet future premium payments) as his or her income permits. Individuals who like to track the investment performance of their insurance product may appreciate the greater consumer information that is disclosed with a universal life product.

Variable Life Insurance

The newest type of permanent life insurance is variable life insurance, commonly sold as variable universal life. If you purchase a variable life insurance policy, you—rather than the insurance company—make the investment selections for your cash value from a specified group of accounts managed either by the insurance company or by an investment firm hired by the insurance company. These accounts are separate from the general institutional funds of the insurance company (which include premiums paid on whole and universal policies), and therefore cannot be accessed by the insurance company's creditors.

If you purchase a variable life policy, you can choose to invest your cash reserve in one or more accounts that have varying investment objectives. For example, there are money market accounts, as well as accounts with investments in stocks, bonds, or other interest-bearing vehicles. Thus, purchasing a variable life insurance product is similar to selecting between a number of mutual funds offered by an investment company. Because of the various investment options available with a variable policy, your potential return (and the buildup of your cash reserve) will obviously vary depending upon your account selection and market conditions. Therefore, although this type of policy has potential for the greatest investment return, you also risk the greatest loss.

Who Should Purchase Variable Life Insurance?

An individual with some investment savvy who desires greater personal control over the investments chosen for his or her cash reserve may wish to purchase a variable life insurance policy. An individual willing to risk more on the fluctuations of the stock market in return for a potentially greater return would be more likely to purchase this type of insurance product.

Single Premium Life Insurance

Most forms of permanent life insurance can be purchased with a single, up-front premium payment. This is typically done by adding a single premium rider to a whole life policy. A *rider* is merely an extra provision added to a basic policy. The rider may provide extra options (e.g., the option to make only one premium payment) or extra benefits (e.g., waiver of the premium in the event of your disability). An extra premium, however, is often required with a rider.

Who Should Purchase a Single Premium Life Insurance Policy?

Younger individuals with lower incomes may not be able to afford a single premium life insurance product. Depending on the age of the insured and the amount of the policy, such insurance can be very expensive. However, an individual who is considering purchasing an insurance policy in order to provide surviving family members with a source of cash to pay estate taxes and expenses upon his or her death might choose this type of policy. An individual purchasing a single premium policy for this purpose could then transfer ownership of the policy to his or her spouse or children in order to remove the proceeds from his or her taxable estate without worrying about the ability or willingness of the new owner or owners to make future premium payments. This will be discussed in more detail later in this chapter.

Second-to-Die (Joint) Life Insurance

Second-to-die or joint life insurance insures the lives of two individuals, typically a husband and wife. As the name implies, a death benefit is paid only upon the death of the survivor of the two individuals. At the first death, no proceeds are paid and, in fact, the surviving spouse will often have to continue paying premiums for as long as he or she lives. Premiums, however, should be lower for a second-to-die policy than for a policy insuring the life of only one individual. The premiums will, of course, depend on the ages and health of the couple purchasing the policy.

A couple may wish to purchase a second-to-die policy if they are concerned about estate taxes being due upon the death of the second spouse to die. You can leave all of your property to your husband (and he to you) without worrying about estate taxes being due at the first spouse's death because of the unlimited marital deduction discussed in Chapters 4 and 5. The surviving spouse's estate will owe taxes if the survivor owns more than $600,000 of assets outright. If you and your husband purchase a second-to-die life insurance policy that pays a death benefit approximately equal to the amount of tax that will be due and have your children or a trust own that policy, those policy proceeds can be used to pay the tax. By having these proceeds available for taxes, your heirs will not be forced to liquidate assets just to pay taxes.

Example: Glenn and Peggy are a married couple who together own assets worth $3 million—$1,500,000 each. Glenn's will directs that at his death, $600,000 (as indexed) of his assets will be divided between their two children, and $900,000 will pass to Peggy. Peggy's estate is worth $2,400,000 at her death (her $1,500,000, plus the $900,000 she received from Glenn). She can also leave $600,000 (as indexed) tax-free to the children. However, that still leaves $1,800,000 to be taxed. The tax bill on $1,800,000 is $690,800. If Glenn and Peggy purchase a second-to-die policy in a life insurance trust or transfer the ownership of the policy to their children, the children's inheritance will not be reduced by the $690,800 tax. Instead, the insurance proceeds can be used to pay the tax bill, and the children will receive their full inheritance. If Glenn and Peggy had not had this insurance, the executor of Peggy's estate could have been forced to sell stock or real estate when the markets were down or liquidate other assets which the children might have preferred to keep, just to have enough cash to pay the estate taxes.

Who Should Purchase a Second-to-Die Life Insurance Policy?

A couple with assets in excess of $1,200,000 who will have to pay estate taxes may wish to purchase a second-to-die policy in order to provide their heirs with the financial resources to pay the tax bill without having to sell other assets in the estate. Owners of a family business in which only some of the children participate may wish to purchase a second-to-die policy as part of a business continuation plan. All of the children may share equally in inheriting the business (all children treated equally), and the insurance proceeds payable at the death of the second spouse can be used by those children actively involved in the business to buy out the interests of their brothers and sisters.

First-to-Die Life Insurance

A first-to-die life insurance policy insures the lives of two or more individuals, but as its name implies, it pays a death benefit upon the death of the first insured. First-to-die policies are commonly used by business partners or co-owners as part of a business continuation plan. The partnership or company may purchase a policy insuring the partners' or co-owners' lives. If several individuals are insured under one policy this way, the premiums will be lower than if the company had purchased a separate policy on each individual, because only one death benefit will be paid. When the first partner dies, the company or partnership (or the surviving co-owner or partner) will receive the death benefit and can use the proceeds to either purchase the interest of the deceased partner (or co-owner) from his or her family or, if the family wishes to participate in the business, to use the policy proceeds as an emergency fund during the period of ownership transition. Because many companies do not have much ready cash on hand on any given business day, having insurance money available for either of these purposes can provide a degree of financial security to a business suffering the loss of a key individual.

Who Should Purchase a First-to-Die Life Insurance Policy?

Partners or co-owners of a business may wish to purchase a first-to-die policy in order to have funds readily available to purchase the interest of a deceased partner or co-owner or to provide additional financial resources as the company's ownership shifts to the deceased individual's family. Spouses who both work and have children may wish to purchase a first-to-die rider for their basic insurance policy so that their family will receive benefits to replace the income lost if either spouse should die before the children finish school. Individuals who are not citizens of the United States are not entitled to the full marital deduction for property transferred to a non-citizen spouse unless the property is transferred to a special, restrictive type of trust (the QDOT trust discussed in Chapter 8). This means that, if at least one spouse is a non-citizen, there may be estate tax due upon the death of the first spouse. Therefore, a woman who is not a citizen of the United States (or whose husband is not a citizen of the United States) may wish to purchase a first-to-die policy to provide funds with which to pay the estate tax in the event that the U. S. citizen spouse dies first and leaves funds to the non-citizen spouse in a way that does not qualify for the marital deduction.

ANNUITIES

A commercial annuity is a contract under which you agree to pay the issuing insurance company a certain premium in exchange for the insurance company agreeing to pay you or your designated beneficiary a certain amount of cash each month (or year) for life or a term of years. You may purchase an annuity to provide yourself (or your spouse or other beneficiary after your death) with a fixed, guaranteed income stream for life, or to provide, after your death, several payments over an extended period to beneficiaries (such as young, inexperienced, or fiscally irresponsible children, or elderly parents in poor health) whom you believe would not be able to handle one large lump sum payment of cash. Of course, these same objectives may be met in other, potentially more flexible, ways. Retirement income can be generated from individual retirement accounts (IRAs) or retirement plans sponsored by your company. Or you can create a trust and name a family member, trusted friend, or secure financial institution to manage money and produce income for a surviving spouse, a young or inexperienced child, or an elderly parent. However, a commercial annuity is an option you may find attractive for its relative simplicity.

There are several categories of annuities and, depending upon the company from which you purchase the annuity, there are even more variations within each category. Some of these options include:

- *Immediate annuity.* If you purchase an immediate annuity, you make one lump sum payment to the insurance company, and annuity payments to you or your designated beneficiary begin immediately.

- *Deferred annuity.* You may purchase a deferred annuity with one lump sum payment or in installments. If you purchase a deferred annuity, the annuity payments do not begin until some time in the future.

- *Fixed annuity.* When you purchase a fixed annuity, you are purchasing the right to receive a guaranteed, fixed amount for life. The amount paid to you depends upon your sex, the age at which the payments are to start, and certain interest assumptions established on the annuity tables used by the company from which you are purchasing the annuity. These assumptions will vary from company to company and, therefore, the amount you can receive also will vary from company to company.

- *Variable annuity.* If you purchase a variable annuity, the issuing company will invest your premium in stocks and bonds, and the annuity you receive will vary according to the performance of these investments.

INSURANCE FOR DISABILITY OR OTHER LIFETIME NEEDS

After careful consideration of the present and future financial needs of your family, you might decide that you do not need life insurance. However, there are other insurance products, created to meet more present needs, that deserve your review and consideration.

Disability Insurance

Disability insurance pays a benefit in the event that you are unable to work in your profession due to an accident or illness. Disability insurance is often expensive, but if you are young or self-employed, it may be more important than life insurance. Some employers provide disability insurance as part of employee benefits packages, but most group disability policies do not replace 100 percent of your lost earnings. In the first year of disability, group disability insurance policies will typically pay up to 60 percent of lost income. Thereafter, if you can perform *any* job, even if it requires additional education or training, you may no longer be considered disabled and policy payments may stop. For this reason, the definition of disability stated in the policy you purchase is extremely important. There have been oral surgeons who collected disability payments for their entire lifetimes even though, after their "disability," they were able to practice general dentistry. They were able to do this because they paid attention to their policies' definitions of disability (in this case, any disability that prevented them from practicing as oral surgeons).

Accelerated Pre-Death Benefits

Accelerated pre-death benefits (sometimes called living benefits) are not a separate form of life insurance but rather an option you may purchase as a rider with some life insurance policies. If you have a life insurance policy that pays accelerated pre-death benefits, you may be able to receive a portion of your death benefit if you have a terminal illness, need long-term or permanent nursing home care, or if you have been diagnosed with a serious disease or condition.

Long-Term Care Insurance

It is estimated that there will be 52 million Americans age 65 or older by the year 2020.[1] According to the Health Insurance Association of America, by 2020, more than 12 million of these older Americans will need some type of long-term care, either nursing home care or in-home care.[2] And approximately one-half of all women and one-third of all men now age 65 will spend some time in a nursing home.[3] Although the average stay in a nursing home is a year or less, the current average annual cost of nursing home care is approximately $40,000.[4] Full-time professional home care can be even more expensive. Even if full-time home care is provided by a family member, there may still be adverse financial consequences for the family, particularly if the caregiver was a wage earner. In addition, full-time caregiving for a family member can be both emotionally and physically taxing.

As the financial, emotional, and physical burdens of long-term caregiving shouldered by families mount, the government continues to decrease its share of the burden. Medicaid currently pays about one-half of all nursing care costs, but it is likely that this share will decrease as the government strains to balance the federal budget.[5] Medicare does not cover all the costs of home care and very few of the costs of all nursing home care.[6] Furthermore, Medicaid, Medicare, Medigap, and even employer-provided health insurance plans do not pay any portion of the expenses of custodial care.[7] (*Custodial care* is assistance with the daily tasks of living, including eating, bathing, and dressing, and is usually provided in the individual's home or in an assisted living facility.)

Increasing numbers of older individuals find themselves disqualified for government assistance based on the size of their incomes. Qualification for Medicaid requires meeting poverty guidelines for income and assets. In hopes of preserving their children's inheritance or their own retirement resources from total depletion, some individuals have attempted to transfer assets to children and grandchildren, either outright or in trust, in order to meet the poverty guidelines for Medicaid purposes. Lawmakers have caught on to such schemes, however, and have made it increasingly difficult, if not impossible, for individuals to protect their assets in this way while qualifying for government assistance.

The rapidly rising costs of health care and these gaps in the traditional means of financing long-term health care costs have led many women (and men) to begin evaluating their need for long-term care insurance. More than 120 life insurance companies currently offer long-term care insurance coverage, and today there are more than 3.5 million long-term care insurance policies in effect.[8] Recently enacted tax legislation has made owning long-term care insurance even more attractive for some individuals.[9] Beginning in 1997, for income tax purposes, the premiums paid for long-term care insurance will be fully deductible as medical expenses (if total medical expenses incurred in any one tax year are equal to or more than $7\frac{1}{2}$ percent of the insurer's adjusted gross income), and the benefits paid to the insured under the policy will be excludable from his or her gross income.[10]

Although coverage varies from policy to policy, long-term care policies can cover functional infirmities, physical impairment, and cognitive impairment. Functional infirmities are conditions that impair your ability to dress, bathe, and feed yourself. A stroke is an example of a common physical impairment that can necessitate either home care or nursing home care. Alzheimer's disease is a cognitive impairment that often requires around-the-clock care, sometimes for years.

A long-term care policy pays a daily benefit, typically around $100, but, you can purchase benefits of $200 or more per day. One insurer offers more expensive policies that pay monthly benefits ranging from $1,500 to $6,000 for nonprofessional care (i.e., care provided by family members or other unlicensed personal assistants). The daily benefit usually covers not only nursing home care but also home care. Policies may cover all levels of care, including skilled care provided in a nursing home or by a nurse or therapist in the home, intermediate care in an assisted living facility or in the home, and custodial care provided by a nonprofessional assistant in the home.

When purchasing a long-term care policy, you choose not only the amount of the daily benefit, but also the benefit period. Typical benefit periods range from two to five years although lifetime coverage can be purchased. In addition, when selecting a benefit period, you will probably want to choose a policy that does not require you to be admitted into a hospital before payments commence.

Long-term care insurance can be an expensive proposition. If you are going to purchase it, you should do so when you are young, because premiums typically triple from age 50 to 70.[11] When you purchase a policy, renewal is usually guaranteed; however, premiums, which initially are fixed, may be raised later. The premiums charged for long-term care coverage are based upon the age of the individual (younger purchasers get lower premiums), the amount of daily benefit to be provided, the length of the benefit period, and the elimination period. The elimination period is the basis of your deductible. The longer you are willing to wait for the coverage to begin (i.e., the longer you are willing to pay for care yourself), the lower your premium will be.

Who Should Purchase Long-Term Care Insurance?

Individuals whose families have a history of stroke, cancer, Parkinson's disease, or Alzheimer's disease, which often require extended long-term care, may wish to purchase long-term care insurance. Individuals with relatives living nearby who are willing to provide in-home care should the need ever arise may want to purchase home care coverage. However, individuals who are alone, whose family members live far away, or who prefer not to rely on family members for care may wish to purchase nursing home care coverage as well as home care coverage. Women typically outlive men and are more likely to spend longer periods of time in nursing homes; therefore, women may determine that they have a greater need for long-term care insurance. Couples whose combined net worth is $100,000 to $250,000 (not including the value of their residence if it is important to them to keep the residence for their lifetimes) or individuals whose net worth is $50,000 to $100,000 may find their assets depleted by the costs of long-term care. Therefore, they may be good candidates for long-term care coverage. Couples and individuals with more assets who may be able to pay for long-term care without insurance may nevertheless wish to purchase it as an extra measure of security against the depletion of their children's inheritance.

HOW MUCH LIFE INSURANCE COVERAGE DO I NEED?

Insuring a life is the business of placing an economic value on that life. In the world of insurance, the value of your life is based on the total financial needs of your family and the percentage of those needs that your income meets and is expected to meet over your lifetime. Thus, the amount of insurance coverage you buy should reflect your present and anticipated future contributions to the family. If you are the sole or primary breadwinner in the family, the amount of coverage you purchase should at least equal the estimated lifetime needs of your surviving family members. But how do you project these needs?

1. Estimate Immediate Expenses

Certain expenses, such as funeral expenses, last medical bills not covered by insurance, and unpaid debts, are due immediately after your death. Other expenses, including income taxes, property taxes, and estate taxes, are due shortly thereafter. These needs require that cash be immediately available to your estate and surviving family members.

Example: Wanda estimates that if her husband Mickey were to die this year, his funeral would cost $10,000, the property taxes owed on their home would be $5,000, and their income taxes could be almost $20,000. This means that Wanda would need almost immediate access to $35,000 in cash just to meet these expenses.

2. Estimate Major Obligations

The amount of cash necessary to meet certain major financial obligations, such as private school or college tuition, will depend upon several factors. To estimate the amount of money needed to start (or supplement) a college fund, for example, time is a major factor. If your children are young, you can purchase insurance that pays out enough death benefit to start a college investment fund. The amount of insurance will depend upon how long your spouse will have to invest before your oldest child reaches college age. If your children are teenagers, there will obviously be less time to invest; therefore, more immediate cash may be required. Estimate the cost of tuition and living expenses at the school of your child's choice by looking at a current college catalog. Assume that tuition will increase at the same rate that it traditionally has at that school. With a little research, other expenses, such as orthodontist bills, piano lessons, summer camp tuition, and wedding expenses, can also be estimated.

Example: Wanda and Mickey have one son, Brad, who is 17 and wants to go to Harvard next year. Tuition, room, and board at Harvard are currently $30,000 per year and have increased at a rate of 10 percent per year in the past. Brad is one year away from going to college. Brad's college expenses can be estimated as follows:

Estimated Harvard Costs for Brad

Now	$30,000
One year from now	$33,000 (Brad is a freshman.)
Two years from now	$36,300 (Brad is a sophomore.)
Three years from now	$39,930 (Brad is a junior.)
Four years from now	$43,923 (Brad is a senior.)
Total expenses for tuition, room, and board at Harvard for Brad	**$153,153**

---

3. Estimate Basic Family Living Expenses

You should next estimate your family's basic living expenses and the amount of capital needed to generate enough cash to cover these needs. If you have an annual family budget, you should have a good idea of your family's financial needs on a day-to-day basis. Your calculation of basic family expenses might include mortgage and car loan payments. With respect to a mortgage or other substantial debt, you should base your cash need estimate on the size of the current debt, the size of the payments, and how often they come due. You should also consider whether you want to provide your spouse with enough cash to pay off the debt in full at your death or provide only a seed fund which your spouse will invest to generate enough income to meet the debt payments as they come due.

When estimating basic family living expenses, you can subtract social security benefits payable to your survivors (children are entitled to social security benefits upon the death of a parent until they reach age 18) and the projected income earned by your surviving spouse if he or she works. If your spouse does not work, include in your estimate an amount of ready cash that would give your spouse the time to gain the education or skills necessary for him or her to enter into the work force. Remember to include child care expenses if they will be necessary in order for your surviving spouse to enter the work force after your death.

Example: Wanda and Mickey have living expenses totaling $6,000 per month, or $72,000 per year. Wanda is 45 years old and does not work. If Mickey were to die, she would not be able to get social security for 15 years (until she is age 60). Wanda estimates that, if Mickey were gone, she could live comfortably on $5,000 per month (83 percent of current income), or $60,000 per year.

After calculating the living expenses of your family, figure out what amount of capital would be needed to generate enough cash to meet those needs if the capital were to become available at your death (or at your husband's death). If your surviving spouse is likely to choose stocks and bonds as investments, use an average return for these investments as your basis in calculating the potential return.

Example: Wanda and Mickey have traditionally been able to generate a 10 percent yield on their investment assets. Therefore, $600,000 invested at 10 percent would generate the $60,000 needed by Wanda each year if Mickey died.

4. Subtract Other Assets and Insurance

Subtract the value of any other assets, such as stocks, bonds, and checking and savings accounts that you currently own. These assets could be liquidated to meet your family's financial needs after your death. If you are already insured, either through work or through other individual policies, subtract the value of these policies as well.

Example: Mickey has a $250,000 insurance policy through his employer. Wanda and Mickey have $200,000 in stocks, bonds, and cash. Therefore, their total insurance needs are calculated as follows:

Total Insurance Needs of Wanda and Mickey Williams

Short-term cash needs (funeral expenses, taxes)	$ 35,000
Plus: Brad's college expenses (tuition, room, board)	$153,153
Plus: Capital needed to produce income for basic needs	$600,000
Less: Insurance policy provided by Mickey's employer	(250,000)
Less: Investments Wanda and Mickey own	(200,000)
Total insurance needed	**$338,153**

5. Periodically Review and Recalculate

The amount of insurance coverage an individual needs will vary substantially over time. For example, your family's needs will decrease as mortgages are paid off, children graduate from college, your earnings increase, and your savings and investments grow. Therefore, it is important to periodically recalculate your family needs. Perhaps you'll decide to purchase an additional term policy until your mortgage is paid off or your children finish school, or that you can afford to reduce premiums in return for a smaller death benefit because your income and investment returns have substantially increased and your expenses have decreased.

Of course, the question of how much coverage you need may very well boil down to how much coverage you can afford. This is why it is important to discuss your objectives, your family's needs, and your financial capacity to meet those goals with an insurance professional who can assist you in finding an insurance product that will provide the coverage you need at the price you can currently afford to pay.

HOW DO I CHOOSE AN INSURANCE COMPANY?

An insurance policy is a contractual arrangement with an insurance company, and you should obviously choose to enter into such an arrangement only with a company that is more likely than not to be around to honor its commitment to your beneficiaries after your death. With more than 2,000 insurance companies in the United States from which to choose, selecting the right company may be as difficult as selecting the right policy.

Although the entire insurance sector was once considered financially stable, increased competition in recent years has prompted some companies to make risky investments, often in real estate and "junk" bonds (high-yield but also high-risk). More than 100 insurers have failed since 1988. Of course, there are also a large number of rock-solid insurance companies, which you can find with just a little research. A healthy insurance company is an insurance company with a healthy portfolio. The way an insurance company makes money is by investing your premiums. Your return and death benefit are functions of an insurance company's projected and realized return on its investments. The insurance company needs to earn more than it offers to you so that it can make its annuity payments, pay death benefits, and make a profit.

To assist you in your evaluation, there are firms that rate the financial stability of insurance companies. The four largest rating firms are A. M. Best, Standard & Poor's, Duff & Phelps, and Moody's Investor Services. Standard & Poor's and Moody's rate only those companies that apply for evaluations, whereas A. M. Best evaluates 1,750 companies. Although the firms' evaluation scales vary to some extent (because each firm uses slightly different evaluation criteria), the actual differences in the scales and the ratings scored are slight. *A++* ("Superior/Very Little Risk") is the best possible rating offered by A. M. Best; *F* ("Nonviable" or "In Liquidation") is the worst. Standard & Poor's and Duff & Phelps' equivalent to A. M. Best's *A++* is *AAA*; Moody's equivalent is *Aaa*. Standard & Poor's and Duff & Phelps offer *D* and *DDD*, respectively, as the lowest ratings (also being "Nonviable" or "In Liquidation"). Moody's bottoms out at *C*. Regardless of how high or low the rating given to an insurance company by a rating firm, keep in mind that a rating *is simply the opinion* of that rating firm, so it would be wise to get a second opinion from a second rating firm before settling on a company.

A. M. Best publishes *Best Insurance Reports,* which can be found in many public and college libraries. You can also call A. M. Best customer service department at (908) 420-0400 and request an insurance company's identification number. Once you have this number, you can call another A. M. Best service number—(900) 420-0400—and for approximately

$2.50 per minute (for a call that will last for two to three minutes), get the insurance company's A. M. Best rating and an explanation of this rating.

The other three rating firms also offer publications that usually can be found in your local library, as well as customer service departments that offer ratings over the telephone. You can reach Standard & Poor's at (212) 208-1527, Duff & Phelps at (312) 368-3157, and Moody's at (212) 553-0377.

HOW DO I KEEP INSURANCE PROCEEDS OUT OF MY TAXABLE ESTATE?

If you purchase a life insurance policy, you may discover that the insurance proceeds payable at your death make up the largest single asset in your estate. For some people, insurance proceeds alone push them over the $600,000 (as indexed) estate tax limit. Other people may already have had taxable estates and purchase life insurance for the sole purpose of paying estate taxes. These individuals certainly do not want to increase the size of their taxable estates by the amount of the insurance proceeds. If you are the owner of a policy at your death, the proceeds will be included in your taxable estate regardless of who actually receives the payment from the insurance company (unless your spouse is the beneficiary, which will generate a marital deduction).

One way to exclude insurance proceeds from your taxable estate is to transfer the ownership of the policy to the beneficiary. If your estate (combined with your spouse's estate) is over $1,200,000 (as indexed), and if the beneficiary of your insurance policy is your spouse, you need to transfer ownership of the policy to a trust that names your spouse as trustee. If your children are the beneficiaries, you may simply transfer ownership to your children (or to a trust for their benefit). However, if you transfer the ownership of a policy, you must live for three years after the gift is made or the IRS will disregard your gift and include the proceeds in your taxable estate.[12] In addition, when you transfer the ownership of your policy, you must give it *all* away. The IRS will not permit you to retain any "incidents of ownership" in the policy. This means that, after you give the policy away, you cannot:

■ name or change beneficiaries.

■ borrow against the policy or pledge its cash value (if any).

■ cash in the policy.

■ surrender, cancel, or convert the policy.

■ select the beneficiary payment option (lump sum or installment).

The policy does not have to be paid up when you transfer it. After transferring the policy, you can indirectly pay the premiums by giving cash gifts to the new owner for the purpose of paying the premiums, regardless of whether the new owner is an individual or a trust.[13]

The transfer of an existing policy and policy premiums to an irrevocable trust may have gift tax implications. However, as explained in Chapter 5, with the assistance of an estate planning attorney, your irrevocable life insurance trust can be drafted to take advantage of the $10,000 per trust beneficiary per year present interest gift tax exclusion ($20,000 for married persons who split gifts) in order to minimize, if not altogether eliminate, taxation of your policy and premium gifts.

NOTES

1. U.S. Senate Committee on Aging, "Aging America: Trends and Projections," S. Prt. No. 59, 101st Cong., 1st Sess. 1, 3 (1989).

2. See Kerry Capell, "Long-Term Care: Sizing Up New Wrinkles," *Business Week*, Dec. 4, 1995, at 128.

3. See Ronaleen R. Roha, "Considering Long-Term Care," *Kiplinger's Personal Finance Magazine*, Mar 1996 at 111.

4. *Id.*

5. *Id.* at 112.

6. English, *supra* n. 2 at 495.

7. *Id.*

8. Roha, *supra* n. 3 at 112.

9. The Health Insurance Portability and Accountability Act of 1996 ("Kassebaum-Kennedy Bill"), P.L. No. 104-191 (8/21/96), sections 321-323, 325-326, amending Section 213(d) of the Internal Revenue Code of 1986, and enacting Code Sections 4980C, 6050Q, and 7702B.

10. I.R.C. §§ 7702B(b)(2), 7702B(d).

11. Capell, *supra* n.2.

12. I.R.C. § 2035.

13. I.R.C. § 2042.

CHAPTER 14

Saying "I Do" the Second Time Around

Tips for the Bride-to-Be

We must be willing to get rid of the life we've planned,
so as to have the life that is waiting for us.

—Joseph Campbell

After divorce or the death of a spouse, you may find a new Mr. Right and hear wedding bells in your future. However, this time around your concerns are much different from those you had as a first-time bride-to-be. You may have children, for example, who are worried about your new husband winding up with their inheritance. To protect your family, your wealth, and yourself, there are three key things you should do before saying "I do" the second time around: review your will and other estate planning documents, review your beneficiary designations, and consider a prenuptial agreement.

REVIEWING YOUR WILL AND OTHER ESTATE PLANNING DOCUMENTS

In some states, marriage will invalidate your will unless your will expressly states that it was made in contemplation of such an event.

Example: This will is made in contemplation of my marriage to Edward D. Simpson and shall not be revoked by the occurrence of such event.

If your will does not include such language (and it probably doesn't unless you just executed it), you will need to make a new will or at least execute a codicil reaffirming the terms of your old one and stating that you are executing the codicil to reaffirm your will in contemplation of your anticipated marriage. Of course, if you are remarrying, you may wish to change the terms of your old will anyway. In addition, trusts, financial powers of attorney, living wills, and health care powers of attorney may need to be amended or re-executed to include your new spouse. You should check with an attorney in your state regarding the effect of remarriage on these documents.

REVIEWING YOUR BENEFICIARY DESIGNATIONS

After your death, life insurance policies, annuities, retirement plans, and other similar assets pass to the beneficiary (or beneficiaries) named on the policy, contract, or beneficiary designation form. Unless your estate is named as the beneficiary of the policy or plan, the benefits paid at your death will not pass by the terms of your will. Instead, they will pass outside of your probate estate directly to the beneficiary named.

Example: Suzanne, a divorcee, recently remarried and rewrote her will. Her new will leaves one-third of her property to her new husband, Alan, and two-thirds to her daughter, Michelle. Suzanne's estate is currently worth about $375,000. In addition, she owns a $600,000 life insurance policy that she wants to pass to her spouse at her death. However, the beneficiary of her policy is still her ex-husband, Richard. If Suzanne were to die today, her husband would receive $125,000, her daughter $250,000, and her ex-husband $600,000. In addition, the policy proceeds of

$600,000 are part of her taxable estate, and since they would pass to her ex-husband instead of her current husband, there would be no marital deduction to shield that sum from tax. Thus, even if her full unified credit exemption amount were available, Suzanne's estate would still owe taxes on $250,000 ($950,000 – $125,000 marital bequest – $600,000 unified credit), and the tax of $70,800 would be paid from the share passing to her daughter.

By contacting your insurance agent, your employer's benefits coordinator, your bank representative, or your broker, you can confirm that the proper person is designated as the beneficiary of your life insurance policy or retirement assets or, if you wish, you can change your beneficiary designations to reflect the change in your marital status.

PRENUPTIAL AGREEMENTS

A *prenuptial* (*premarital* or *antenuptial*) agreement is an agreement between two individuals who intend to marry. It is made in contemplation of marriage and is effective upon the marriage of the individuals executing it.[1] By executing a prenuptial agreement, you and your fiance can define and distinguish the separate property owned by each of you at the time of your marriage, as well as agree upon how you will treat earnings, inheritances, and gifts received during your marriage. You also can create a plan for the disposition of your separate and joint property in the event of separation, divorce, annulment, or death.

A prenuptial agreement is not a will and should only be used in addition to a will. Neither is a prenuptial agreement a divorce settlement and, although it may be adopted as part of a divorce decree, a court may make modifications to the agreement if it is successfully challenged by either spouse.

A *postnuptial* (*postmarital*) agreement also is an agreement between spouses. A postnuptial agreement is executed after marriage. It is effective at the time it is signed or at any later date set forth in the agreement. A postnuptial agreement is made for the same reasons as a prenuptial agreement. It is not an agreement made because of the separation of the spouses or in anticipation of divorce. Neither is it a will, although it does define the property interests of the spouses.

Prenuptial agreements are recognized by statute in most states.[2] Postnuptial agreements, however, are expressly prohibited by statute in some states, and in other states, they may be struck down by the courts as promoting separation or divorce. The modern trend in many courts is to uphold postnuptial agreements if they do not promote separation and if there is adequate "compensation" exchanged by the executing parties. The act of marriage itself is sufficient consideration for a prenuptial agreement. For postnuptial agreements, however, marriage cannot serve as consideration (as it has already occurred). For this reason, it often is more difficult to prove that there is sufficient consideration to uphold a postnuptial agreement. In upholding postnuptial agreements, courts have accepted the exchange of mutual promises,[3] the relinquishment of rights in the individual's spouse's estate,[4] and the transfer of property from one spouse to another[5] as adequate consideration.

> Example: In consideration of Robert's *promise* to *transfer* the property located at 200 Main Street, Smalltown, Georgia, to Elizabeth at the time of his death, Elizabeth agrees to waive and *relinquish* all of her marital rights in the remainder of Robert's estate.

State Law Requirements

In general, the requirements for executing prenuptial agreements and the enforceability of such agreements will vary from state to state. As a general rule, however, prenuptial agreements must meet the basic requirements of all contracts. In states that recognize postnuptial agreements, these requirements apply to them as well as to prenuptial agreements.

Statutes in most states require that the prenuptial agreement, like any other contract, be in writing and signed by both parties.[6] Following are descriptions of other basic contractual requirements that typically apply throughout the states and that must be met in order for a prenuptial agreement to be valid and binding.

Ability to Contract

The prenuptial agreement will not be valid unless the individuals executing it have the ability to contract. Minors and mentally incapacitated persons, by law, are not capable of making contracts and, therefore, these persons cannot execute valid prenuptial agreements.

Voluntary Execution

The two persons executing the prenuptial agreement must do so voluntarily. If one individual has been coerced into signing the agreement or has signed the agreement under duress or as a result of undue influence, the agreement will be void.

Exchange of Consideration

As already mentioned, as a matter of contract law, there must be adequate consideration exchanged between individuals executing a prenuptial agreement in order for the agreement to be valid.

In evaluating prenuptial agreements, courts are typically most concerned that each person (1) know the extent of the other's property and finances; (2) understand his or her rights, as a spouse, in the property of the other; and (3) understand the effects of his or her waiving such rights to his or her spouse's property.[7] Many people are unfamiliar with their rights to their spouse's property under state law. All states, both community property states and non-community property states (which have elective or spousal shares, dower rights, curtesy rights, or the right to a year's support), have laws governing the property rights of married persons unless those persons contract otherwise between themselves. (See Chapter 3 for a more complete discussion of marital property rights.) Thus, it is important for you and your intended spouse to have separate legal representation to explain your rights to you, to protect your interests, and to guide you in the negotiation, drafting, and execution of your prenuptial agreement.

Invalid Prenuptial Agreements

The courts have recognized several defenses to the enforceability of a prenuptial agreement which can serve as safeguards of your interests and rights: misrepresentation, fraud, undue influence and duress, and unconscionability.

Misrepresentation

A prenuptial agreement may be declared void if one spouse signs the agreement because of misrepresentations made by the other. By misrepresenting the facts and circumstances upon which the provisions of the agreement are based, one person impairs the ability of the other to make an informed decision about the advisability of entering into the agreement. You and your intended spouse may avoid the dangers of misrepresentation by making full disclosures of your assets and liabilities when the agreement is prepared. Some states require full disclosure prior to execution. In other states, the courts consider evidence of such disclosures (in the form of statements that such disclosure was made or schedules of assets and liabilities included as part of the agreement) in examining the issue of misrepresentation. Finally, in many states, even if full disclosure is required by law, an agreement may still be upheld if the court finds that the individuals knew or should have known of each other's financial situation at the time the agreement was signed.

Fraud

A prenuptial agreement may be declared void if the court determines that it is based on fraud. The contractual requirements are meant to provide protection to the contracting individuals against fraud between them. Between engaged or married individuals, fraud is essentially the same as misrepresenting facts. However, together, spouses may execute a prenuptial or postnuptial agreement by which they attempt to defraud their creditors or other third parties. Courts will not uphold such agreements if spouses are transferring assets between themselves in an attempt to shield the assets from known creditors.

Undue Influence and Duress

A court will not uphold a prenuptial agreement which was signed under duress or as a result of undue influence being exerted over one spouse by another. In examining the issue of undue influence, one factor the court may consider is whether each person had the opportunity to consult with legal counsel of his or her own choosing or obtain independent advice as to the terms of the agreement. Undue influence may be found if there is:

- a large difference in the ages, experience, or sophistication of the parties.

- a substantial difference in the parties' levels of business experience.

- evidence that one party is more vulnerable than the other due to illness, pregnancy, or threat of loss of job.

- evidence that one party has threatened to call off the wedding or sue for divorce.[8]

Lack of separate legal representation also may be evidence of undue influence. Duress is similar to undue influence. In examining the issue of duress, courts will consider the bargaining positions of both parties and the ability of the party with less property to review the terms of the agreement and evaluate his or her rights under such an agreement. Thus, once again it is important to remember that you and your fiance should have separate legal representation in order to protect against the possibility of one spouse some-day challenging the agreement on any of these grounds.

Unconscionability

Finally, even if there is no evidence of fraud, misrepresentation, undue influence, or duress, a court still may not uphold a prenuptial agreement if it determines that the agreement is not fair and reasonable to both parties or is *unconscionable*. Although there is no set standard of reasonableness or unconscionability, one definition of "unconscionability" is the "overreaching concealment of assets or relevant information and sharp dealing not consistent between partners who share a confidential relationship."[9] Again, in making such determinations, the court will consider whether both parties made full disclosures to each other or had (or should have had) sufficient knowledge of the other's financial circumstances when the agreement was made.

CONTENTS OF A PRENUPTIAL AGREEMENT

You may think that a prenuptial agreement is a device used primarily by financially suc-cessful, overprotective fathers who are concerned about gold-digging young men stealing their family fortunes by marrying and then divorcing their daughters. In fact, prenuptial agreements may have the most value for those remarrying later in life, especially when the newlyweds have children from previous marriages. Prenuptial agreements can be used to accomplish a variety of financial planning goals for married couples of all ages.

Disposition of Property

A prenuptial agreement can fix the disposition of property in the event of separation, divorce, or death.

Example: Rick and Elissa agree that, if they should divorce, all separate property owned by each of them at the time of their marriage should remain separate prop-erty. Rick and Elissa execute a prenuptial agreement that states that, upon the dis-solution of their marriage by divorce and during any separation, each one of them agrees not to make any claim, and expressly waives all right to make any claim, upon the separate property of the other for alimony, maintenance, support, or a property settlement for his or her maintenance or support, temporary or otherwise.

In addition, the agreement also provides that, in the event of dissolution of the marriage by divorce or the entry of a decree of legal separation, all property other than their separate property shall be divided between them in accordance with their respective contributions to the purchase of that property. (In other words, if Rick contributes 30 percent and Elissa contributes 70 percent to the purchase of an asset titled in both names, then on dissolution of the marriage or separation, 30 percent shall be distributed to Rick and 70 percent to Elissa.)

Record of Ownership

A prenuptial agreement may serve as a written record of property ownership.

Example: Anne owns stocks and bonds worth about $750,000. Her fiance, Charles, has investments that are worth approximately $1,500,000. Once they marry, Anne and Charles plan on commingling these assets for investment purposes, but they will divide earnings proportionately based on each one's contribution to the investment fund. In the event of divorce, they wish to divide the investments in the same manner. Charles and Anne execute a prenuptial agreement setting forth provisions to accomplish these goals. In addition, the agreement includes an itemized list of the investments each one of them owns at the time of their marriage.

Estate Preservation

Individuals will often execute prenuptial agreements in order to preserve individual estates and family harmony.

Example: Sam, a widower, is 60 years old and has one daughter, Sarah, age 34. Sam inherited most of his net worth (approximately $3 million) from his late wife. Sam now wants to marry Ellen, an old family friend, and his daughter is not pleased with this decision. Sam's existing estate plan generously includes his daughter and her family, and he now wants to reassure Sarah that his upcoming marriage will not change his long-term plans for her and her family. Ellen has a substantial estate of her own and four children. She does not want or need an inheritance from Sam. In addition, she does not plan on leaving Sam anything, since she wants her children to share the wealth earned and invested by their father during his lifetime. Sam and Ellen execute a prenuptial agreement, waiving all rights to each other's property at death or in the event of divorce.

Community Property Rights

The terms of a prenuptial agreement may address community property rights and obligations. Even if you do not currently live in a community property state, there is always a chance that you may move to one in the course of your marriage, so, including provisions addressing these rights is safe planning.

Example: Josh and Margaret, both attorneys, live in Texas, a community property state. However, since they each have children from previous marriages and do not plan on having children together, Josh and Margaret would prefer that all of their property remain separate, even if earned during their marriage. Furthermore, they wish for their individual investments to remain separate, even though Margaret, who has more investment experience, will probably be managing both of their investment accounts. Therefore, Josh and Margaret execute a prenuptial agreement in which they "opt out" of the Texas community property laws and agree that all of their property, regardless of when earned or by whom managed and invested, will remain separate. They also each agree not to make any claims against the earnings or income of the other.

Basic Marital Property Rights

Regardless of where you live, your prenuptial agreement should define your rights to your own property and the property of your spouse.

Example: Jay, a widower and father of two, plans to marry Kristine. Jay's children are grown and have successful careers of their own. Therefore, at his death, Jay plans to leave his cash and investments to Kristine. The majority of Jay's wealth, however, is in land he inherited from his first wife. The land belonged to her family, and Jay wants his children to own the land after his death. As his wife, however,

Kristine would have certain rights under state law to at least a portion of this land. To reassure Jay that she will not ever challenge his decision to give the land to his children, Kristine signs a prenuptial agreement in which she agrees to release all of her rights in the land.

Asset Protection

Your prenuptial agreements can be drafted to protect your fiance's assets from existing creditors.

Example: Alexander is paying off approximately $150,000 of student loans from medical school. He plans to marry Deborah in two months. Deborah has a successful career as an advertising executive. Alexander is adamant that Deborah's income not be used to pay off his creditors and wishes to protect her money as much as possible. They execute a prenuptial agreement that defines their separate property and states that Deborah will not be held liable for Alexander's personal debts in existence prior to their marriage and that her separate property will not be used to pay off those debts.

Goal-Setting

A prenuptial agreement may define personal or marital goals.

Example: Todd, a stockbroker, and Mary, a nurse, are marrying in July and plan to have two children over the first four years of their marriage. Todd and Mary have agreed that Mary will stop working to stay at home with the children. However, if Todd should later decide to return to graduate school, Mary would prefer to return to work part-time and have Todd share the child care and maintenance of the household. As long as Todd is working and Mary is not, Todd has promised to establish an IRA for Mary and plans on periodically purchasing other investments in her name. Todd and Mary execute a prenuptial agreement that sets forth this arrangement.

Note that Todd's agreement to transfer property to Mary is in consideration of her quitting her job and is not provided to her as compensation for her domestic services. Prenuptial agreements that attempt to compensate one spouse for providing domestic services or nursing care are typically declared void for being against public policy.[10]

Inducement to Marriage

Sometimes a prenuptial agreement is used to create an inducement to marriage.

Example: Cheryl is a widow receiving a substantial monthly income from a trust created by her late husband. She is now contemplating marrying Mark, who has promised to take care of her financially for life. However, if Cheryl, who has no separate property of her own, marries Mark, she will no longer receive the stream of income from her deceased husband's trust. Cheryl is concerned that, if Mark should die before her, his children would challenge any bequests he leaves to her, leaving her with nothing in her later years. To reassure her (and to convince her to marry him), Mark tells her that he is willing to transfer property outright to her during his lifetime. Mark and Cheryl execute a prenuptial agreement which states that Mark agrees to transfer $200,000 of assets outright to Cheryl at the time of their marriage and that he will also transfer $50,000 of assets outright to her at the end of the second, fifth, and tenth years of their marriage.

Handling Special Concerns

You may have special concerns or objectives if you are executing a prenuptial agreement in anticipation of a second marriage, particularly one occurring later in life. There are several options you may wish to consider as you, your fiance, and your estate planning attorney negotiate and draft your agreement.

Cash Payments to One Spouse at Death or Upon Divorce

Some prenuptial agreements provide for cash to be paid in a lump sum to the less-wealthy spouse at the death of the other spouse or in the event of divorce. One option for making such a payment would be to increase the size of the payment depending upon the length of the marriage.

Example: If divorce should occur any time during the first five years of marriage, Lucy shall receive $100,000. If divorce should occur any time after five years of marriage, Lucy shall receive $100,000 plus $10,000 for each additional year of marriage over five years.

If the payment is to be made at death, you may opt to give a percentage of your estate rather than a specific cash sum. In this way, appreciation or depreciation may be factored into the gift. Your executor would then have the option of transferring assets other than cash, thereby foregoing the time and expense of liquidating your property before distributing it.

Example: Upon the death of Jill, Gary shall receive 5 percent of the value of the remainder of Jill's estate.

You may also use a combination percentage-cash bequest to cap the amount given to the second spouse so that residuary bequests to other family members are not substantially decreased.

Example: Upon the death of Jill, Gary shall receive 5 percent of the value of the remainder of Jill's estate or $150,000, whichever is less.

Of course, the recipient spouse will desire a provision in the agreement that prohibits the donor spouse from making sales of property, lifetime gifts, or specific bequests that deplete the estate so that there is nothing left for the recipient spouse. In addition, there may be tax consequences to making a lump sum transfer or gift to a spouse (or ex-spouse) in this manner. The possible tax implications should be reviewed with each party's attorney as the agreement is being negotiated and drafted.

Survivor Trusts Created for a Less-Wealthy Second Spouse

Instead of making a lump sum payment to a surviving spouse, the prenuptial agreement can provide for property to be transferred at the death of the wealthier spouse to a trust for the lifetime benefit of the surviving spouse. (This trust, the QTIP trust, is discussed in Chapter 5.) This arrangement may be particularly attractive in a second marriage between individuals of disparate wealth who have children from previous marriages, because the wealthier spouse can retain control of the ultimate disposition of his or her assets. The lifetime needs of the surviving spouse can be met through distributions of trust income and/or principal, and the deceased spouse's children can be named as the remainder beneficiaries of the trust property. Of course, this planning option will delay the ultimate distribution of some or all of the decedent's estate to his or her children until the end of the surviving spouse's lifetime. In addition, conflicts may arise between the surviving spouse, children, and trustee as the trustee attempts to balance the interests of the spouse and the children. This situation may be exacerbated if a child or the spouse is named as the trustee or the spouse and a child are named as co-trustees.

Life Insurance Policies

Sometimes an individual's estate is composed primarily of illiquid assets such as real estate or stock in a family-owned business. Many times, an individual would prefer to leave such assets to his or her children rather than to a second spouse. If you have these types of assets in your estate, one way to pass them to your children and also provide for your surviving spouse is to purchase a life insurance policy that names your spouse as the beneficiary. The policy proceeds would pass outside the probate process, thus making it less likely that your children would challenge this gift to your spouse. Another way to give life insurance is through a life insurance trust that holds the proceeds for the benefit of the surviving spouse for life and then distributes the remainder to children. (See Chapter 5 for more on life insurance trusts.) If you are considering including life insurance in your prenuptial agreement, you should consult with both parties' advisors in the planning process.

Family Residence and Vacation Home

The family residence is the largest asset in many estates. Although you may want your children to be the ultimate recipients of the family residence after your death, you would also like your second spouse to be able to live in the house as long as he or she desires. The same may be true of your family's vacation home: you want your surviving spouse, your children, and your grandchildren to be able to use it. You might consider giving your spouse rent-free occupancy of your family residence for as long as he or she wishes to live there, or the right to occupy the house for a specified period of time after your death during which he or she can find another place to live. Regardless of which option you choose, you should also prepare a contingency plan in case your spouse either does not want to remain in the house or needs to remain there longer than the time specified. In addition, you must decide who will be financially responsible for property taxes, normal upkeep, major repairs, and insurance. If your spouse is to pay for these things, you may want to provide funds for him or her to do so. If your estate or a trust is to pay, you may want to compensate your other beneficiaries for the loss of these funds. Whatever your choices, the use of your family residence and vacation home should be addressed by your prenuptial agreement, with full consideration of the income and estate tax implications of any decisions you make.

Retirement Plan Benefits

It has become common for individuals to accumulate large amounts of wealth in their retirement plans. If you or your fiance has a substantial amount of wealth accumulated in a retirement plan, your prenuptial agreement will need to address the disposition of these retirement plan benefits. The Employee Retirement Income Security Act of 1974, which protects individuals' rights in the retirement plan benefits of their spouses, provides that federal law will supersede state law in all areas affecting retirement plan benefits.[11] Therefore, the provisions of your prenuptial agreement addressing the disposition of your retirement plan benefits will not control their allocation if those provisions conflict with federal law.[12] If you and your fiance both have retirement plans, you may both agree to waive your rights (including rights to an annuity payout and the pre-retirement survivor benefit) in each other's plan. In waiving your rights, however, you must take care to comply with the requirements established by the Retirement Equity Act of 1984. Therefore, in your prenuptial agreement, you can only *agree* to waive those rights and agree to complete, at the appropriate time, all documentation required by federal law in order to execute a valid waiver of those rights.[13] Of course, this language certainly should be included in your agreement as it will establish your intent to waive these rights and meet the requirements of federal law in doing so. If you have a large retirement plan, it is extremely important for you and your spouse to seek professional assistance in crafting your prenuptial agreement for the disposition of your retirement plan assets because this is an extremely complicated area of the law.

TAX IMPLICATIONS OF A PRENUPTIAL AGREEMENT

Remember that the property ownership decisions of you and your intended spouse set forth in your prenuptial agreement will have income, gift, and estate tax consequences. The reclassification or transfer of property according to a prenuptial agreement executed in accordance with state law will be recognized by the IRS as valid for income tax purposes.[14] In addition, for income tax purposes, a properly executed prenuptial agreement between individuals living in a community property state will be an effective reclassification of both property ownership and prospective rights to income.[15]

Generally, prenuptial agreements do not provide for the immediate transfer of property, because the terms of the agreement are effective only upon the subsequent marriage of the parties. If title to property is transferred pursuant to the terms of the agreement, or if an interest in property is created under the terms of the agreement itself, a gift is made. However, because the gift is from one spouse to another, there is no gift tax due on the transfer.[16] Even if you transfer substantial amounts of property to your spouse, you are still not required to file a federal gift tax return to report the transfer to the IRS.[17]

In an estate tax context, if the property transferred otherwise qualifies, the estate of the deceased spouse will be entitled to an estate tax marital deduction for the value of the property so transferred pursuant to the terms of the prenuptial agreement.[18] What happens if the deceased spouse fails to provide for the surviving spouse as agreed in the prenuptial contract? If the surviving spouse successfully files suit against the estate of the deceased spouse to enforce the terms of their agreement, the surviving spouse's claim against the estate cannot be deducted for estate tax purposes.[19] However, the property transferred to the surviving spouse pursuant to court order enforcing the agreement may qualify for the estate tax marital deduction.[20]

You and your fiance should consult with experienced estate planning attorneys and your other tax advisors in the process of negotiating and drafting your prenuptial agreement.

NOTES

1. See Section 1(1) of the Uniform Premarital Agreement Act of 1983.

2. Marital agreements are recognized under the common law of Alaska, Arizona, Illinois, Indiana, Michigan, Missouri, Pennsylvania, Oregon, and Virginia. They are recognized expressly by statute in Alabama, California, Colorado, Montana, Nevada, New Mexico, Ohio, Oklahoma, and South Dakota. Marital agreements are recognized as one type of contract which may be executed by a woman on her own under the Married Women's Property Acts which have been adopted in Connecticut, Delaware, Florida, Hawaii, Kansas, Maine, Maryland, Massachusetts, Nebraska, New York, North Dakota, Rhode Island, South Carolina, and West Virginia. In Idaho, Louisiana, Texas, and Wisconsin there are statutes which authorize married couples to organize their separate and community property by contract. Finally, in Georgia, Iowa, Kentucky, Minnesota, Mississippi, New Hampshire, New Jersey, and Utah, the validity of marital agreements is inferred from other statutes that regulate property contracts entered into by spouses.

3. *Chapman v. Corbin*, 316 S.W. 2d 880 (Mo. App. 1958)[Missouri]; *In re Estate of Bradley*, 179 Kan. 539, 297 P. 2d 180 (1956)[Kansas]; *McQuate v. White*, 389 S.W. 2d 206 (Mo. 1965); *In re Nickolay's Estate*, 249 Wis. 571, 25 N.W. 2d 451 (1946)[Wisconsin].

4. *First National Bank of Clearwater v. Morse*, 248 So. 2d 658 (Fla. App.), *cert. denied*, 253 So. 2d 706 (Fla. 1971)[Florida]; *Rockwell v. Estate of Rockwell*, 24 Mich. App. 593, 180 N.W. 2d 498 (1970)[Michigan]; see also *In re Estate of Kester*, 486 Pa. 349, 405 A. 2d 1244 (1979)[Pennsylvania].

5. *Clark v. Clark*, 228 S.W. 2d 828 (Mo. App. 1950)[Missouri].

6. See Section 2 of the Uniform Premarital Agreement Act of 1983.

7. *Id.* at 6-20.

8. Springs, Clare H. and Jackson M. Bruce, Jr. "Marital Agreements: Uses, Techniques, and Tax Ramifications in the Estate Planning Context," *University of Miami Law Center, Philip E. Heckerling Institute on Estate Planning* at 6-21 (1987).

9. *Id.* at 6-23.

10. See *Brooks v. Brooks*, 48 Cal. App. 2d 347, 119 F. 2d 970 (1941).

11. Springs, *supra*, at 6-95.

12. *Id.* at 6-96.

13. *Id.* at 6-99.

14. Springs, *supra*, at 6-63.

15. *Id.*

16. I.R.C. § 2523.

17. I.R.C. § 6019.

18. Springs, *supra*, at 6-49 citing Revenue Ruling 54-446, 1954-2 C.B. 303 and Revenue Ruling 68-271, 1968-2 C.B. 409.

19. Springs, *supra*, at 6-51.

20. *Id.*

Handling the Death of a Loved One

A Step-by-Step Guide

Make your own recovery the first priority in your life.

—Robin Norwood

This chapter will take you through all the things you will need to handle if your husband (or other loved one) passes away. Because most women marry men slightly older than themselves, and because women, on average, live seven years longer than men, this is a situation most married women will find themselves in at some point or another. This chapter is intended to help you avoid some of the pitfalls I have seen clients encounter and to pass along some practical tips I have picked up from some astute and conscientious financial advisors during my 21 years of practice.

CONTACTING THE FUNERAL HOME OR CREMATORIUM

The first thing you must do if a loved one dies is dispose of the body. Although wills are not generally read until after this is done, I suggest that you make every effort to determine whether your loved one had any special wishes with respect to disposition of his or her body. I usually recommend that my clients complete a questionnaire (like the one that follows) concerning their wishes about the funeral.

The will may sometimes have a brief statement with respect to whether burial or cremation is desired. Some people want to be buried in a certain cemetery next to a specific family member. I have had two calls in my career that went something like: "What are we going to do? We just read Dad's will and found out that we buried him in the wrong cemetery!" Believe me, it is not easy to move a body once it is buried. It is quite expensive, and permission from the health department is necessary. This is why I advise you to try to determine (even though it may not be uppermost in your mind), what the deceased's wishes are.

After dealing with the funeral home or crematorium, you will also need to place an obituary in the local newspaper, notify friends and relatives who will want to come to the funeral or memorial service, and make arrangements for out-of-town family members. In addition, you will need to meet with the pastor, rabbi, or other religious leader to plan the service itself.

THE MEMORIAL OR FUNERAL SERVICE

The most beautiful funeral and memorial services I have attended are truly celebrations of the decedent's life. I always enjoy hearing close friends and relatives speak about their loved one, recounting what he or she accomplished, how he or she inspired others, and how blessed we were to have had the person among us for a while. Not long ago, I attended the funeral of a former pastor of mine. He was 88, and his children are my contemporaries. We grew up together under his spiritual leadership. Three other pastors (from the same denomination as the deceased) each spoke of one aspect of this remarkable man's life. One called him a man of vision, and reminded us that, because of his vision, many homes for senior citizens were built. (My mother-in-law happens to live in one of them today.) Another pastor said that he was a man of hope. Even though there wasn't money to build these homes for senior citizens, he continued to be hopeful, talking about his vision and encouraging people to give. He never became despondent, never lost hope. Eventually the money came, and now many senior citizens have a safe, secure, and warm place to live. The final speaker called him a man of faith, and reminded us that because of his faith, he was inspired to work diligently to see that these homes for senior citizens were built all over our state. In fact, this man himself lived in one of the very homes he had worked so hard to build in the last few months immediately prior to his

SAMPLE FORM FOR FUNERAL ARRANGEMENTS

Name_____ Date _____

These are my wishes concerning my funeral:

I. A. That there be no public viewing of the body _____
   or

   B. That there be a public viewing of the body _____

II. A. That the service be held in church with the body present _____
   or

   B. That a memorial service be held in the church or synagogue some time after burial

   or cremation _____
   or

   C. That the service be held in a funeral home _____

   Funeral home I prefer is _____

III. A. That the following hymns be sung:

   _____

   _____

   B. That the following scripture be read:

   _____

   _____

   C. Other instructions concerning the service:

   _____

   _____

   D. That the following preacher or rabbi conduct the service:

   _____

IV. A.   That internment be in _____

               Deed for cemetery can be found in _____

               or

    B.   That I be cremated _____

               That my ashes be _____

V. A.   That costs be held to a minimum _____

               or

    B.   Other instructions on costs of funeral:

               _____

               _____

               _____

VI.   That, in lieu of flowers, family and friends may make contributions to

               _____

               _____

                                     (name)

VII.   That _____ is to have final authority concerning my funeral and has the right to change any of the above arrangements if necessary.

VIII.   Other special instructions:

               _____

               _____

               _____

               _____

               Signed _____

               Social Security Number _____

death. This was a celebration, a victory service and thanksgiving for a long, full productive life. We all left inspired and encouraged.

Another funeral I recently attended was that of the 26-year-old son of close personal friends. This young man died of muscular dystrophy, but he lived 10 years beyond his predicted life expectancy because of the quality of care given to him by his parents. For years, we had watched this young man, confined to a wheelchair, unable to run and play with the other children. He couldn't even attend college for health reasons. Yet he was artistic, creative, bright, and funny—a gift and a blessing to everyone who knew him. His funeral service was a celebration of his tremendous spiritual victory through a body crippled with disease. Although outwardly debilitated, this young man was inwardly strong and vibrant. One of the pastors who conducted the service reminded us, "In this young man, we saw perseverance and hope produce a beautiful character." His life was a shining light for all around him to see. Because he lived among us, we are all better people. If he could do such wonderful things through a body crippled with disease, how much more could *we* do? These are the kinds of funerals that help and touch me.

DEALING WITH LOSS

Before you start taking care of business, take care of yourself. If you have lost a husband (or other loved one), you have suffered a devastating blow. There are support groups in almost every community. If you feel you need the support of other people, ask around and join one. A number of good books on coping with death are also available. Psychological counseling can often be helpful during times of loss. Don't hesitate to seek out professional help; all of us need it during certain times in our lives. Ask around for recommendations from people you respect.

Professionals who deal with grief tell us that recovery is a process, and there are certain critical stages in the process. Generally, the days immediately following the death of a loved one are like emotional anesthetic. We are numb. Reality hasn't really hit yet, but it will. The worst time, according to those who regularly counsel the grieving, is about three to four weeks following the death of a loved one. Keep in mind that no two people are alike, however. As psychologist Mary R. Donahue explains, "Different widows heal in different periods of time, depending on the circumstances of the husband's death, the widow's preexisting mental health, the available emotional support from friends and family, and her financial knowledge. Progress cannot be charted on a straight upward line. Just when a widow thinks she has it all together, she may have a relapse."[1] Be prepared, and because you know yourself better than anyone else, plan to take care of yourself in a special way during this period of time.

Because you will be in a state of emotional turmoil for a year or two following the death of your husband (or child), try to avoid making any major decisions for at least a year following such a loss. For example, unless you need to because of dire financial conditions, don't sell your house for at least a year. Go slowly on all financial decisions, including choosing your financial advisors. (More about this later.) Go slowly in investing money you may have received in a lump sum from insurance or in some kind of wrongful death claim, settlement, or judgment. Take time to learn, and don't rush into any decisions. Keep lump sums of cash in a bank certificate of deposit or money market account until you are back on your feet and able to make decisions without being consumed by emotion. Ask people for help. There is wisdom in many counselors.

SELECTING AN ATTORNEY FOR THE ESTATE

Review Chapter 2 for tips on selecting an attorney. The attorney is usually the first advisor you will see following the death of your husband or other loved one. At the first meeting with the attorney, you may want to have a friend or family member along with you to help you remember everything the attorney tells you. You might also ask the attorney to send you a letter summarizing the meeting and the steps that need to be taken.

Some of the questions you might want to ask the attorney at your meeting include how long it will take to settle the estate, when distributions can be made to the beneficiaries of the estate, what the attorney's fees will be. Attorneys usually charge either on an hourly basis or, in some states, a percentage of the assets of the estate. If an attorney charges on a percentage basis, you may want to shop around. Even though, in certain states (such as New York), it is customary for attorneys to charge a percentage of the assets to handle the estate, you can always negotiate another fee arrangement. If an attorney you are talking to will not negotiate, another attorney might be willing to negotiate an hourly basis that could, depending on the assets of the estate, work out to be far better for you.

If an attorney quotes you a flat fee, make sure you understand what that flat fee includes. For example, if an attorney says, "We can handle the probate for five hundred dollars," this may only cover the preparation of the petition to the court and not include such things as transferring title to assets. Also discuss with the attorney how often invoices will be sent. Request invoices on a regular basis (preferably monthly), so that you can question anything that appears out of line.

ON TO BUSINESS

Depending on the size of your husband's estate, the nature of the assets in the estate, and your family situation (not to mention your law), the steps you will need to take will vary from very simple to quite complex.

Your husband probably had assets in his name, and these will need to be transferred to someone else (probably to you or to trustees who hold it for the benefit of family members). This process is called *probate*.

You must determine if your husband had a will (we certainly hope so). If so, read it to see who is appointed as the executor or executrix. Most husbands appoint their wives as executrix. If you are named as executrix, then you will need to take the will (the original) to an attorney who specializes in the probate and estate area and have him or her prepare the forms necessary to present the will to the local probate court and have you officially appointed executrix by the court. If you are not named as executrix, then you need to make sure that whoever is appointed starts the probate process.

If there is no will, then you will need to petition (through an attorney) to be appointed as the administratrix or personal representative (PR) of your husband's estate. Without a will, your husband's assets will pass according to the laws of the state where you live. An attorney knowledgeable about probate matters in your state can advise you with respect to how assets pass.

In order to probate a will or administer an estate, all heirs must generally be notified. If signatures of the decedent and witnesses to the will were not notarized, then testimony of at least one of the witnesses will likely be required.

After this information is assembled, the person responsible for administering the estate—whether executrix, administratrix, or PR—goes to the local probate court and is sworn in. At that point, the court issues a document (in Georgia, it is called "Letters Testamentary") authorizing the PR to transfer title to assets, notify and pay creditors, pay taxes, and otherwise handle the winding up of the decedent's affairs.

RENDERING UNTO CAESAR

One of the jobs of the PR is to determine whether the decedent has filed his or her income tax returns (both federal and state) for prior years. If the decedent dies between January and April, there is a good chance this will not have been done for the immediately preceding year, and one of the PR's first jobs will be to file (or hire an attorney or accountant to file) this return. If your state has an intangibles tax, this return will also have to be filed. The best thing to do if you are not an expert in this area, is hire a professional (preferably the accountant the decedent used prior to death).

If the value of the decedent's estate was more than $600,000 (as indexed) then an estate tax return (IRS Form 706) will have to be filed within nine months of the date of death. Again, a professional should be hired to file this return, unless you happen to have expertise in this area. An estate planning attorney or accountant can file it for you. The professional should apply for a tax identification number for the estate and notify the IRS that you are the PR (so that any correspondence that would otherwise have been sent to the decedent will now be sent to you).

The attorney you hire to prepare the probate petition should advise you with respect to any other state requirements. One of these is to notify any known creditors and publish a notice in a newspaper in the county where the decedent died for the benefit of unknown creditors. This notice should state that anyone who thinks the decedent owed him or her money should notify you, the PR. Under the law of your state, creditors will have a certain amount of time to notify you that they think the decedent owed them money. If they fail to do so within this period of time, their claims are generally barred.

You will also want to open an estate bank account in order to keep track of expenses that will be deductible on either the estate tax return (if one is filed) or the estate's income tax return. Examples of deductible expenses include legal and accounting fees, appraisal fees, court costs and fees, medical expenses, funeral expenses, and fees and expenses of the executor. You also will want to cancel magazine and newspaper subscriptions and notify the post office that the decedent has died if he or she did not live in the same home as you. You should also make sure that insurance on automobiles, houses, and other valuables is kept in place until the transfer to beneficiaries is completed.

SOCIAL SECURITY AND INSURANCE BENEFITS

Even if you are not the PR of your husband's will, if you are named as beneficiary of any insurance on his life, you may obtain that insurance directly from the insurance company by contacting the company and submitting the information requested (the death certificate, the policy itself, or anything else the company needs). If the estate was the beneficiary and you are not the PR, then the PR will have to do this.

As a surviving spouse, you may claim any social security benefits due. Generally speaking, you may receive benefits if you are at least age 60, although the benefits will be reduced if you elect to begin receiving them before age 65. Everyone may receive a $255 lump sum death payment. If your husband was receiving social security and you were not, or if his social security was greater than yours, then you may receive his social security check.

Family members who are eligible to receive social security upon death of a family member include:

- unmarried children under age 16
- disabled children if disabled before the age of 22
- a spouse caring for a child under age 16 or a disabled child who was disabled before age 22
- a disabled spouse at age 50
- a spouse at age 65 (age 60 for reduced benefits)
- dependent parents age 62 or over

A divorced spouse qualifies for a benefit if he or she was married to the decedent for 10 years. The benefit is the same as that payable to a spouse. However, if the divorced spouse remarries before age 60, benefits are not payable unless a subsequent marriage ends. Remarriage after the attained age of 60 does not prevent or stop entitlement to benefits.[2]

Please note that the benefits for a widow or widower caring for a nondisabled child stop when that child becomes age 16. Benefits do not start again until the widow (or widower) reaches age 60 (50 if disabled). During this "blackout" period, the need for income protection through a professionally designed insurance plan is great.

If your husband was a veteran, you might be able to obtain some minor benefits from the Veterans' Administration. He probably has a small insurance policy ($5,000 to $10,000), and you might be eligible to receive some assistance with burial or cremation expenses. You may also be eligible for a pension for yourself or your children. For information about veterans' benefits, contact the Department of Veterans Affairs.

DEALING WITH THE PROBATE COURT

If your husband had a will that relieved the PR of filing periodic reports with the probate court, then the PR may not have to deal with this at all. If the will did not relieve the PR of filing periodic returns, then the PR will most likely have to file annual returns with the probate court, reporting on the estate's assets.

Bond is another requirement that most wills waive for the PR. Bond is a premium paid for insurance that the PR will not abscond with the estate's assets. Bond is quite expensive, and almost all wills waive the requirement of bond.

Even if you have been relieved by the will of filing periodic reports with your local probate court, you will probably want to file a petition to dismiss yourself as PR when the estate administration has been completed. This closes the estate and gives you protection from people (such as beneficiaries or creditors) later filing suits against the estate or its PR.

FILING THE ESTATE TAX RETURN

If your husband's estate is valued at more than $600,000 (as indexed), a federal estate tax return will have to be filed on IRS Form 706. This return is time-consuming and requires a great deal of patience. Because the form requests information about all assets owned by the decedent, it is useful for helping you to learn what assets your husband owned and which of them are passing to you either outright or in trust. Professional appraisals will likely have to be obtained if this form is required, although if your husband's estate takes advantage of the unlimited marital deduction and no tax is due, the appraisals can be greatly abbreviated. One of the first things that you should do as PR of an estate is contact appraisers who can begin the process of appraising real estate, partnership interests, family businesses, and other hard-to-value assets. You need to let the appraiser know why the appraisal is being requested and any due date. For example, your estate planning attorney may want all appraisals in seven months from date of death so that he or she can have the estate tax return ready with all attachments nine months from date of death. Even appraisers specialize, so be sure to contact an appraiser who appraises the type of property in question. For example, some real estate appraisers only appraise residential property, and some appraise only commercial.

Another attachment to Form 706 is provided by insurance companies for life insurance paid at the decedent's death. IRS Form 712 must be attached to the estate tax return for any insurance owned by the decedent at the date of his or her death. It is a good idea to contact insurance companies that paid proceeds immediately at the decedent's death, because it takes companies a little while to prepare the forms.

Other forms you should be gathering include a certified copy of the will filed with the probate court, copies of trust documents executed by the decedent, the death certificate, and a certified copy of the court order supporting the executrix or administrator or PR.

THE ESTATE'S INCOME TAX RETURNS

An estate is a taxpayer just like you. When the decedent dies, his or her estate springs into existence. An estate, unlike you and me, may select a noncalendar year as its taxable year. The only requirement is that an estate's taxable year must end on the last day of a month. Hence, an estate has 12 choices for its calendar year-end.

Example: Jim died on August 3, 1996. Kay, his wife, is the PR of his estate. She may select any month as the estate's year-end. She may elect to choose July 31 of the following year (1997), for example. (The first year-end must be no more than 12 months from the date of the decedent's death.)

The selection of a fiscal year-end for the estate is important because it allows for income tax deferral. Any income paid out to the beneficiaries of an estate during its calendar year is deemed to be paid on the last day of that calendar year.

Example: Following Jim's death in August 1996, Kay decides (after consultation with the estate's attorney) to make a distribution to the estate's beneficiaries on December 31, 1996. However, this distribution is deemed to be made to the beneficiaries on the following July 31, 1997—the estate's year-end. The estate's beneficiaries do not have to report the distribution as taxable income until they prepare their 1997 income tax returns and do not have to pay tax on it until April 15, 1998.

Every year the estate remains open, an estate income tax return will have to be filed on IRS Form 1041. Generally, the estate has the same kinds of deductions you and I have, but there are some exceptions. You will want to engage an accountant or the estate's attorney to prepare this return for you.

POST-MORTEM ESTATE PLANNING

In the event that your husband did not have a will that sought to reduce estate taxes at the death of the survivor of the two of you, you may want to discuss with your attorney what can be done on the "back end." For example, suppose your husband's will left everything to you. You now have an estate tax problem, because you own assets in excess of $600,000. If you are fortunate enough to have plenty to live on (more than you anticipate you will need), you may disclaim $600,000 of your husband's assets and let them go immediately at his death to your children. A disclaimer must generally be filed with the local probate court within nine months, but check with an attorney to see what the statute of limitations is for a disclaimer in your state. This way, you can take advantage of your husband's $600,000 exemption amount, even though he didn't do so in his will. Of course, it also means you will not have the assets, but at least they will not be taxed in your estate, and with this type of disclaimer you can make sure that both estates are able to take advantage of the full exemption amount. The best assets to disclaim are illiquid assets such as land, non-income-producing real estate, and tangibles (art, antiques, etc.). In all probability, these are not assets you are going to use to live on.

If your husband's will has a flaw in it due to a drafting error, or perhaps your husband simply named someone you don't think you can work with, as trustee of a trust of which you are the beneficiary, much can be done by a talented and experienced estate planning attorney to correct these problems. Many marital deductions have been preserved through consent orders filed with courts or disclaimers filed by children. If any of these problems exist, it is very important that you work with an experienced, knowledgeable, and highly recommended estate planning attorney.

TRANSFERRING TITLE TO ASSETS

Ultimately, the PR will want to get assets out of the name of the decedent and into the names of individuals, trusts, or charitable organizations in accord with the decedent's will. The first question that usually arises is: When is title transferred? If there are beneficiaries outside of yourself and your immediate family, it is possible that they will put pressure on you to transfer assets to them before the estate has been completely administered. Remember, though, if you are the PR, you have personal liability for taxes, creditors' claims, and debts of the decedent. To transfer title prior to payment of these claims could mean that you bear the burden of these liabilities yourself. Therefore, it is important to be extremely cautious about not transferring title to assets too soon.

A PR will sometimes make distributions of a percentage of the estate's assets prior to all taxes and other claims being paid. Check with your estate attorney to see if this is possible. This gives the beneficiaries some money early on, yet retains the bulk of the assets until you, as PR, are satisfied that all taxes and claims are paid and met. In general, you should not transfer title to the bulk of the estate's assets until the statutory period for creditors making claims has run and, if you had to file an estate tax return, until you receive a closing letter from the IRS.

Once you are ready to transfer title to the bulk of the assets in the estate, the following issues may arise:

- If several people are to share in the distribution of an asset or category of assets (for example, the children are to receive the decedent's personal effects), then the PR will have to design a plan whereby the division and distribution can be done fairly. Such a plan may or may not be set out in the will. Some PRs have come up with plans that involve, with respect to tangible personal property (remember, this is furniture, jewelry, clothing, cars, books, guns, and collectibles), letting the children choose items in order of age, and then repeating the process after each child has chosen one item.

- If trusts are to receive assets, then a careful selection of assets to fund the trusts (provided the will leaves this up to the PR) should be made. If the decedent's will establishes a credit shelter trust, then the assets in this trust will not be taxed in the surviving spouse's estate. Therefore, it would make sense to put assets that are expected to appreciate most rapidly into this trust, protecting them from later taxation when the surviving spouse passes on.

Example: Carl died in 1997 with $600,000 of blue-chip stocks and $400,000 of CDs. His wife, Jeannette, decided to fund his credit shelter trust with the $600,000 in blue-chip stocks because she figured that these assets would appreciate more rapidly than the CDs held by Carl's estate. She also knew that, if she transferred the CDs directly to herself (Carl's will left $600,000 to the trust and the rest to Jeannette), she would be able to cash the CDs and use them for her living expenses. She is hoping that the $600,000 in stocks can grow in a manner not to be taxed in her estate so that, at her death, her children can receive $600,000 plus all growth estate tax-free.

- Some assets may bear income tax liability. Suppose, for example, that the decedent's will left everything equally to his second spouse and his two children by a prior marriage. Each beneficiary receives one-third. The decedent's assets were a mortgage worth $200,000, a CD worth $200,000, and a house worth $200,000. If the wife gets the house, and Child A gets the CD, these assets are approximately equal. If Child B receives the mortgage (meaning that he or she receives the right to collect payments on a promissory note secured by an interest in real property for the remaining term of the note), that child will have to pay income tax as mortgage payments are received. Part of the payment will likely be capital gain and part ordinary income (interest). This means that Child B is in a worse position than either Child A or the spouse because, after the mortgage payments are received, tax must be paid (not to mention the fact that Child B does not receive the money up front, but simply the right to receive the money over a period of time).

- Assets nobody wants may sometimes be included in a decedent's estate. For example, hazardous waste real estate is something that could cost more to clean up than the land is worth. If you are unfortunate enough to be PR of an estate that includes this type of asset, it is essential that you seek professional guidance.

MOVING ON

Once the assets have been distributed, you are ready to enter the next phase of your life. If you have been a wife (or daughter, or whatever) whose husband (or father, mother, or other loved one) has taken care of you, don't think you can't learn how to take care of yourself and your own finances. You can. Numerous resources are available to help you get started. For example, *On Your Own* by Alexandra Armstrong (a financial planner) and Mary R. Donahue (a psychologist) provides advice about how to move on both psychologically and financially. Everything from finding a support group to calculating your net worth, making a budget, and choosing financial advisors is covered.

Take your time. Don't rush. Learn everything you can about investing—by attending seminars, reading books, talking to knowledgeable (and wealthy) friends, and any other means you can think of. Have confidence in yourself. Over time, you can—and will—learn a great deal about investing.

You will probably want to select your own advisors. You may need your own attorney, your own accountant, and your own financial planner. You may want to select advisors as occasions arise, such as the need for an educational trust when a grandchild is born. Information on finding an estate planning attorney can be found in Chapter 2. To find an accountant, you might want to contact one or more of the following organizations:

The American Institute of Certified Public Accountants
1211 Avenue of the Americas
New York, NY 10036-8755
(212) 596-6200

Haverside Financial Center
201 Plaza 3
Jersey City, NJ 07311-3881
(201) 938-3000

National Association of Enrolled Agents
200 Orchard Ridge Drive, Suite 302
Gaithersburg, MD 20878
1 (800) 424-4339

To find a financial planner, you may want to contact:

Registry of Financial Planning Practitioners
c/o CFP Board of Standards
1660 Lincoln Street, Suite 3050
Denver, CO 80264

International Association for Financial Planning
5775 Glenridge Drive, N.E., Suite B
Atlanta, GA 30328-5364
1 (800) 945-IAFP

Institute of Certified Financial Planners (CFP)
7600 East Eastman Avenue, Suite 301
Denver, CO 80231-4397
(303) 751-7600

Choose advisors you feel comfortable talking with. There are many advisors to choose from in each of these specialties, so there is no need for you to deal with anyone who is not pleasant to work with, timely, and reasonable.

If you have lost your husband, you are now in charge of the family financial ship. It is up to you to plan your estate (which may include your husband's assets as well, if he did not do his own planning) for the benefit of yourself first, and then your children and grandchildren. If you happen to have members of Generation X as children or grandchildren, remember: they may never see Social Security. Their entire futures may depend on how well you plan using the techniques described in this book.

NOTES

1. Alexandra Armstrong and Mary R. Donahue, *On Your Own,* Dearborn Financial Publishing, Inc. 1993, 1996, page ix.

2. *Guide to Social Security and Medicare,* the Prudential Life Insurance Company 1966 Guide.

Index